Roman Dementiev

Algorithm Engineering for Large Data Sets

Roman Dementiev

Algorithm Engineering for Large Data Sets

Hardware, Software, Algorithms

VDM Verlag Dr. Müller

Bibliografische Information der Deutschen Nationalbibliothek:
Die Deutsche Nationalbibliothek verzeichnet diese Publikation in der Deutschen Nationalbibliografie; detaillierte bibliografische Daten sind im Internet über http://dnb.d-nb.de abrufbar.

Das Werk ist einschließlich aller seiner Teile urheberrechtlich geschützt. Jede Verwertung außerhalb der engen Grenzen des Urheberrechtsgesetzes ist ohne Zustimmung des Verlages unzulässig und strafbar. Das gilt insbesondere für Vervielfältigungen, Übersetzungen, Mikroverfilmungen und die Einspeicherung und Verarbeitung in elektronischen Systemen.

Alle in diesem Buch genannten Marken und Produktnamen unterliegen warenzeichen-, marken- oder patentrechtlichem Schutz bzw. sind Warenzeichen oder eingetragene Warenzeichen der jeweiligen Inhaber. Die Wiedergabe von Marken, Produktnamen, Gebrauchsnamen, Handelsnamen, Warenbezeichnungen u.s.w. in diesem Werk berechtigt auch ohne besondere Kennzeichnung nicht zu der Annahme, dass solche Namen im Sinne der Warenzeichen- und Markenschutzgesetzgebung als frei zu betrachten wären und daher von jedermann benutzt werden dürften.

Copyright © 2007 VDM Verlag Dr. Müller e. K. und Lizenzgeber
Alle Rechte vorbehalten. Saarbrücken 2007
Kontakt: VDM Verlag Dr. Müller e.K., Dudweiler Landstr. 125 a,
D-66123 Saarbrücken, Telefon 0681/9100-698, Telefax 0681/9100-988,
Email: info@vdm-verlag.de
Coverbild: copyright www.purestockx.com
Zugl.: Saarbrücken, Saarland University, Diss., 2006

Herstellung:
Schaltungsdienst Lange o.H.G., Zehrensdorfer Str. 11, D-12277 Berlin
Books on Demand GmbH, Gutenbergring 53, D-22848 Norderstedt

ISBN: 978-3-8364-4741-6

Preface

Massive data sets arise naturally in many domains: geographic information systems, computer graphics, database systems, telecommunication billing systems [Hum02], network analysis [DLL+06], and scientific computing [Moo00]. Applications working in those domains have to process *terabytes* of data. However, the internal memories of computers can only keep a small fraction of these huge data sets. During the processing the applications need to access the external storage (e.g. hard disks). One such access can be about 10^6 times slower than a main memory access. For any such access to the hard disk, accesses to the next elements in the external memory are much cheaper. In order to amortize the high cost of a random access one can read or write contiguous chunks of size B. The I/O becomes the main bottleneck for applications dealing with large data sets, therefore one tries to minimize the number of I/O operations performed. In order to increase I/O bandwidth, applications use multiple disks in parallel. In each I/O step the algorithms try to transfer D blocks between the main memory and disks (one block from each disk). This model has been formalized by Vitter and Shriver as the Parallel Disk Model (PDM) [VS94] and it is the standard theoretical model for designing and analyzing I/O-efficient algorithms.

Theoretically, I/O-efficient algorithms and data structures have been developed for many problem domains: graph algorithms, string processing, computational geometry, etc. Some of them have been implemented: sorting, matrix multiplication [VV96], search trees [Chi95, PAAV, AHVV99, AAG03], priority queues [BCFM00], text processing [CF02]. However, there is an ever increasing gap between theoretical achievements of external memory algorithms and their practical usage. Several external memory software library projects (LEDA-SM [CM99] and TPIE [ABH+03]) have been started to reduce this gap. They offer frameworks which aim to speed up the process of implementing I/O-efficient algorithms, abstracting away the details of how I/O is performed.

The TPIE and LEDA-SM projects are excellent proofs of the concepts of the external memory paradigm, but they do not implement many practice-relevant features which speed up I/O-efficient algorithms (parallel disks, pipelining, explicit overlapping between I/O and computation). This led us to start the development of a performance–oriented library of external memory algorithms and data structures STXXL [1], which tries to avoid those obstacles. The STXXL library is one of the *main* results of this work.

In the framework of this book we build cost-effective multidisk experimental

---

[1] http://stxxl.sourceforge.net

computer systems with excellent I/O bandwidth characteristics. Furthermore, this work is intended to provide research experience and support for designing other systems.

In the main part of this book we design the STXXL library and show how high-performance features are supported: disk parallelism, explicit overlapping of I/O and computation, external memory algorithm pipelining to save I/Os, improved utilization of CPU resources. The high-level algorithms and data structures of our library implement interfaces of the well known C++ Standard Template Library (STL) [SL94]. This allows to elegantly reuse the STL code such that it works I/O-efficiently without any change, and to shorten the development times for the people who already know STL. Our STL-compatible I/O-efficient implementations include the following data structures and algorithms: unbounded array (vector), stacks, queue, deque, priority queue, search tree, sorting, etc. They are all well-engineered and have robust interfaces allowing a high degree of flexibility. Sorting is the core tool of almost all I/O-efficient algorithms, defining at a large extent the overall performance. We develop a fast parallel disk sorter, whose I/O cost approaches the lower bound and can guarantee almost perfect overlapping of I/O and computation. In this book we provide results of numerous benchmarks proving that our library (at least) competes with the best practical implementations.

In the second part of this book we show which impact the STXXL library has on engineering I/O-efficient algorithms for graphs and text processing: minimum spanning forests, spanning forests, connected components, breadth first search, listing all triangles in graphs and suffix array construction problems are studied. We overview the algorithmic aspects and present the most important computational results achieved with STXXL. To evaluate the performance of the STXXL implementations many real-world and synthetic inputs have been used. It is shown that external memory computation for these problems is *practically feasible* now.

Then, we study external memory algorithms for coloring graphs. The main contributions are simple and fast heuristics for general graphs. One of these heuristics — Batched Smallest-Degree-Last — turns out to be a 7-coloring algorithm for planar graphs having the I/O complexity of sorting only: It needs $\mathcal{O}(\text{sort}(m))$ I/Os, where m is the number of edges in the input graph. This work is the first experimental study of algorithms that can color huge graphs exceeding the size of the main memory. We run our implementations on several architectures and on various random and real-world data sets.

Finally, it is explained how to port some parallel and internal memory algorithms for graphs to *external memory*, making them I/O-efficient.

IV

Contents

1 Introduction   **1**
    1.1   I/O-Efficient Algorithms and Models 3
    1.2   Disk Parallelism in Storage Technologies 4
    1.3   Memory Hierarchies 6
    1.4   Algorithm Engineering for Large Data Sets 9
    1.5   C++ Standard Template Library 9
    1.6   The Goals of STXXL 10
    1.7   Software Facts 11
    1.8   STXXL Users 12
    1.9   Related Work 13
    1.10 Outline 15

2 Building Experimental Parallel Disk Systems   **19**
    2.1   Hardware Disk Interfaces 21
    2.2   Busses, Controllers, Chipsets 22
    2.3   Our First System 24
    2.4   Other Systems 26
    2.5   File System Issues 26

3 The STXXL Library   **29**
    3.1   STXXL Design 29
    3.2   AIO Layer 32
        3.2.1   AIO Layer Implementations 33

	3.3	BM Layer	36
	3.4	STL-User Layer	39
		3.4.1 Vector	39
		3.4.2 Stack	39
		3.4.3 Queue	44
		3.4.4 Deque	44
		3.4.5 Priority Queue	45
		3.4.6 Map	50
		3.4.7 General Issues Concerning STXXL Containers	59
		3.4.8 Algorithms	60
	3.5	Parallel Disk Sorting	62
		3.5.1 Multi-way Merge Sort with Overlapped I/Os	65
		3.5.2 Implementation Details	69
		3.5.3 Experiments	70
		3.5.4 Discussion	78
	3.6	Algorithm Pipelining	79
	3.7	Streaming Layer	79
4	**Engineering Algorithms for Large Graphs**		**85**
	4.1	Overview	85
	4.2	Maximal Independent Set	87
	4.3	Minimum Spanning Trees	92
		4.3.1 Definitions	92
		4.3.2 Related Work and Motivation	92
		4.3.3 Semi-External Algorithm	93
		4.3.4 Node Reduction	93
		4.3.5 Experiments	98
		4.3.6 Conclusions	100
	4.4	Connected Components and Spanning Trees	101
		4.4.1 Introduction	101
		4.4.2 Spanning Forest	101

		4.4.3	Connected Components 102
		4.4.4	Experiments 103
	4.5	Breadth First Search 105
		4.5.1	Introduction 105
		4.5.2	Internal Memory BFS 105
		4.5.3	MR-BFS 106
		4.5.4	MM-BFS 107
		4.5.5	Experiments 110
	4.6	Listing All Triangles in Huge Graphs 113
		4.6.1	I/O-Efficient Node-Iterator Algorithm 113
		4.6.2	Pipelined Implementation 114
		4.6.3	Experiments 116
	4.7	Graph Coloring 117
		4.7.1	Introduction 117
		4.7.2	Greedy Coloring 119
		4.7.3	Highest-Degree-First Heuristic 120
		4.7.4	Batched Smallest-Degree-Last Heuristic 121
		4.7.5	7-Coloring of Planar Graphs 124
		4.7.6	6-Coloring of Planar Graphs 127
		4.7.7	2-Coloring 133
		4.7.8	Experiments 133
		4.7.9	Conclusion and Future Work 141
5	**Engineering Large Suffix Array Construction**		**143**
	5.1	Introduction 143
		5.1.1	Basic Concepts 144
		5.1.2	Overview 144
	5.2	Doubling Algorithm 145
	5.3	Discarding 147
	5.4	From Doubling to a-Tupling 150
	5.5	I/O-Optimal Pipelined DC3 Algorithm 151

5.6	Generalized Difference Cover Algorithm	154
5.7	Checker	156
5.8	Experiments	157
	5.8.1 The Checker	163
5.9	An Oracle PL/SQL Implementation	164
5.10	Conclusion	165

6 Porting Algorithms to External Memory   167

6.1	5-Coloring Planar Graphs	167
6.2	1/2-Approximation of Maximum Weighted Matching	168
	6.2.1 Definitions	168
	6.2.2 The Algorithm	168
6.3	Perfect Matchings in Bipartite Multigraphs	169
	6.3.1 Definitions	169
	6.3.2 Introduction	169
	6.3.3 Euler Partition Algorithm	170
	6.3.4 I/O-Efficient Perfect Matching Algorithm	171

7 Conclusions   173

A Notation   193

Acknowledgments

First of all, I would like to thank my PhD supervisor Peter Sanders for giving me an opportunity to work on this topic. I would like to gratefully acknowledge the time and the attention he always has been giving to me.

I thank Lutz Kettner for the consulting and the collaboration on the design of STXXL. He has revealed the full power of C++ to me. I would like to thank Gerhard Weikum for encouraging comments and his commitment to become a referee of this work.

I have been very lucky to work in the wonderful environment of the Max-Planck-Institut für Informatik (MPII) in Saarbrücken. Most of the work presented in this book has been done at the MPII.

I would like to thank my master and bachelor students Dominik Schultes, Jens Mehnert and Deepak Ajwani for the fruitful collaboration. They have given a valuable feedback on the very first versions of STXXL. Their contribution to the evaluation of STXXL, which is the second part of this book, is enormous. Thanks to all my co-authors who made this work possible.

The last two years I have worked at the chair of Peter Sanders at University of Karlsruhe. I acknowledge the excellent working atmosphere there and all my colleagues for the enjoyable lunches.

I thank Anton Myagotin for the interesting (scientific) conversations which I greatly appreciated.

I wish to thank Johannes Singler and Anja Blancani for accurately and diligently proof-reading this book.

During my graduate studies I have been financially supported by the International Max Planck Research School for Computer Science, and the Future and Emerging Technologies programme of the EU under the contract number IST-1999-14186 (ALCOM-FT).

Finally, I thank my mother, my brother and *my wife* for their love and support.

Chapter 1

Introduction

Massive data sets arise naturally in many domains. Spatial data bases of geographic information systems like GoogleEarth and NASA's World Wind store terabytes of geographically-referenced information that includes the whole Earth. In computer graphics one has to visualize huge scenes using only a conventional workstation with limited memory [FS01]. Billing systems of telecommunication companies evaluate terabytes of phone call log files [Hum02]. One is interested in analyzing huge network instances like a web graph [DLL+06] or a phone call graph. Search engines like Google and Yahoo provide fast text search in their data bases indexing billions of web pages. A precise simulation of the Earth's climate needs to manipulate with petabytes of data [Moo00]. These examples are only a sample of numerous applications which have to process huge amount of data.

The *internal memories* [1] of computers can keep only a small fraction of these large data sets. During the processing the applications need to access the *external memory* [2] (e.g. hard disks) very frequently. One such access can be about 10^6 times slower than a main memory access. Therefore, the disk accesses (I/Os) become the main bottleneck.

The reason for this high latency is the mechanical nature of the disk access. Figure 1.1 shows the schematic construction of a hard disk. The data is stored on a rotating magnetic disk surface. The rotational speed of modern

---

[1] The *internal memory*, or primary memory/storage, is a computer memory that is accessible to the CPU without the use of the computer's input/output (I/O) channels.

[2] The *external memory*, or secondary memory/storage, is a computer memory that is not directly accessible to the CPU, requiring the use of the computer's input/output channels. In computer achitecture and storage research the term of *"external storage"* is used more frequently. However, in the field of theoretical algorithm research the term of *"external memory"* is more established.

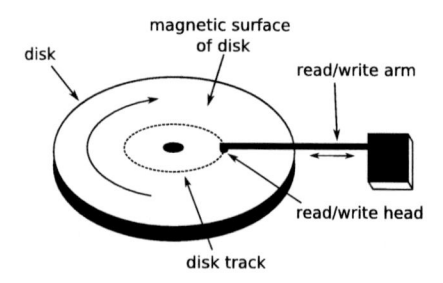

Figure 1.1: Hard disk mechanics [CLR90].

hard disks varies from 4,200 to 15,000 rotations per minute (RPMs). The information is modified by applying a magnetic field from a read/write head that flies very closely to the surface following a concentric trajectory called disk track. In order to read or write the certain position on the disk, the disk controller horizontally moves the read/write arm such that the track with the desired data is under the head. After that, one has to wait until the needed track segment is rotated under the head (rotational latency). Only from this moment reading or writing is possible. The total time needed for finding the data position on the disk is called seek time or (seek) latency and averages to about 3–10 ms for modern disks. The seek time depends on the surface data density and the rotational speed and can hardly be reduced because of the *mechanical* nature of hard disk technology, which still remains the best way to store massive amounts of data. Note that after finding the required position on the surface, the data can be transferred at a higher speed which is limited only by the surface data density and the bandwidth of the interface connecting CPU and hard disk. This speed is called sustained throughput and achieves up to 80 MByte/s nowadays.

In order to amortize the high seek latency one reads or writes the data in chunks (blocks). The block size is balanced when the seek latency is a fraction of the sustained transfer time for the block. Good results show blocks containing a full track. For older low density disks of the early 90's the track capacities were about 16-64 KB. Nowadays, disk tracks have a capacity of several megabytes.

Operating systems implement the so called *virtual memory mechanism* that provides an additional working space for an application, mapping an external memory file (page file) to virtual main memory addresses. This idea supports the Random Access Machine model [Neu45] in which a program has an infinitely large main memory with uniform random access cost. This model has served as the most important basis of computer architecture and programming language development.

Since the memory view is unified in operating systems supporting virtual memory, the application does not know where its working space and program code are located: in the main memory or (partially) swapped out to the page file. This kind of abstraction does not have large running time penalties for applications with a simple sequential data access pattern. The operating system is even able to predict scanning patterns and to load the data in ahead. For more complicated patterns these remedies are not useful and even counterproductive: the swap file is accessed very frequently; the data code can be swapped out in favor of data blocks; the swap file is highly fragmented and thus many random input/output operations (I/Os) are needed even for scanning.

1.1 I/O-Efficient Algorithms and Models

The operating system cannot adapt to complicated access patterns of applications dealing with massive data sets. Therefore, there is a need of explicit handling of external memory accesses. The applications and their underlying algorithms and data structures should care about the pattern and the number of external memory accesses (I/Os) which they cause.

Several simple models have been introduced for designing I/O-efficient algorithms and data structures (also called *external memory* algorithms and data structures). The most popular and realistic model is the Parallel Disk Model (PDM) of Vitter and Shriver [VS94]. In this model, I/Os are handled explicitly by the application. An I/O operation transfers a block of B consecutive bytes from/to a disk to amortize the latency. The application tries to transfer D blocks between the main memory of size M bytes and D independent disks in one I/O step to improve bandwidth. The input size is N bytes which is (much) larger than M. The main complexity metrics of an I/O-efficient algorithm in this model are:

- I/O complexity: the number of I/O steps should be minimized (the main metric),
- CPU work complexity: the number of operations executed by the CPU should be minimized as well.

The PDM has become the standard theoretical model for designing and analyzing I/O-efficient algorithms.

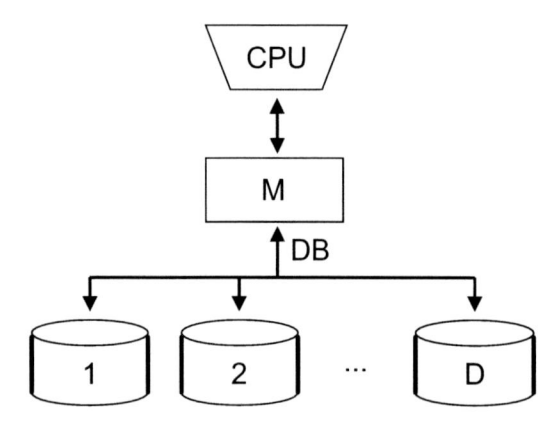

Figure 1.2: Parallel disk model.

For this model the following matching upper and lower bounds for I/O complexity are known:

- Scanning a sequence of N items takes $\text{scan}(n) = \Theta(N/(DB))$ I/Os.

- Sorting a sequence of N items takes $\text{sort}(N) = \Theta(\frac{N}{DB} \log_{M/B}(N/M))$ I/Os.

- Online search among N items takes $\text{search}(N) = \Theta(\log_{DB}(N))$ I/Os.

1.2 Disk Parallelism in Storage Technologies

Parallel disks have been used to achieve high I/O bandwidth and fault tolerance already in 1980s [PGK88]. Patterson et al. [PGK88] and Chen et al. [CLG+94] propose "Redundant Arrays of Inexpensive Disks" (RAID) with seven methods (levels) of organization. The basic RAID-0 level stripes the data blocks over all D disks in a round–robin fashion (see Chapter 2 for more details). Reading and writing is sped up by the factor D in the best case. The data is stored without redundancy: If one disk fails, all the data in the array is lost. At the RAID-1 level (mirroring), the data stored on all D disks is identical: even if $D - 1$ disks fail, the remaining disk contains all information. This level provides high reliability and the read bandwidth that linearly scales with D. However, this comes at the price of D-fold data capacity reduction. The RAID-2 level uses a Hamming code for error correction trying to improve the space usage. The method is not viable, since for a modern computer environment it requires 39 hard disks to be realized. The RAID levels 3–6 are more practical and require only a small amount of parity information to guarantee a high fault tolerance. They differ in how and where the parity data is stored. The best (parallel) performance have the levels 5 and 6 because they distribute the parity data blocks across all D disks, such that there is no bottleneck.

All RAID levels can be realized in software in the framework of the Parallel Disk Model (see for instance the software RAID in Linux). Since the RAID disk parallelism can (partially) mitigate the I/O-bottleneck problem and is very easy to use (a RAID array looks like a single disk for the user), the RAID solutions became standard and are implemented in many *hardware* disk controllers to off-load the CPU. In addition to the standard levels, the (hardware) implementations offer *nested* RAID levels that combine the properties of several levels: A RAID-50 (RAID-5+0) is a RAID-0 striped across superdisks realized as RAID-5 arrays. Other popular combinations are: RAID-01, RAID-10, RAID-30 and RAID-100.

A network-attached storage (NAS) is a data storage technology that can be connected to a computer network to provide centralized data storage for clients [MT03]. NAS can be realized as a dedicated server running a minimal-functionality operating system with support of a file-based protocol like NFS or CIFS to export the data to the clients. NAS has several advantages over the direct attached storage (e.g. local hard disks). Since NAS servers execute only file-serving functions, they are more reliable (going down less frequently) and faster, if the network bandwidth is high. To exploit disk parallelism, NAS servers can use local RAID arrays to store the data.

A storage area network (SAN) is a network designed to attach storage elements (e.g. hard disks, RAID controllers, tapes) to servers [MT03]. In contrast to NAS, the protocols used in a SAN are block-oriented, similar to the protocols used in hardware interfaces like ATA and SCSI. A SAN consists of a communication infrastructure, which provides physical connections, and a management layer, which organizes the connections, storage elements, and computer systems so that data transfer is secure and robust. The data stored in SANs can be striped across hundreds of disks to provide high bandwidth to access to the same files. SAN technology has excellent performance, however, the cost of the SAN equipment (disks, network) is relatively high.

The goal of distributed and parallel file systems (e.g. AFS [HKM+88], Google FS [GGL03], xFS [ADN+96], Swift [CL91], GPFS [SH02], see also references in [MSS03, Chapter 13] and [GGL03]) is to provide high-performance and reliable storage of user files. The file data is split into chunks and a num-

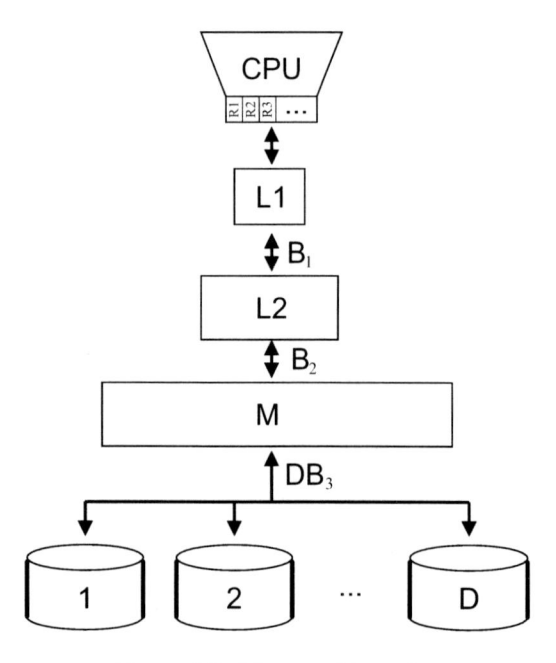

Figure 1.3: Memory hierarchy.

ber of chunk replicas are stored at several computers (storage nodes). This allows to achieve a high fault tolerance: If a disk at the node or the node itself is broken, then the remaining chunk replicas are copied to another nodes to restore the data redundancy. The I/O bandwidth and response time can be improved as well: The chunks of the requested file can be read in parallel from several nodes and the closest replica is requested from the available ones.

1.3 Memory Hierarchies

The PDM measures the transfers between the main memory and the hard disks, however, in modern architectures, the CPU does not access the main memory directly. There are a few levels of faster memory caches in-between (Figure 1.3).

Most processor commands operate on the content of CPU registers: during one processor cycle, a few commands can be executed which read and write

1.3. MEMORY HIERARCHIES

the registers in parallel. When the data is to be loaded from the main memory into the registers, the level one the (L1) cache is checked first to see whether it already contains the content of the needed memory cell (cache hit). Otherwise it must be loaded from the next cache level (cache miss). If a register value is to be stored in memory, it is buffered in the L1 cache. This value will be flushed only if the cache is full and a place for new data is needed. The L1 cache is a small (a few KBytes) and fast memory which allows up to two (or few) accesses per CPU cycle. If the data is not cached in L1, the larger (up to several MBytes with the current technology) level two (L2) cache is accessed. The access time of the L2 cache is about 10 cycles. The transfers between the L1 and L2 caches use block sizes about 16-32 bytes. Both L1 and L2 caches lie on the same chip as the main processor. Some modern processors also have off-the-chip L3 caches, however, they are rather expensive. The transfer block of the main memory and the L2/L3 cache is 128-256 Bytes (i.e. for the Pentium 4).

The main memory is cheaper and slower than the caches. Cheap dynamic random access memory, used in the majority of computer systems, has an access latency up to 60 ns. However, for a blocked access a high bandwidth of several GByte/s can be achieved.

The translation lookaside buffer (TLB) is another caching mechanism in processors. TLBs cache some parts of large tables which store the logical to physical address region mappings. The caching speeds up the virtual memory mechanism of operating systems. TLB misses might be the main bottleneck for algorithms: a TLB miss could be quite expensive (up to 100 CPU cycles); the cache itself is small (32-128 entries) [3].

The memory hierarchy in computer systems is a natural phenomenon: a fast huge memory with uniform memory access cannot exist because the access time is correlated with the speed of light. Therefore the faster memories (caches) are placed closer to the processor. Another reason is cost efficiency: Prices for a byte for L1 caches and hard disks differ in many orders of magnitude. One can only afford to keep a small, most frequently used fraction of the data in fast memory. The number of memory hierarchy levels having different access latencies and speed is growing: in 1986, Intel's 386 processor had a single off-chip cache, nowadays the IBM Power 5 series already has a 144 MByte L3 cache off-chip shared among several processors.

The discrepancy between the speed of CPUs and the latency of the lower hierarchy levels grows very quickly: the speed of processors is improved by

---

[3]The Calibrator tool http://monetdb.cwi.nl/Calibrator/ reports a TLB miss-latency of 54 CPU cycles on our 3.0 GHz Pentium 4 processor with only 32 TLB entries.

about 55 % yearly, the hard disk access latency only by 9 % [Pat04]. Therefore, the algorithms which are aware of the memory hierarchy will continue to benefit in the future and the development of such algorithms is an important trend in computer science.

The PDM only describes a single level in the hierarchy. An algorithm tuned to make a minimum number of I/Os between two particular levels could be I/O-inefficient on other levels. The cache-oblivious model in [FLPR99] avoids this problem by not providing the knowledge of the block size B and main memory size M to the algorithm. The benefit of such an algorithm is that it will be I/O-efficient on all levels of the memory hierarchy across many systems without fine tuning for any particular real machine parameters. Many basic algorithms and data structures have been designed for this model: sorting [FLPR99], matrix transposition and multiplication [FLPR99], priority queues [ABD+02], dictionaries [BDIW02], breadth-first-search [ABD+02, BFMZ04], depth-first-search [ABD+02], shortest paths [BFMZ04], minimum spanning trees [ABD+02], ... A drawback of cache-oblivious algorithms playing a role in practice is that they are only *asymptotically* I/O-optimal. The constants hidden in the $\mathcal{O}()$ notation of their I/O-complexity are significantly larger than the constants of the corresponding I/O-efficient PDM algorithms (on a particular memory hierarchy level). For instance, a tuned cache-oblivious funnel sort implementation [Chr05] is 2.6–4.0 times slower than our I/O-efficient sorter from STXXL (Section 3.5) for out-of-memory inputs [Osi06, AMO07]. A similar funnel sort implementation is up to two times slower than the I/O-efficient sorter from TPIE library (Section 1.9) for large inputs [BFV04]. The reason for this is that these I/O-efficient sorters are highly optimized to minimize the number of transfers between the main memory and the hard disks where the imbalance in the access latency is the largest (up to 10^6 times). Cache-oblivious implementations lose on the inputs, exceeding the main memory size, because (up to a constant factor) they do more I/Os at the last level of memory hierarchy.

In this book we concentrate on extremely large *out-of-memory* inputs, therefore we will design and implement algorithms and data structures efficient in the *PDM*.

1.4 Algorithm Engineering for Large Data Sets

Theoretically, I/O-efficient algorithms and data structures have been developed for many problem domains: graph algorithms, string processing, computational geometry, etc. (see the surveys [MSS03, Vit01]). Some of them have been implemented: sorting, matrix multiplication [VV96], search trees [Chi95, PAAV, AHVV99, AAG03], priority queues [BCFM00], text processing [CF02]. However only few of the existing I/O-efficient algorithms have been studied experimentally. As new algorithmic results rely on previous ones, researchers, which would like to engineer practical implementations of their ideas and show the feasibility of *external memory* computation for the solved problem, need to invest much time in the careful design of unimplemented underlying external algorithms and data structures. Additionally, since I/O-efficient algorithms deal with hard disks, a good knowledge of low-level operating system issues is required when implementing details of I/O accesses and file system management. This delays the transfer of theoretical results into practical applications, which will have a tangible impact for industry. Therefore one of the primary goals of algorithm engineering for large data sets is to create software frameworks and libraries which handle both the low-level I/O details efficiently and in an abstract way, and provide well-engineered and robust implementations of basic external memory algorithms and data structures.

1.5 C++ Standard Template Library

The Standard Template Library (STL) [SL94] is a C++ library which is included in every C++ compiler distribution. It provides basic data structures (called containers) and algorithms.

STL containers are generic and can store any built-in or user data type that supports some elementary operations (e.g. copying and assignment). STL algorithms are not bound to a particular container: an algorithm can be applied to any container that supports the operations required for this algorithm (e.g. random access to its elements). This flexibility significantly reduces the complexity of the library.

STL is based on the C++ template mechanism. The flexibility is supported using compile-time polymorphism rather than the object oriented run-time polymorphism. The run-time polymorphism is implemented in languages like C++ with the help of virtual functions that usually cannot be inlined by C++ compilers. This results in a high per-element penalty of calling a virtual function. In contrast, modern C++ compilers minimize the abstraction penalty of STL being able to inline many functions.

STL containers include: `std::vector` (an unbounded array), `std::list`, `std::priority_queue`, `std::stack`, `std::deque`, `std::set`, `std::multiset` (allows duplicate elements), `std::map` (allows mapping from one data item (a key) to another (a value)), `std::multimap` (allows duplicate keys), ... Containers based on hashing (`hash_set`, `hash_multiset`, `hash_map` and `hash_multimap`) are not yet standardized and distributed as an STL extension.

Iterators are an important part of the STL library. An iterator is a kind of handle used to access items stored in data structures. Iterators allow one to perform the following operations: read/write the value pointed by the iterator, move to the next/previous element in the container, move by some number of elements forward/backward (random access).

STL provides a large number of algorithms that perform scanning, searching and sorting. The implementations accept iterators that posses a certain set of operations described above. Thus, the STL algorithms will work on any container with iterators following the requirements. To achieve flexibility, STL algorithms are parameterized with objects, overloading the function operator (`operator()`). Such objects are called *functors*. A functor can, for instance, define the sorting order for the STL sorting algorithm or keep the state information in functions passed to other functions. Since the type of the functor is a template parameter of an STL algorithm, the function operator does not need to be virtual and can easily be inlined by the compiler, thus avoiding the function call costs.

The STL library is well accepted and its generic approach and principles are followed in other famous C++ libraries like Boost [Kar05] and CGAL [FGK+00].

1.6 The Goals of STXXL

Several external memory software library projects (LEDA-SM [CM99] and TPIE [ABH+03]) were started to reduce the gap between theory and practice in external memory computing. They offer frameworks which aim to speed up the process of implementing I/O-efficient algorithms, abstracting away the details of how I/O is performed. See Section 1.9 for an overview of these libraries.

The TPIE and LEDA-SM projects are excellent proofs of the concepts of the external memory paradigm, but they miss some practice-relevant features which are important for applications. This led us to start the development of a performance–oriented library of external memory algorithms and data structures, namely STXXL, which tries to avoid those obstacles. The STXXL library is the *main* contribution of this work.

The following here are some key features of STXXL:

- Transparent support of parallel disks. The library provides implementations of basic *parallel* disk algorithms. STXXL is the only external memory algorithm library supporting parallel disks. Such a feature was announced for TPIE in [Ven94, ABH+03].

- The library is able to handle problems of a *very large* size (up to dozens of terabytes).

- Improved utilization of computer resources. STXXL explicitly supports *overlapping* between I/O and computation. STXXL implementations of external memory algorithms and data structures benefit from the overlapping of I/O and computation.

- STXXL achieves small constant factors in I/O volume. A unique library feature *"pipelining"* can save more than *half* the number of I/Os performed by many algorithms.

- Shorter *development times* due to well known STL-compatible interfaces for external memory algorithms and data structures. STL algorithms can be directly applied to STXXL containers (code reuse); moreover, the I/O complexity of the algorithms remains optimal in most cases.

1.7 Software Facts

STXXL is distributed under the Boost Software License[4] which is an open source license allowing free *commercial* use. The source code, installation instructions and documentations are available under

---

[4] http://www.boost.org/more/license_info.html

`http://stxxl.sourceforge.net/`. According to the well known SLOC-Count [5] tool of David A. Wheeler, the release branch of the STXXL project not including applications has about 25,000 physical source lines of code (SLOC).

1.8 STXXL Users

Here is a list of active STXXL users we know about:

- University of Karlsruhe, Germany (text processing, graph algorithms, practical courses)

- Max-Planck-Institut für Informatik, Germany (graph algorithms)

- University of Rome "La Sapienza", Italy (connected components)

- University of Texas at Austin, USA (gaussian elimination)

- Bitplane AG, Switzerland (visualization and analysis of 3D and 4D microscopic images)

- Philips Research, The Netherlands (differential cryptographic analysis)

- Dalhousie University, Canada (N-gram extraction)

- Florida State University, USA (construction of Voronoi diagrams)

- Montefiore Institute, Belgium (big sparse matrices)

- University of British Columbia, Canada (topology analysis of large networks)

- Bayes Forecast, Spain (statistics and time series analysis)

- Indian Institute of Science in Bangalore, India (suffix array construction)

- Rensselaer Polytechnic University, USA (suffix array construction)

- Institut français du pèrole, France (analysis of seismic files)

- Northumbria University, UK (search trees)

---

[5] `http://www.dwheeler.com/sloccount/`

- University of Trento, Italy (text compression)

- Norwegian University of Science and Technology in Trondheim, Norway (suffix array construction)

1.9 Related Work

TPIE [Ven94, APV02] was the first large software project implementing I/O-efficient algorithms and data structures. The library provides implementations of I/O efficient sorting, merging, matrix operations, many (geometric) search data structures (B^+-tree, persistent B^+-tree, R-tree, K-D-B-tree, KD-tree, Bkd-tree) and the logarithmic method. The work on the TPIE project is in progress.

LEDA-SM [CM99] external memory library was designed as an extension to the LEDA library [MN99] for handling large data sets. The library offers implementations of I/O-efficient sorting, external memory stack, queue, radix heap, array heap, buffer tree, array, B^+-tree, string, suffix array, matrices, static graph, and some simple graph algorithms. However, the data structures and algorithms cannot handle more than 2^{31} elements. The development of LEDA-SM has been stopped. LEDA releases later than the version 4.2 are not supported by the last LEDA-SM version 1.3. To experiment with LEDA-SM we have used the **g++** version 2.95, since it it is the most recent compiler supported by LEDA-SM 1.3.

LEDA-SM and TPIE libraries currently only offer single disk external memory algorithms and data structures. They are not designed to explicitly support an overlapping between I/O and computation. The overlapping largely relies on the operating system that caches and prefetches data according to a general purpose policy, which cannot be as efficient as the explicit approach. Furthermore, on most of the operating systems, the overlapping based on the system cache requires additional copies of the data, which leads to computational and internal memory overhead.

The list of algorithms and data structures available in TPIE, LEDA-SM and STXXL libraries is shown in Table 1.1.

Database engines use I/O-efficient search trees and sorting to execute SQL queries, evaluating huge sets of table records. The idea of pipelined execution of the algorithms which process large data sets not fitting into the main memory is well known in relational database management systems [SKS01]. The pipelined execution strategy allows one to execute a database query with

Table 1.1: Algorithms and data structures of the external memory libraries.

Function	TPIE	LEDA-SM	STXXL
sorting	√	√	√
stack	√	√	√
queue	√	√	√
deque	—	—	√
array/vector	—	√	√
matrix operations	√	√	—
suffix array	—	√	√(extension)
search trees	B^+-tree, K-D-B-tree persist. B^+-tree R-tree, KD-tree Bkd-tree	B^+-tree buffer tree	B^+-tree
priority queue	—	array heap radix heap	sequence heap
pipelined algorithms	—	—	√

a minimum number of external memory accesses, to save memory space to store intermediate results, and to obtain the first result as soon as possible.

The design framework FG [DC05] is a programming environment for parallel programs running on clusters. In this framework, parallel programs are split into series of asynchronous stages which are executed in the pipelined fashion with the help of multithreading. The pipelined execution allows to mitigate disk latency of external data accesses and communication network latency of remote data accesses. I/O and communication can be automatically overlapped with computation stages by the scheduler of FG environment.

Berkeley DB [OBS00] is recognized as the best open source external memory B^+-tree implementation. It has a dual license and is not free for industry. Berkeley DB has very large user base, among those are amazon.com, Google and Motorola. Many free open source programs use Berkeley DB as their data storage backend (e.g. MySQL data base system).

There are several libraries for advanced models of computation which follow the interface of STL. The Standard Template Adaptive Parallel Library (STAPL) is a parallel library designed as a superset of the STL. It is sequentially consistent for functions with the same name and performs on uni- or multi-processor systems that utilize shared or distributed memory [AJR+01].

MCSTL (Multi-Core Standard Template Library) project [Sin06] was started in 2006 at the University of Karlsruhe. The library is an implementation of the STL which uses multiple processors and multiple cores of a processor with shared memory. It already has implementations of parallel sorting, merging, random permutation, searching, scanning. MCSTL is currently being used to parallelize the internal work of STXXL external memory sorting.

There is a number of libraries which provide *persistent* containers [Unia, Unib, GND99, Nel98, Kni, SKW92]. Persistent STL-compatible containers are implemented in [Ste98, Gsc01]. These containers can keep (some of) the elements in external memory transparently to the user. In contrast to STXXL, these libraries do not guarantee the *I/O-efficiency* of the containers, e.g. the PSTL [Gsc01] library implements search trees as I/O-inefficient red-black trees.

The content of this book is partially based on our contributions which have been already published in a number of refereed conference and journal papers. The design rational of STXXL has been investigated in [DKS05a]. The extended version of this paper has appeared as a technical report [DKS05b]. The results on engineering algorithms for large *graphs* have been published in [DSSS04] (minimum spanning forests) and in [ADM06] (breadth first search). I/O-efficient algorithms for construction of suffix arrays are the subject of the paper [DMKS05]. An extended version will appear as a journal publication [DKMS06].

1.10 Outline

This book is organized as follows.

Chapter 2 considers hardware architectures for experimenting with parallel disk algorithms. We overview the possible bandwidth bottlenecks in systems with a large number of disks. We build a very cheap system which supports the full bandwidth of eight hard disks (375 MByte/s). The experience, obtained during the construction of this machine has helped us to build and configure other more powerful systems for our experiments, mentioned in Chapter 2. We believe that this knowledge will find further application.

The *main contribution* of the book, the STXXL library, is presented in Chapter 3. We introduce the library design including its layers, explaining design decisions taken in the development. We show how portability is provided by moving the operating system issues to a separate layer and explain how the PDM model is emulated using files on independent parallel disks. The design of external memory data structures implementing the STL interface is discussed. We compare the performance of our containers with the performance of data structures of LEDA-SM, TPIE and Berkeley DB using various benchmarks. Examples of the compatibility and combined usage of STL algorithms and STXXL containers will be demonstrated. In Section 3.5, we engineer a parallel disk sorting that has almost perfect overlap of I/O and computation and has an I/O cost approaching the lower bound. Previous algorithms have either a suboptimal I/O volume or cannot guarantee that I/O and computation can always be overlapped. We compare its performance with the performance of LEDA-SM and TPIE sorters. Furthermore, we introduce the idea of external algorithm pipelining in the context of an external memory software library and show how pipelining is implemented in the STXXL Streaming layer via objects with an iterator-like interface. A small example demonstrates the I/O savings gained by the use of pipelining.

STXXL has been successfully applied in implementation projects that studied various I/O-efficient algorithms from the practical point of view (Chapters 4 and 5). The fast algorithmic components of the STXXL library gave the implementations an opportunity to solve problems of very large sizes on a low-cost hardware in record time.

The chapter starts with a small benchmark (maximal independent set computation), which we implement using TPIE, LEDA-SM and STXXL. We run these implementations to compare the performance of some components of the library on a real graph application.

Furthermore, we investigate the feasibility of minimal spanning forest computation in external memory. Due to the STXXL, our external memory MSF implementation is only 2–5 times slower than a good internal algorithm with sufficient memory space. We modify the minimum spanning forest algorithm to derive a fast I/O-efficient algorithm for computing connected components and/or spanning forests.

The next study, investigating the feasibility of external memory breadth-first search (BFS), is surveyed in Section 4.5. The study compares two implementations of the external memory BFS algorithms [MR99, MM02]. The implementations heavily use STXXL pipelining and can compute BFS decompositions for very large real and synthetic graphs within hours on a modest PC.

In Section 4.6 we design a practical algorithm that lists and counts all triangles in huge graphs. The triangle information is used to analyze the properties of (social) networks, like "clusterness" and transitivity. With the help of STXXL we find all triangles of a huge web crawl graph in a few hours.

The last graph application we have designed in this book is coloring (Sec-

1.10. OUTLINE

tion 4.7). External memory coloring can be used to compute a schedule for executing a huge number of parallel jobs using only a single computer. Our main contributions are simple and fast heuristics for general graphs. One of these heuristics — Batched Smallest-Degree-Last — turns out to be a 7-coloring algorithm for planar graphs performing only $\mathcal{O}(\text{sort}(n))$ I/Os, where n is the number of nodes in the graph. Our work is the first experimental study of algorithms that can color huge graphs exceeding the size of the main memory. We run our implementations on several architectures and on various random and real-world data sets.

In Chapter 5 we present STXXL-pipelined implementations of suffix array construction algorithms. We compare the performance of numerous algorithms and their variants on many huge random and real-world text instances. We precisely compute the I/O costs of the implemented algorithms using pipelined data flow graphs. We also analyze the I/O volume of a generalized difference cover algorithm. An implementation of doubling algorithm, which uses the Oracle XE data base engine, has been investigated and compared with an STXXL implementation. The bottom line of the experiments is that we can construct suffix arrays for 4 billion characters overnight on a low cost PC. This achievement is partially due to the high performance of the STXXL.

Chapter 6 ports some graph-related algorithms designed originally for internal memory and parallel computers to *external memory*. We make them run I/O-efficiently exchanging their underlying subprocedures by our own and already existing I/O-efficient versions.

The common notations used in this book are summarized in Appendix A.

Chapter 2

Building Experimental Parallel Disk Systems

Experiments with *single* disk external memory algorithms do not require a special hardware to be run on. All off-the-shelf desktop computers are equipped with at least one hard disk which stores an operating system and keeps the working space of applications. Such systems are readily fit for experimenting with I/O-efficient algorithms designed for a single disk.

The I/O bandwidth of a modern hard disk is limited to 70–80 MB/s, the bandwidth of transfers between memory and CPU is much higher: several *gigabytes* per second. The relatively low disk bandwidth can be the bottleneck of an external memory algorithm. This bottleneck can be mitigated or even eliminated when by using a RAID.

The RAID (redundant array of independent disks; originally redundant array of inexpensive disks) array level 0 (RAID-0 for short) is a way of storing data distributed over multiple disks [CLG+94]. Usually, all disks of a RAID are identical. A RAID acts as a single logical disk to the operating system. RAID-0 employs the technique of striping, which involves partitioning each drive's storage space into units of size c bytes (usually a power of two, ranging from 4 KBytes to 128 KBytes). Each chunk of size $s = D \times c$ of the RAID logical space is called *stripe*, where D is the number of disks in the RAID. Stripes are mapped in an interleaved fashion to the disks: logical RAID disk position x is mapped to position $c\lfloor \frac{x}{s} \rfloor + (x \bmod c)$ on disk $\lfloor \frac{x \bmod s}{c} \rfloor$ (see Figure 2.1). This mapping can be performed by a special device controller, called RAID-controller, or via software by the RAID emulation driver (e.g. the Linux software RAID driver). If an application reads a block from RAID-0 or writes a block to RAID-0 and the size of the block is a (big) multiple of

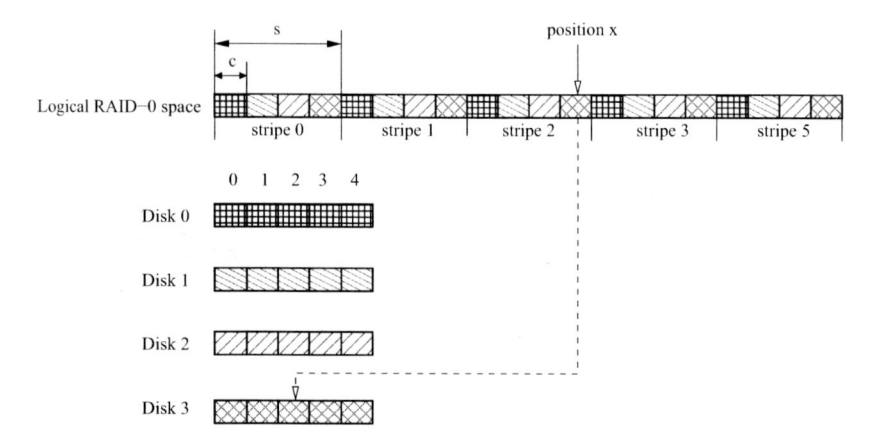

Figure 2.1: RAID-0 on four disks with five stripes

the stripe size s, then the bandwidth of this transfer should (theoretically) approach $D \times BW$ bytes per second, where BW is the maximal bandwidth of the single disk. However, in practice, the real bandwidth can be less than $D \times BW$ because of the overheads and inefficiencies of hardware RAID boards and software RAID drivers.

Despite that, the bandwidth-bound single disk I/O-efficient algorithms can benefit from the increase of the bandwidth. For example, adding the second disk can almost halve the total running time of an application. This significantly improves the performance/cost ratio of the system, since the price of a fast modern disk is much less than the total price of the system.

Many *parallel disk* external memory algorithms need *independent* access to the disks to be optimal [DS03]. In some situations, running such algorithms on a RAID-0 would require the reduction of the physical block size by factor D, which increases the number of I/Os by a constant factor, and thus increases the seek time. In general, the simple RAID-0 striping cannot guarantee speed-up D when using D disks for external memory parallel disk algorithms. The speedup can only be achieved using the disks independently. Building such a system which enables independent access to many disks with high speed was one of the goals of this work. This system would enable real experimentation with the parallel disk I/O-efficient algorithms.

The practical performance of algorithms designed for PDM (Section 1.1) on real systems with many disks has been studied for the first time in this book, to the best of the authors's knowledge. All previous studies have *simulated* the parallel disks in software.

2.1 Hardware Disk Interfaces

Currently, there are two types of hardware interfaces which connect hard disks with computers: IDE (Integrated Drive Electronics) and SCSI (Small Computer Systems Interface). Several versions of the IDE interface were standardized under the name ATA (Advanced Technology Attachment). The original ATA hard disks use 40 or 80 wire cables (parallel ATA). A newer version of the ATA standard enables transferring the information over a cable with the same speed or faster using only a few wires (*serial* ATA = SATA). The parallel ATA (PATA) permits to assign two disks to the same channel, which can result in less than expected parallel disk performance, even if the ATA bus rate is higher than the total maximum bandwidth of the two disks. The reason is that the original IDE/ATA interface protocol was not designed for concurrent access to the disks, the disks "must take turns". A parallel ATA channel permits transfer rates up to 133 MByte/s.

Serial ATA has some crucial differences to parallel ATA that improve performance. Since the cost of an additional channel controller on a circuit is small, and a little space is required for cables and cable headers, SATA specifies only a single device per channel to be used. Another feature is the hardware support of disk request queuing (native command queuing): A hard disk can receive more than one I/O request at a time and decide on its own in which order the requests will be served. This allows a lot of optimizations, provided the knowledge about the seek times and rotational position. A SATA channel can sustain a bandwidth up to 150 or 300 MByte/s depending on the used standard.

Low-cost or middle range PCs have an on-board controller with at least two ATA or four SATA channels. They can theoretically support two/four disks at full speed (the maximum sustained transfer rate of modern disks is 60–80 MB/s). The logic of an IDE controller is kept simple to reduce the price of hardware, therefore many low level details of the ATA protocol are implemented in software and executed by the main CPU.

SCSI standard has been initially developed to support many disks which can be accessed concurrently at high speed. One Ultra320 SCSI (U320) channel can connect up to 15 disks and has a bandwidth of 320 MB/s. The SCSI bus controller is capable of controlling the hard disk drives without any work by the CPU. Native support of command queuing already existed in very early versions of the SCSI standard. Also, all drives on a SCSI channel are able to operate at the same time due to the advanced protocol logic, implemented in hardware. Therefore one U320 channel can support up to four modern disks at almost full speed (60–80 MByte/s).

The SCSI interface has apparent advantages over IDE/ATA one, however, the price of SCSI hardware (controllers and hard disk drives) is *3–8 times* higher than the price of comparable IDE/ATA equipment. We have tried to find out whether it is possible to build an *affordable* high performance multi disk system using IDE/ATA technology.

2.2 Busses, Controllers, Chipsets

As above mentioned, an *ordinary PC* can already support four hard disks connected to the on-board PATA controller. However, in order to avoid bottlenecks and channel contention, it is better to have only one disk per IDE channel. Thus, only two ATA drives can be supported at full speed.

In order to support more disks one has to use more controllers, which are installed in a PCI bus slot of the PC. There are several variants of PCI busses, the older version of the bus protocol can transfer 32 bits in a cycle and has a cycle frequency of 33 MHz, giving the maximum transfer rate of 133 MByte/s. Theoretically, this would be enough for only two disks with a transfer rate of 66 MByte/s (we take 66 MByte/s as the bandwidth of one disk in calculations), but in practice, due to the bus control overhead, the sustained bandwidth could be less. Cheap desktop systems usually have only one 32bit/33MHz bus. The chipset schema of such a system is presented in Figure 2.2. This system can support four (S)ATA disks at most at full speed: two disks connect to the onboard Serial ATA controller, the other two require a PCI bus (S)ATA controller. The Intel hub connection between the memory controller hub (MCH) and the I/O controller hub (ICH) chips is fast enough to sustain the bandwidth of four disks.

Some chipsets/mainboards do include an additional hardware RAID controller with two (S)ATA channels. The Intel 875P chipset has such an option (see Figure 2.2). The RAID controller could be configured for independent access to the disks, i.e. RAID is switched off. This means that this cheap system can already support up to *six* (S)ATA disks without bottlenecks in the busses.

Newer PCI standards allow larger bus widths of 64 bits and/or higher cycle frequencies 66, 100 or 133 MHz. A 64bit/133MHz PCI controller can transfer

2.2. BUSSES, CONTROLLERS, CHIPSETS 23

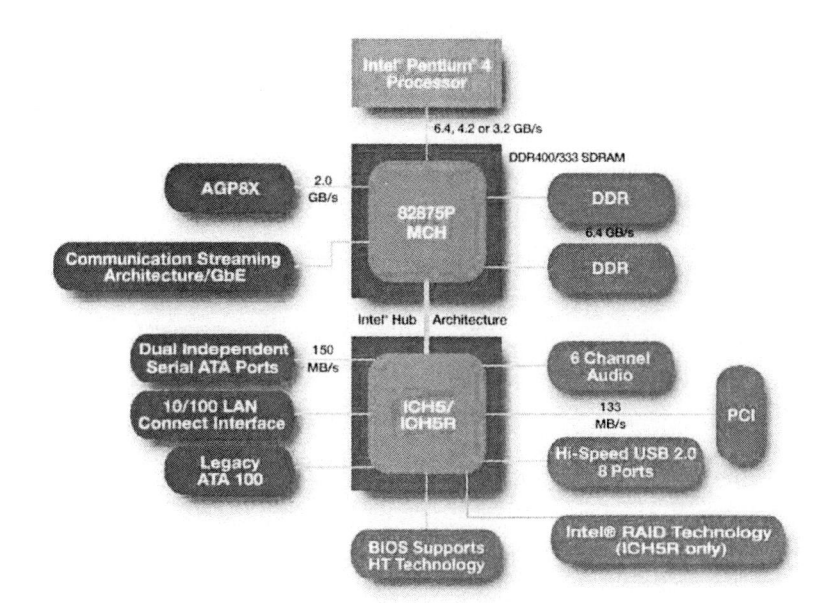

Figure 2.2: The schema of Intel 875P chipset [Int].

at a speed of 533 MB/s, this bandwidth is enough for eight hard disk drives with a bandwidth of 66 MB/s. SATA controllers with many ports have been released *recently*: The Promise SATAII150 SX8 has eight SATA ports, each operating at a speed up to 150 MB/s. The manufacturer reports more than 500 MB/s sustained throughput for sequential access for the controller.

Another approach would be to connect conventional two-port ATA controllers to several independent PCI busses. This was the only alternative for us, since multiport serial ATA controllers appeared only in 2003. An example of the chipset that has many PCI busses is the Intel E7500 chipset, as shown in Figure 2.3. This chipset is the basis of the SUPER P4DP6 dual Xeon processor motherboard. The chipset has two 133 MHz 64-bit PCI busses, one 100 MHz 64-bit PCI bus, and one 66 MHz 64-bit PCI bus. The PCI busses 1, 2 and 3 have only one slot each for a controller, bus 4 has three slots. Affordable ATA controllers are 32-bit ones and work at a 66 MHz bus frequency (for example the Promise Ultra133 TX2). This means that the PCI busses have to work in 32-bit 66 MHz mode also. This mode can achieve at most 266 MB/s, which is equivalent to four disk drives with a maximum bandwidth of 66 MB/s. In total, a P4DP6 motherboard can support up to 12 hard disks (bandwidth 66 MB/s): two disks are connected to the onboard ATA controller, three ATA controllers are inserted into the PCI busses 1–3, two controllers are inserted into PCI bus 4, each controller supports two disks. The total maximum rate of disks at PCI bus 3 and 4 can be at most $66 \cdot 6 = 400$ MB/s which is less than the bandwidth of the connection between the memory controller hub (MCH) and the PCI 64-bit hub (1 GB/s). The total maximum bandwidth of all 12 disks is about 800 MB/s, which is less than the throughput of the 3.2 GB/s memory channel. The bandwidth constraints in all bus connections are satisfied, this means that at least from *a hardware point of view*, the 12 hard disks can work at full speed.

2.3 Our First System

We built an experimental parallel disk system on the basis of the SUPER P4DP6 mainboard in summer 2002. The system had nine IBM disks (120 GXP series), one system disk and eight disks for external memory experiments. The maximum bandwidth of one disk is 48 MB/s. The maximum measured sustained throughput of the eight disks was 375 MB/s in sequential reading. When building the machine, we had to solve another engineering problem: the cabling. The original parallel ATA cables are about 6 cm wide, it is impossible to have 12 cables connecting 12 disks, in the cramped space

2.3. OUR FIRST SYSTEM

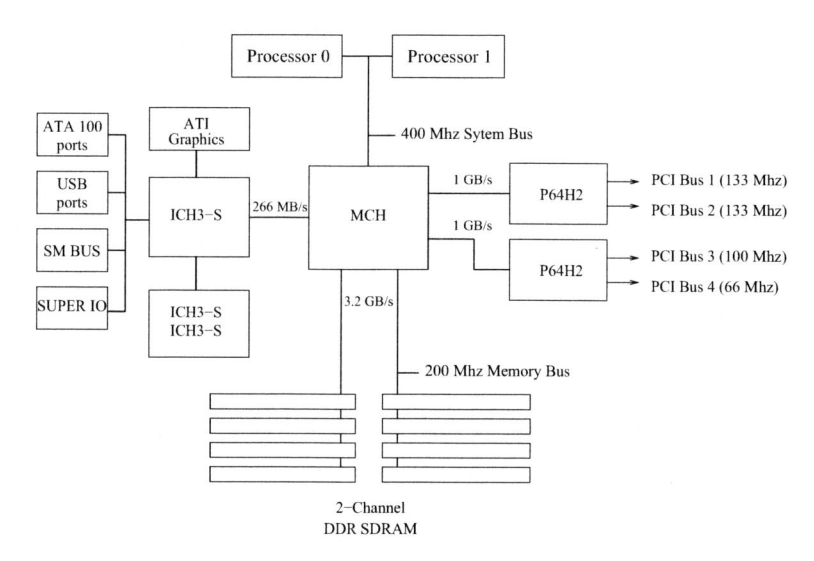

Figure 2.3: The schema of the Intel E7500 chipset [Int].

of a PC case. Instead, we used round cables which are much more robust and only 1 cm in diameter. The usage of this type of cable also improved the airflow and thus the temperature conditions inside the case. If such a system would be set up today we would choose the *serial* ATA standard since it has much thinner cables.

This high performance system cost only about 3000 Euro in 2002. The list with detailed information about the system components is presented in Table 2.1. The photograph of the computer is shown in Figure 2.4.

Table 2.1: Hardware components of our experimental computer.

Item	#	Euro/Item
Motherboard SUPER P4DP6	1	400
Xeon 2.0 GHz processor	2	400
IBM IC35L080AVVA07 80 GB disk	9	100
Promise Ultra133 TX2 parallel ATA controller	5	35
512 MB DDR2 memory	2	200
Case/chassis	1	400

Figure 2.4: Our multidisk experimental computer.

2.4 Other Systems

Guided by the experience gathered while constructing the Xeon machine in Section 2.3, we have recently built new multidisk machines, using modern hardware components. These machines are specified in Table 2.2 as *SCSIOpteron* and *SATAOpteron*. MPIXeon is the system from Section 2.3. We will refer to these systems in experimental sections throughout this book.

2.5 File System Issues

In order to achieve the best I/O-performance one should carefully choose the file system to use. One of the oldest and most favorite Linux file systems is ext2. Its extension ext3 has added the support of file operation journaling.

The ext2/ext3 file systems use linear bitmap structures for tracking free and allocated blocks. Finding regions of contiguous space in such bitmaps in large files is not efficient. For external memory algorithms this might become a significant bottleneck in the performance. The XFS file system solves this problem using a B^+−tree to index disk regions. Besides that, XFS *preallocates* the free space needed for a file to avoid file system fragmentation. Performance is increased as the contents of a file are not distributed all over the file system.

2.5. FILE SYSTEM ISSUES

Table 2.2: Specifications of our multidisk disk systems.

Code name	MPIXeon	SCSIOpteron	SATAOpteron
Processor	2×Xeon 2.0GHz	4×Opteron 1.8GHz	Dual-Core Opteron 2.0GHz
Main memory	1 GByte	8 GBytes	4 GBytes
Exp. disks	8	10	4
Disk interface	PATA	SCSI	SATA
Number of controllers	6	3	1
Disk manufacturer	IBM	Seagate	Seagate
Disk RPM	7200	15000	7200
Single disk capacity	80 GBytes	70 GBytes	250 GBytes
Measured max. bandwidth of a disk	48 MByte/s	75 MByte/s	79 MByte/s
Total max. bandwidth achieved	375 MByte/s	640 MByte/s	214 MB/s
Approx. price (year)	3000 EURO (2002)	15000 EURO (2005)	3500 EURO (2006)

In most of our experiments we have used the XFS file system because of its good performance and scalability.

Chapter 3

The STXXL Library

The material covered in this chapter has been published partially in [DKS05a, DKS05b, DS03].

3.1 STXXL Design

STXXL is a layered library consisting of three layers (see Figure 3.1). The lowest layer, the Asynchronous I/O primitives layer (AIO layer), abstracts away the details of how asynchronous I/O is performed on a particular operating system. Other existing external memory algorithm libraries only rely on synchronous I/O APIs [CM99] or allow reading ahead sequences stored in a file using the POSIX asynchronous I/O API [ABH+03]. These libraries also rely on uncontrolled operating system I/O caching and buffering in order to overlap I/O and computation in some way. However, this approach has significant performance penalties for accesses without locality. Unfortunately, the asynchronous I/O APIs are very different for different operating systems (e.g. POSIX AIO and Win32 Overlapped I/O). Therefore, we have introduced the AIO layer to make porting STXXL easy. Porting the whole library to a different platform requires only reimplementing the AIO layer using native file access methods and/or native multithreading mechanisms.

STXXL already has several implementations of the AIO layer which use different file access methods under POSIX/UNIX and Windows systems (see Table 3.1). Porting STXXL to Windows took only a few days. The main effort was to write the AIO layer using native Windows calls. Rewriting the thread-related code was easy provided the Boost thread library; its interfaces are similar to POSIX threads. There were little header file and compiler-specific incompatibilities; those were solved by conditional compilation using

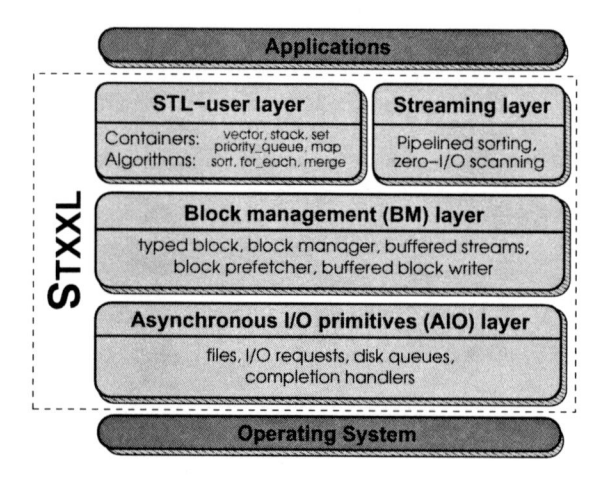

Figure 3.1: Structure of STXXL

the C++ preprocessor. The POSIX version of STXXL had run immediately on the all listed operating systems after changing some Linux-specific header file includes to more common POSIX headers.

The Block Management layer (BM layer) provides a programming interface emulating the *parallel* disk model. The BM layer provides an abstraction for a fundamental concept in the external memory algorithm design — a block of elements. The block manager implements block allocation/deallocation, allowing several block-to-disk assignment strategies: striping, randomized striping, randomized cycling, etc. The block management layer provides an implementation of parallel disk buffered writing [HSV01], optimal prefetching [HSV01], and block caching. The implementations are fully asynchronous

Table 3.1: Supported operating systems.

STXXL version	POSIX	MS Visual C++
OS	Linux, Cygwin, SunOS, Solaris, FreeBSD, NetBSD, MacOS	Windows 2000, Windows XP
Compiler	g++ 3.3+	MS VC++ 7.1+
Dependencies	Posix Threads	Boost library

3.1. STXXL DESIGN

and designed to explicitly support overlapping between I/O and computation.

The top of STXXL consists of two modules. The STL-user layer provides external memory sorting, external memory stack, external memory priority queue, etc. which have (almost) the same interfaces (including syntax and semantics) as their STL counterparts. The Streaming layer provides efficient support for *pipelining* external memory algorithms. Many external memory algorithms, implemented using this layer, can save a factor of 2–3 in I/Os. For example, the algorithms for external memory suffix array construction implemented with this module [DMKS05] require only 1/3 of the number of I/Os which must be performed by implementations that use conventional data structures and algorithms (either from STXXL STL-user layer, LEDA-SM, or TPIE). The win is due to an efficient interface that couples the input and the output of the algorithm–components (scans, sorts, etc.). The output from an algorithm is directly fed into another algorithm as input, without needing to store it on the disk in-between. This generic pipelining interface is the first of this kind for external memory algorithms.

3.2 AIO Layer

The purpose of the AIO layer is to provide a unified approach to asynchronous I/O. The layer hides details of native asynchronous I/O interfaces of an operating system. Studying the patterns of I/O accesses of external memory algorithms and data structures, we have identified the following functionality that should be provided by the AIO layer:

- To issue read and write requests without having to wait for them to be completed.

- To wait for the completion of a subset of issued I/O requests.

- To wait for the completion of at least one request from a subset of issued I/O requests.

- To poll the completion status of any I/O request.

- To assign a callback function to an I/O request which is called upon I/O completion (asynchronous notification of completion status), with the ability to co-relate callback events with the issued I/O requests.

The AIO layer exposes two user objects: `file` and `request_ptr`. Together with the I/O waiting functions `wait_all`, `wait_any`, and `poll_any` they provide the functionality mentioned above. Using a `file` object, the user can submit asynchronous read and asynchronous write requests (methods `file::aread` and `file::awrite`). These methods return a `request_ptr` object which is used to track the status of the issued request. The AIO layer functions `wait_all`, `wait_any`, and `poll_any` facilitate tracking a set of `request_ptr`s. The last parameter of the methods `file::aread` and `file::awrite` is a reference to a callback function object (callback functor). The functor's `operator()(request_ptr )` method is called when the I/O request is completed.

As a part of the AIO layer, the STXXL library provides various I/O performance counters (`stats` class). The class counts the number and the duration of the performed I/O operations as well as the transferred volume. Read and write operations are counted separately. STXXL also measures the time spent by the processing thread(s) waiting for the completions of I/Os (I/O wait time). This metric helps to evaluate the degree and the impact of overlapping between I/O and computation in an application.

Listing 3.1 shows a simple example of how to use AIO objects to perform asynchronous I/O. All STXXL library objects are defined in the namespace

3.2. AIO LAYER

stxxl. For convenience, in Line 1 we bring all names from the STXXL namespace to the local scope. In Line 9 a file object `myfile` is constructed. `syscall_file` is an implementation of the STXXL file interface which uses UNIX/POSIX `read` and `write` system calls to perform I/O. The file named "storage" in the current directory is opened in read-only mode. In Line 11 an asynchronous read of the 1 MB region of the file starting at position 0 is issued. The data will be read into the array `mybuffer`. When the read operation is completed, `my_handler::operator()` will be called with a pointer to the completed request. The execution stops at Line 13 waiting for the completion of the issued read operation. Note that the work done in the function `do_something1()` is overlapped with reading. When the I/O is finished, one can process the read buffer (Line 14) and free it (Line 15).

Listing 3.1: Example of how to program with the AIO layer.

```
1  using namespace stxxl;
2  struct my_handler { // I/O completion handler
3      void operator () (request_ptr ptr) {
4          std::cout << "Request '"<< *ptr <<"' completed."
5              <<std::endl;
6      }
7  };
8  char * mybuffer = new char[1024*1024]; // allocate 1MB buffer
9  syscall_file myfile("./storage", file::RDONLY );
10 request_ptr myreq = myfile.aread(mybuffer, 0,
11     1024*1024,my_handler());
12 do_something1(); //do_something1() is overlapped with reading
13 myreq->wait();   //wait for read completion
14 do_something2(mybuffer);// process the read buffer
15 delete [] mybuffer; // free the buffer
```

3.2.1 AIO Layer Implementations

There are several implementation strategies for the STXXL AIO layer. Some asynchronous I/O related APIs (and underlying libraries implementing them) already exist. The most well known framework is POSIX AIO, which has an implementation on almost every UNIX/POSIX system. Its disadvantage is that it has only limited support for I/O completion event mechanism [1]. The Linux AIO kernel side implementation [2] of POSIX AIO does not have this deficit, but is not portable since it works under Linux only.

---

[1] The Linux `glibc` implementation of POSIX AIO also has a performance drawback. It launches one user thread for each I/O operation. STXXL starts one thread for each disk during the library initialization, avoiding the thread start-up overhead for each I/O.

[2] http://freshmeat.net/projects/linux-aio/

The STXXL AIO layer follows a different approach. It does not rely on any asynchronous I/O API. Instead we use synchronous I/O calls running asynchronously in separate threads. For each file there is one read and one write request queue and one thread. The main thread posts requests (invoking `file::aread` and `file::awrite` methods) to the file queues. The thread associated with the file executes the requests in FIFO order. This approach is very flexible and it does not suffer from limitations of native asynchronous APIs.

Our POSIX implementation of the AIO layer is based on POSIX threads and supports several Unix file access methods: the `syscall` method uses `read` and `write` system calls, the `mmap` method uses memory mapping (`mmap` and `munmap` calls), the `sim_disk` method simulates I/O timings of a hard disk provided a big internal memory. To avoid superfluous copying of data between the user and kernel buffer memory, the `syscall` method has the option to use unbuffered file system access. These file access methods can also be used for raw disk I/O, bypassing the file system. In this case, instead of files, raw *device handles* are open. The `read/write` calls using direct access (`O_DIRECT` option) have shown the best performance under Linux. The disadvantage of the `mmap` call is that programs using this method have less control over I/O: In most operating systems 4 KBytes data pages of a `mmap`ed file region are brought to the main memory "lazily", only when they are accessed for the first time. This means if one `mmap`s a 100 KBytes block and touches only the first and the last element of the block then *two* I/Os are issued by the operating system. This will slow down many I/O-efficient algorithms, since for modern disks the seek time is much longer than the reading of 100 KBytes of contiguous data.

The POSIX implementation does not need to be ported to other UNIX compatible systems, since POSIX threads is the standard threading API on all POSIX-compatible operating systems.

Our Windows implementation is based on Boost threads, whose interfaces are very similar to POSIX threads.

AIO file and request implementation classes are derived from the generic `file` and `request` interface classes with C++ pure virtual functions. These functions are specialized for each access method in implementation classes to define the read, write, wait for I/O completion and other operations. The desired access method implementation for a file is chosen dynamically at running time. One can add the support of an additional access method (e.g. for a DAFS distributed filesystem) just providing classes implementing the `file` and `request` interfaces. We have decided to use the virtual function mechanism in the AIO layer because this mechanism is very flexible and *will not sacrifice* the performance of the library, since the virtual functions of the AIO layer need to be called only once per *large* chunk of data (i.e. B bytes). The inefficiencies of C++ virtual functions are explained in Section 1.5. Similar to STL, the higher layers of STXXL do not rely on run-time polymorphism with virtual functions to avoid the high per–element penalties.

3.3 BM Layer

As already mentioned above, the BM layer provides an implementation of the central concept in I/O efficient algorithms and data structures: a block of elements (`typed_block` object). Besides, it includes a toolbox for allocating, deallocating, buffered writing, prefetching, and caching of blocks. The external memory manager (object `block_manager`) is responsible for allocating and deallocating external memory space on disks. The manager supports four parallel disk allocation strategies: simple striping, fully randomized, simple randomized [BGV97], and randomized cycling [VH01].

The BM layer also delivers a set of helper classes that efficiently implement frequently used sequential patterns of interaction with the (parallel disk) external memory. The optimal parallel disk queued writing [HSV01] is implemented in the `buffered_writer` class. The class operates on blocks. The `buf_ostream` class is built on top of `buffered_writer` and has a high level interface, similar to the interface of STL output iterators. Analogously, the classes `block_prefetcher` and `buf_istream` contain an implementation of an optimal parallel disk *prefetching* algorithm [HSV01]. The helper objects of the BM layer support overlapping between I/O and computation, which means that they are able to perform I/O in the background, while the user thread is doing useful computations.

The BM layer views external memory as a set of large AIO files — one for each disk. We will refer to these files as *disks*. The other approach would be to map a related subset of blocks (e.g. those belonging to the same data structure) to a separate file. This approach has some performance problems. One of them is that since those (numerous) files are created dynamically, during the run of the program, the file system allocates the disk space on demand, that might in turn introduce severe disk space fragmentation. Therefore we have chosen the "one-large-file-per-disk" approach as our major scheme. However, the design of our library does not forbid data structures to store their content in separate user data files (e.g., as an option, `stxxl::vector` can be mapped to a user file, see Section 3.4).

The external memory manager (object `block_manager`) is responsible for allocating and deallocating external memory space on the disks. The `block_manager` reads information about available disks from the STXXL configuration file. This file contains the location of each disk file, the sizes of the disks, and the file access methods for each disk. When allocating a bunch of blocks, a programmer can specify how the blocks will be assigned to disks, passing an allocation strategy function object. The `block_manager` implements the "first-fit" allocation heuristic [BS03]. When an application

3.3. BM LAYER

requests several blocks from a disk, the manager tries to allocate the blocks contiguously. This reduces the bulk access time. On allocation requests, the `block_manager` returns BID objects – Block IDentifiers. An object of the type BID describes the physical location of an allocated block, including the disk and offset of a region of storage on disk. One can load or store the data that resides at the location given by the BID using asynchronous `read` and `write` methods of a `typed_block` object.

The full signature of the STXXL "block of elements" class is `typed_block<RawSize,T,NRef,InfoType>`. The C++ template parameter RawSize defines the total size of the block in bytes. Since block size is not a single global constant in STXXL, a programmer can simultaneously operate with several block types having different blocks sizes. Such flexibility is often required for good performance. For example, B^+-tree leaves might have a size different from the size of the internal nodes. We have made the block size a template parameter and not a member variable for the sake of efficiency. The values of the template parameters are known to the compiler, therefore for the power of two values (a very common choice) it can replace many arithmetic operations, like divisions and multiplications, by more efficient *binary shifts*. A critical requirement for many external memory data structures is that a block must be able to store links to other blocks. An STXXL block can store NRef objects of type BID. Additionally, one can equip a block with a field of the type `InfoType`, that can hold some per-block information. Block elements of type T can easily be accessed by the array `operator []` and via random access iterators. The maximum number of elements available a block depends on the number of links and the sizes of T, `InfoType` and BID types. contains a This number is accessible as `typed_block<...>::size`.

In Listing 3.2, we give an example of how to program block I/O using objects of the BM layer. In Line 2 we define the type of block: its size is one megabyte and the type of elements is `double`. The pointer to the only instance of the singleton object `block_manager` is obtained in Line 5. Line 7 asks the block manager to allocate 32 blocks in external memory. The `new_blocks` call writes the allocated BIDs to the output iterator, given by the last parameter. The `std::back_inserter` iterator adapter will insert the output BIDs at the end of the array `bids`. The manager assigns blocks to disks in a round-robin fashion as the `striping()` strategy suggests. Line 8 allocates 32 internal memory blocks. The internal memory allocator `new_alloc<block_type>` of STXXL allocates blocks on a virtual memory page boundary, which is a requirement for unbuffered file access. Along lines 9–11 the elements of blocks are filled with some values. Then, the blocks are submitted for writing (lines 12–13). The request objects are stored in an `std::vector` for

Listing 3.2: Example of how to program using the BM layer.

```
using namespace stxxl;
typedef typed_block<1024*1024,double> block_type;
std::vector<block_type::bid_type> bids;//empty array of BIDs
std::vector<request_ptr> requests;
block_manager * bm = block_manager::get_instance ();
bm->new_blocks<block_type>(32,striping(),
    std::back_inserter(bids));
std::vector<block_type,new_alloc<block_type> > blocks(32);
for (int ii = 0; ii < 32; ii++)
    for (int jj=0; jj < block_type::size ; jj++)
        blocks[ii][jj] = some_value(ii,jj);
for (int i = 0; i < 32; i++)
    requests.push_back( blocks[i].write(bids[i]) );
do_something(); // do_something() is overlapped with writing
//wait until all I/Os finish
wait_all(requests.begin(), requests.end());
do_something1(bids.begin(),bids.end());
// deallocate external memory
bm->delete_blocks(bids.begin(), bids.end());
```

the further status tracking. As in the AIO example, I/O is overlapped with computations in the function do_something(). After the completion of all write requests (Line 16) we perform some useful processing with the written data (function do_something1()). Finally we free the external memory space occupied by the 32 blocks (Line 19).

3.4 STL-User Layer

When we started to develop the library we decided to equip our implementations of external memory data structures and algorithms with well known generic interfaces of the Standard Template Library, which is a part of the C++ standard. This choice would shorten the application development times, since the time to learn new interfaces is saved. Porting an internal memory code that relies on STL would also be easy, since interfaces of STL-user layer data structures (containers in the STL terminology) and algorithms have the same syntax and semantics.

We go over the containers currently available in STXXL.

3.4.1 Vector

The most universal STXXL container is `stxxl::vector`. Vector is an array whose size can vary dynamically. The implementation of `stxxl::vector` is similar to the LEDA-SM array [CM99]. The content of a vector is striped block-wise over the disks, using an assignment strategy given as a template parameter. Some of the blocks are cached in a vector cache of fixed size (also a parameter). The replacement of cache blocks is controlled by a specified page-replacement strategy. STXXL has implementations of LRU and random replacement strategies. The user can provide his/her own strategy as well. The STXXL `vector` has STL-compatible Random Access Iterators. One random access costs $\mathcal{O}(1)$ I/Os in the worst case. Sequential scanning of the vector costs $\mathcal{O}(1/DB)$ amortized I/Os per vector element.

3.4.2 Stack

An I/O efficient stack is perhaps the simplest external memory data structure. Four different implementations of a stack are available in STXXL. Some of the implementations (e.g. `stxxl::grow_shrink_stack2`) are optimized to prefetch data ahead and to queue writing, efficiently overlapping I/O and computation. The amortized I/O complexity for **push** and **pop** stack operations is $\mathcal{O}(1/DB)$.

We compare the performance of STXXL stack with performance of LEDA-SM and TPIE stacks in a simple test: we insert records to the stacks and afterwards delete them all. We try 4- and 32-byte records to evaluate different CPU processing overheads. For the experiments we used a 3.00 GHz Pentium 4 processor, 1 GB of main memory and a SATA disk dedicated to the experiments. The measured maximum I/O bandwidth of the hard disk was 72 MB/s for writing and 65 MByte/s for reading. Before the insertion, we allocated a 768 MByte array and filled it with zeros to prevent this memory to be used for file system buffering, which would distort the measurements. This also simulates the memory consumption of other algorithms and data structures used in a real application. The rest of the memory was used for buffer blocks for stacks in the libraries and for operating system buffers in the case of LEDA-SM and TPIE. STXXL has used its own buffer and prefetching mechanism. The block size was set to two MBytes. Preliminary experiments have shown that larger blocks did not help any of the libraries. The LEDA-SM implementation could only be compiled with the g++ compiler version 2.95. STXXL and TPIE implementations have been compiled with g++ 3.3. The compiler optimization level was set to -O3 for both codes.

Figures 3.2–3.5 show the bandwidth achieved in the experiments, which was computed as $n \cdot \text{sizeof(T)}/t$, where n is the number of elements to insert/delete, T is the data type and t is the time to insert/delete all n elements (in seconds). The experiments were conducted on input volumes of 1-8 GBytes. Since we have only registered insignificant variations, the average bandwidths are presented. We considered the following stack implementations (from left to right in Figures 3.2–3.5):

- STXXL grow_shrink_stack2 (GS2) using block pools for asynchronous prefetching and buffering. The name of this stack stems from the access pattern it supports with the best efficiency: An empty stack is first filled with elements up to the maximum number of elements and then all elements are removed one after another. In the first step the implementation is operating in the "grow" mode, using a pool of blocks for buffering the incoming elements. In the second step it is operating in the "shrink" mode, reading ahead some number of blocks (user-defined value) using a prefetch block pool. This type of access (or similar) is frequently used in applications, see e.g. Section 4.3. grow_shrink_stack2 and grow_shrink_stack1 implementations differ in the usage mode of the block pools: the former uses pools, shared between (possibly) several STXXL data structures, the latter has an exclusive access to its own pools.

- STXXL normal_stack is a classical implementation with synchronous reading and writing,

- LEDA-SM stack implementation,

- TPIE stack implementation using the mmap function for disk access,

3.4. STL -USER LAYER

- TPIE stack implementation using standard Unix calls for disk access.

TPIE stack operations on 4-byte elements are CPU-bound as seen in Figures 3.2 and 3.3. STXXL stacks have the best bandwidths and achieve 57 MB/s even for this small record size. GS2 stacks perform better than STXXL normal stacks because of the better overlapping of I/O and computation. The LEDA-SM stack performs significantly better than the TPIE stack as it is probably less CPU-bound, but still its performance is worse than the performance of the STXXL stacks, since it does not use direct I/O and relies on system buffering which incurs superfluous data block copying.

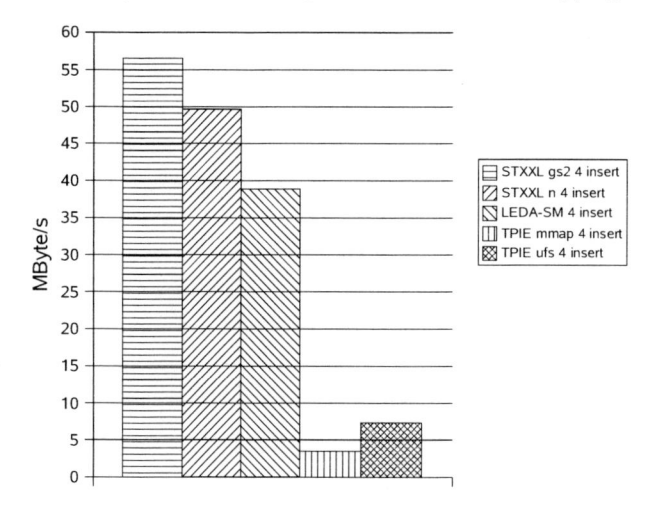

Figure 3.2: Inserting 4-byte elements into the stacks.

Experiments with a larger record size (32 bytes) decrease the per-record CPU overhead (Figures 3.4 and 3.5). This helps TPIE to improve the bandwidth: almost 37 MByte/s could be achieved for writing. This again indicates that the TPIE stack is highly CPU-bound. Note that for our system the `mmap` access method was not the best for TPIE implementations (but the `ufs` access method that is similar to the STXXL `syscall`). The TPIE stack achieves the performance of normal STXXL in inserting. STXXL writes records at 67 MB/s which is 93 % of maximum disk bandwidth.

Figures 3.6 and 3.7 show the results of the above described tests on the SATAOpteron system (Section 2.4) with one GByte of main memory. The measured maximum single disk bandwidths were 79 and 59 MByte/s for writing and reading respectively. We see that almost perfect speedups could

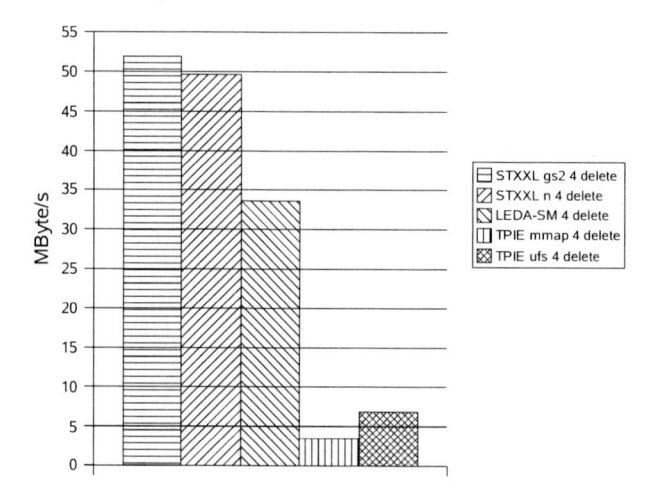

Figure 3.3: Deleting 4-byte elements from the stacks.

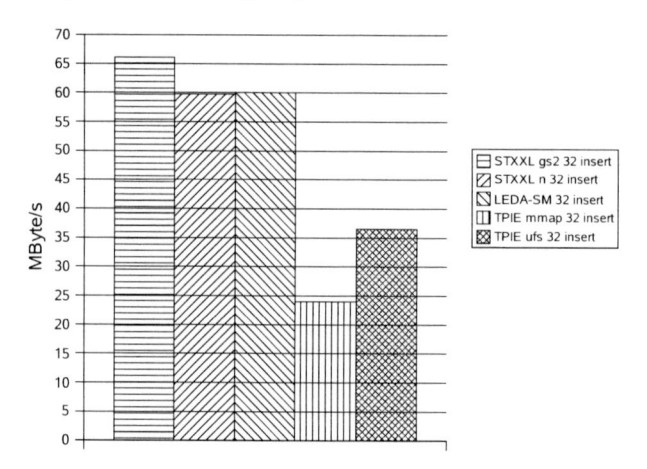

Figure 3.4: Inserting 32-byte elements into the stacks.

be obtained. Only for the deletions running on four disks the speedup was about 3.7.

The stack benchmarks underline the advantages of the STXXL library, which contribute to the leadership in the performance:

- low CPU overhead,

3.4. STL -USER LAYER

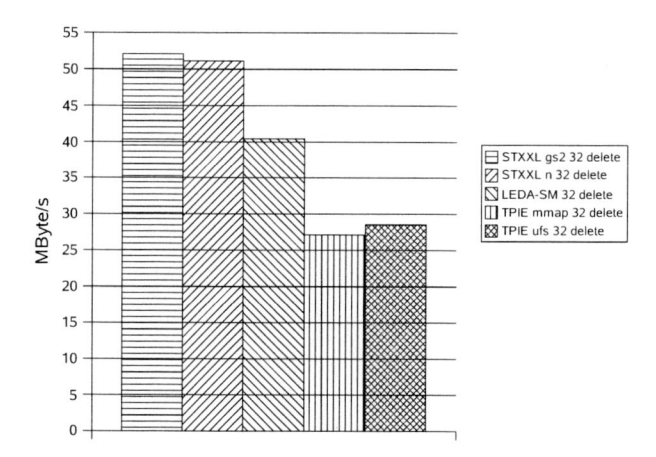

Figure 3.5: Deleting 32-byte elements from the stacks.

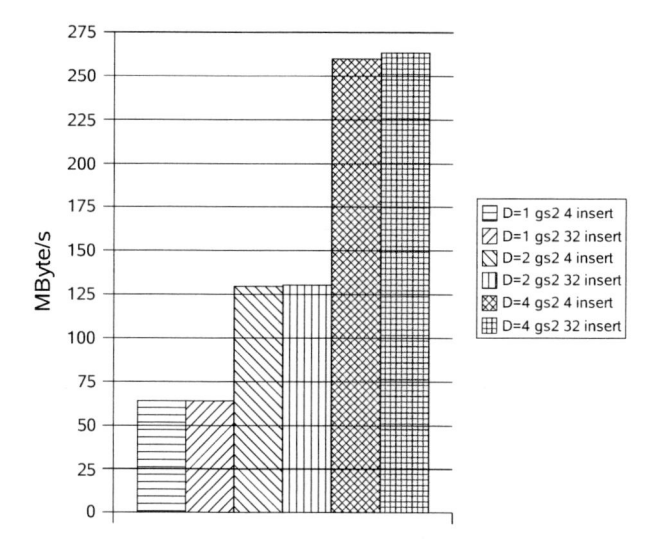

Figure 3.6: Inserting elements into GS2 stacks (multiple disks).

- use of direct I/O to avoid unneeded data copying,
- use of own prefetching/buffering mechanisms for overlapping I/O and computation,
- support of parallel disks.

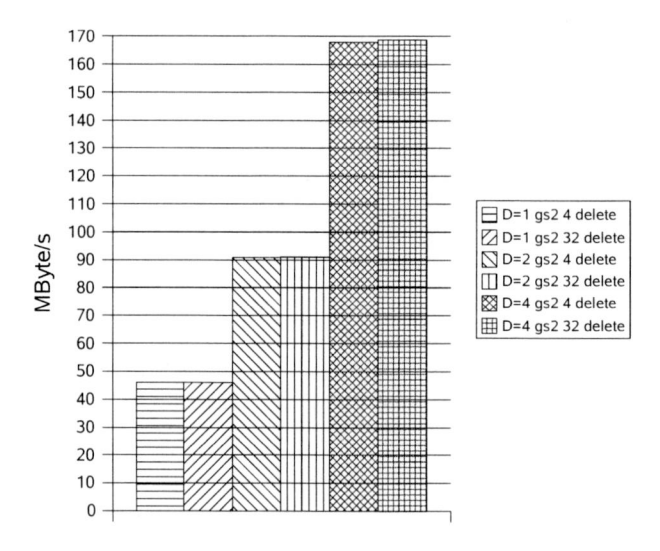

Figure 3.7: Deleting elements from GS2 stacks (multiple disks).

The source code of all stack tests described above is distributed with the STXXL library.

3.4.3 Queue

STXXL also has an implementation of external memory FIFO `queue`. Its design is similar to `stxxl::grow_shrink_stack2`. The implementation holds the head and the tail blocks in the main memory. Prefetch and write block pools might be used to overlap I/O and computation during `queue` operations.

3.4.4 Deque

The STXXL implementation of external memory `deque` is an adaptor of an (external memory) vector. This implementation wraps the elements around the end of the vector *circularly*. It provides the pop/push operations from/to the both ends of the `deque` in $\mathcal{O}(1/DB)$ amortized I/Os if parameterized with a properly configured `stxxl::vector`.

3.4.5 Priority Queue

External memory priority queues are the central data structures for many I/O efficient graph algorithms [Zeh02, CGG+95, MSS03]. The main technique in these algorithms is time-forward processing [CGG+95, Arg95], easily realizable by an I/O efficient priority queue. The output of the processing is another node labelling: The output label of node v is computed from its input label and the messages received from the incoming edges. After computing the output label, node v sends messages along its outgoing edges. I/O efficient priority queues also find application in large-scale discrete event simulation and online sorting. The STXXL implementation of priority queues is based on [San00]. Any operation of this priority queue, called sequence heap, takes $\mathcal{O}\bigl(\frac{1}{B}\log_{M/B}(I/B)\bigr)$ amortized I/Os, where I is the total number of insertions into the priority queue. This queue needs less than a third of I/Os used by other similar cache (I/O) efficient priority queues (e.g. [BCFM00, FJKT97]).

A sequence heap, shown in Figure 3.8, maintains R *merge groups* $G_1,\ldots, G_R$ where G_i holds up to k sorted sequences of size up to mk^{i-1}, $m << M$. When group G_i overflows, all its sequences are merged, and the resulting sequence is put into group G_{i+1}. Each group is equipped with a *group buffer* of size m to allow batched deletion from the sequences. The smallest elements of these buffers are deleted in small batches and stored in the *deletion buffer*. The elements are first inserted into the *insertion priority queue*. On deletion, one checks the minimum elements stored in the insertion priority queue and the deletion buffer.

The difference between our implementation and [San00] is that a number of larger merge groups are explicitly kept in external memory. The sorted sequences in those groups only hold their *first* blocks in the main memory. The implementation supports parallel disks and overlaps I/O and computation. As in [San00], the internal merging is based on loser trees [Knu98]. However, our implementation does not use *sentinel* elements.

In the following we compare the performance of the STXXL priority queue with the general-purpose array heap implementation of LEDA-SM [BCFM00]. TPIE does not provide an I/O-efficient priority queue in the distributed library version. We run the implementation on synthetic inputs following [BCFM00]. The comparison of the data structures in a real graph algorithm is presented in Section 4.2, where we implement an I/O-efficient maximal independent set algorithm.

The first test performs n insertions, followed by n delete-min operations. The elements inserted are pairs of key data 4-byte integers drawn randomly from

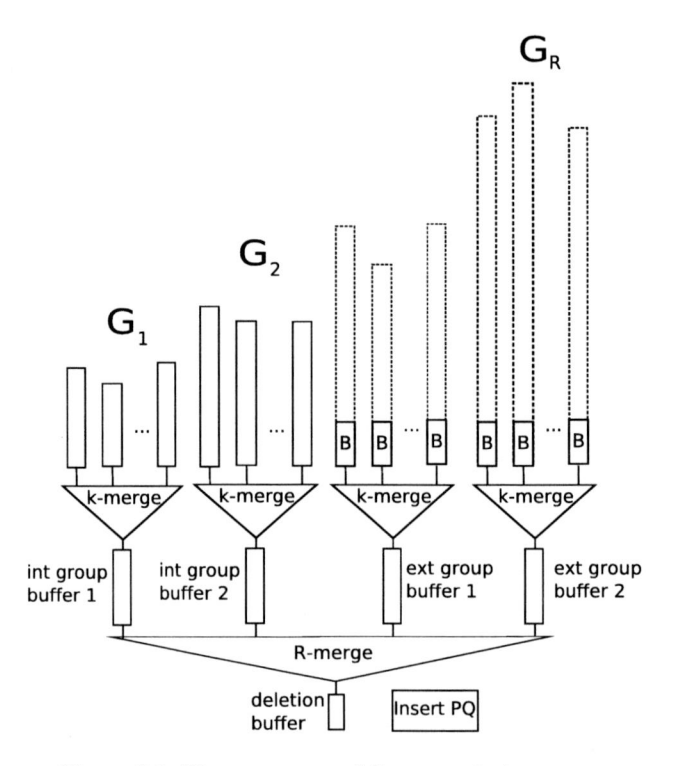

Figure 3.8: The structure of STXXL priority queue.

the range $[0, 2^{31} - 1]$. Figure 3.9 shows the running time of this experiment running on a system with a 3.00 GHz Pentium 4 processor, 1 GB of main memory and a SATA disk dedicated to the experiments. The priority queues were given 512 MB of main memory at their disposal, the rest was used by the Linux operating system for buffering in the case of LEDA-SM and for prefetch and write pools in the case of STXXL . The LEDA-SM implementation could only be compiled with the g++ compiler version 2.95. STXXL implementation was compiled with g++ 3.3. The compiler optimization level was set to -O3 for both codes. We have tuned the external memory block size (256 KB) for LEDA-SM to obtain the best running times for the array heap. However, the differences in running times with different block sizes were negligible, which is a symptom of its CPU-boundness. The STXXL priority queue used 2 MByte blocks. Note the drop of the LEDA-SM delete curve after $n = 2^{23}$ is not an artifact of the measurements; it has been also reported in the original study [BCFM00]. However, we do not devote much attention to the results with

3.4. STL -USER LAYER

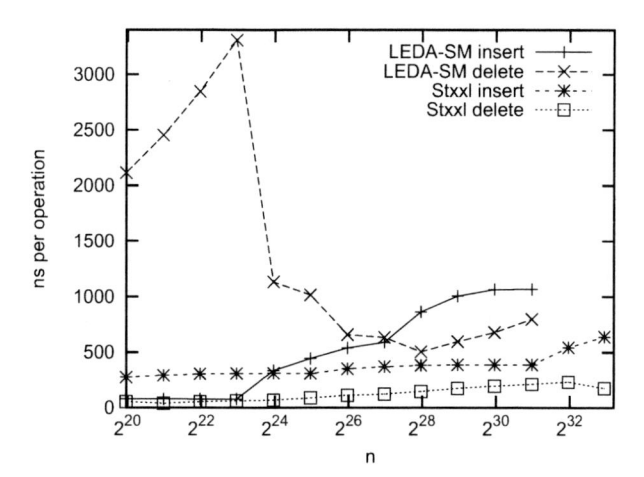

Figure 3.9: The running time of the insert-all-delete-all test for priority queues.

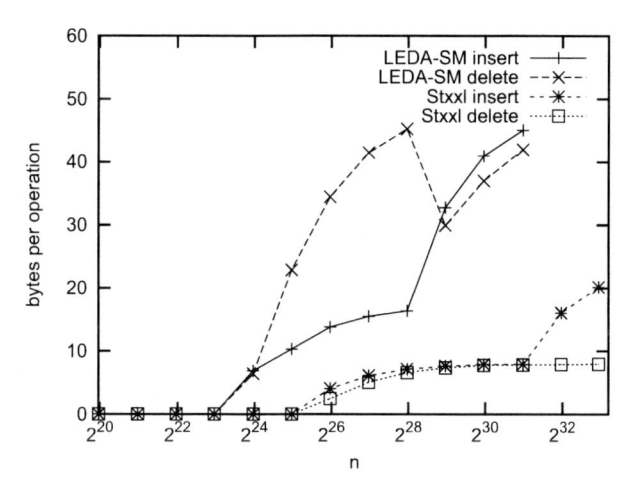

Figure 3.10: The I/O volume of the insert-all-delete-all test for priority queues.

$n \leq 2^{24}$ since those inputs fit in the internal memory. LEDA-SM containers cannot hold more than $2^{31} - 1$ items, therefore we have stopped at input size $n = 2000 \cdot 2^{20}$, which corresponds to about 16 GByte of data. This input is 32 times larger than the main memory size and it is reasonable to be handled in external memory. The STXXL priority queue is up to 2.7 times and 3.7 times faster for insertions and deletions respectively. This can be explained by more expensive CPU work taking place in the LEDA-SM implementation and also better *explicit* overlapping of I/O and computation of STXXL. Note that LEDA-SM relies on (general purpose) operating system caching and buffering. The insertion and deletion phases for the STXXL priority queue need almost the same number of I/Os for $n \leq 2^{31}$. The insertion phase has also the advantage that writing is faster than reading, nonetheless it is almost two times slower than the deletion phase. This is explained by the higher CPU work needed for merging and filling the buffers during insertions. The insertion phase is highly CPU-bound which is confirmed by the I/O-wait time counter, whose value was close to zero. According to the I/O-wait time counter, the deletion phase is less CPU-bound. For $n \geq 2^{32}$ the insertion phase needs to merge and insert *external* sequences, which implies more I/O operations and results in the observed running time escalation. This is confirmed by Figure 3.10, which also shows that the I/O volume of STXXL priority queue is 2–5.5 times smaller than the I/O volume of the LEDA-SM array heap. This difference has been predicted in the original paper [San00].

Figure 3.11 presents the running times of another synthetic test: we insert n random elements into the priority queues and then measure the running time of n operations: We insert a random pair with probability $\frac{1}{3}$ and delete the minimum with probability $\frac{2}{3}$. The behavior of the LEDA-SM curve is similar to the deletions. The STXXL curve has two steps: The first step occurs when the internal sequences have to be merged and put into the external memory for the first time ($n = 2^{25}$), the next step happens at $n = 2^{31}$ when sequences from the first external merger have to be merged and put into a sequence of the second external merger for the first time (see Figure 3.12). These steps are hardly seen in Figure 3.9 (insertions) because of the different access pattern and amortization (n versus $\frac{4n}{3}$ insertions).

Figures 3.13, 3.14 and 3.15 show the results of the above described tests on a system with a 2.0 GHz Opteron Dual-Core Processor and one GByte of main memory and four IDE hard disks (SATAOpteron system from Section 2.4). We could not run LEDA-SM since it compiles only with the old g++ 2.95 compiler, available only for 32-bit architectures. One can see that insertions are highly CPU-bound till $n = 2^{31}$ and cannot benefit from disk parallelism (we ran the implementation on 1,2 and 4 identical independent disks). Also,

3.4. STL -USER LAYER

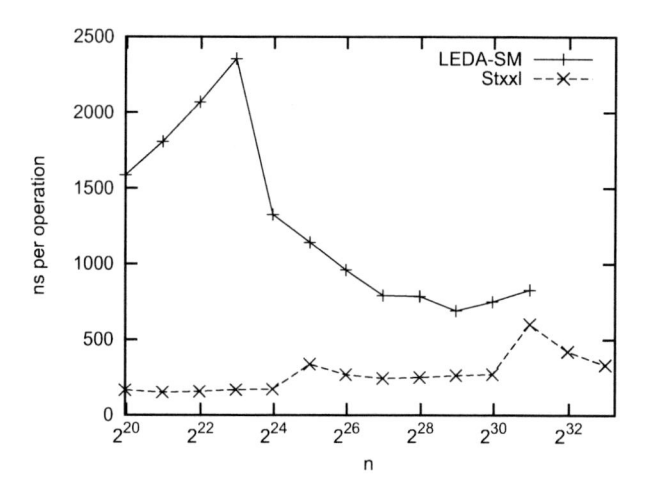

Figure 3.11: The running times of intermixed insertions with deletions (priority queues).

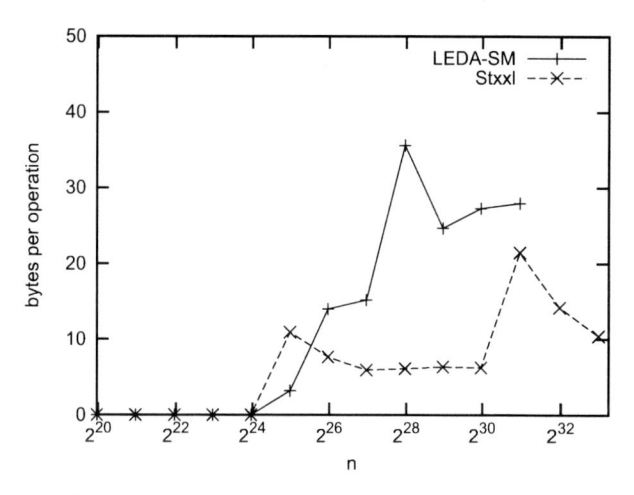

Figure 3.12: The I/O volume of intermixed insertions with deletions (priority queues).

for larger inputs, where large external sequences have to be merged more frequently, we could not achieve a speedup larger than 1.4 for four disks, because of the CPU-boundness. The delete operation is less CPU-expensive, therefore we can already see a small speedup for $n \geq 2^{27}$ (Figure 3.14). The steps in the running time in Figure 3.15 are more prominent compared to Figure 3.11 because the I/O plays a greater role on the faster 64-bit Opteron CPU.

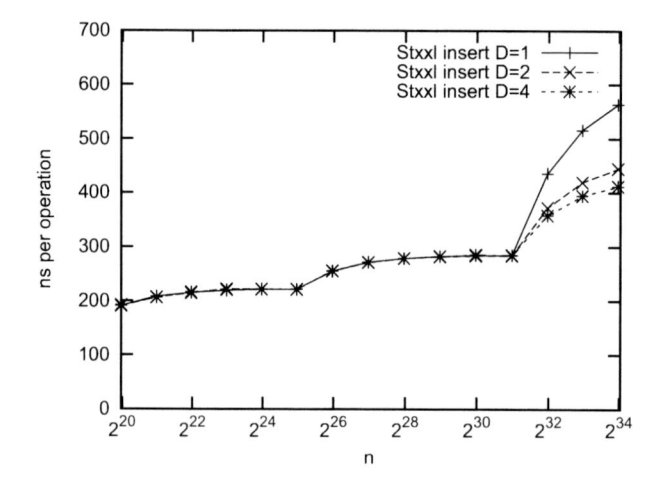

Figure 3.13: Insertions (priority queue with multiple disks).

3.4.6 Map

map is an STL interface for search trees with unique keys. Our implementation of map is a variant of a B$^+$-tree data structure [BM72] supporting the operations insert, erase, find, lower_bound and upper_bound in optimal $\mathcal{O}(\log_B(n))$ I/Os. Operations of map use *iterators* to refer to the elements stored in the container, e.g. find and insert return an iterator pointing to the data. Iterators are used for range queries: an iterator pointing to the smallest element in the range is returned by lower_bound, the element which is next to the maximum element in the range is returned by upper_bound. Scanning through the elements of the query can be done by using operator++ or operator-- of the obtained iterators in $\mathcal{O}(R/B)$ I/Os, where R is the number of elements in the result. Our current implementation does not exploit disk parallelism. The flexibility of the iterator-based

3.4. STL -USER LAYER

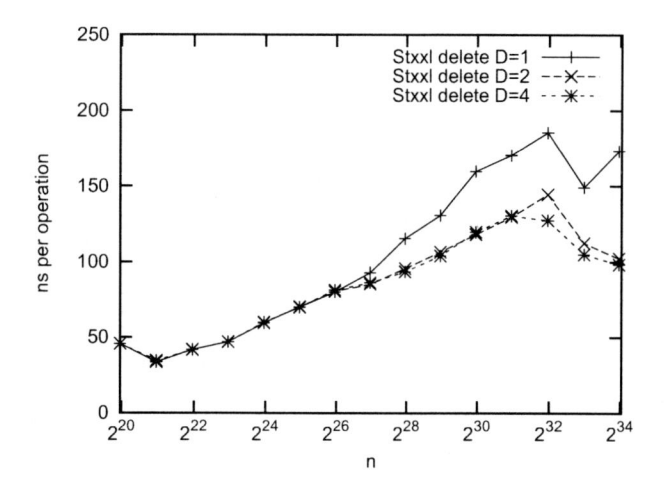

Figure 3.14: Deletions (priority queue with multiple disks).

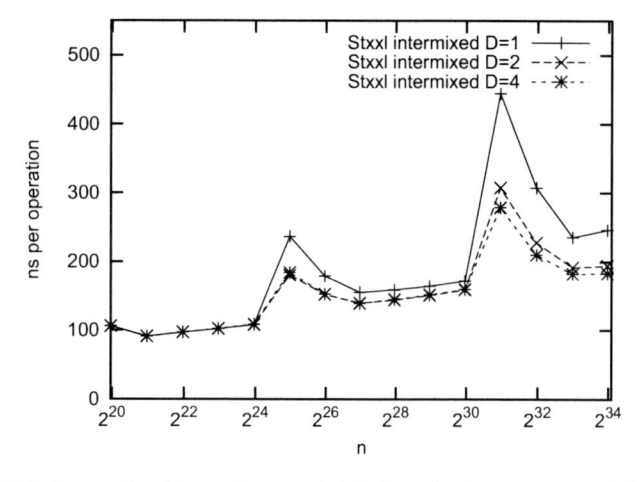

Figure 3.15: Intermixed insertions and deletions (priority queue with multiple disks).

access has some complications for an external memory implementation: iterators must return correct data after reorganizations in the data structure even when the pointed data is moved to a different external memory block.

The way how iterators are used for accessing a map is similar to the use of database *cursors* [OBS99]. STXXL is the first C++ template library that provides an *I/O-efficient* search tree implementation with iterator-based access.

In the following we briefly describe the architecture of the STXXL B$^+$-tree implementation. A simplified UML class diagram of the implementation is depicted in Figure 3.16. Our design allows one to use different implementations for leaves and (internal) nodes. For example, leaves could be represented internally as sparse arrays [BDIW02] (currently, only the classic sorted array implementation is available). Leaves and nodes can have different external memory block sizes. Each leaf has links to the predecessor and successor leaves to speed up scanning. Our B$^+$-tree is able to prefetch the neighbor leaves when scanning, obtaining a higher bandwidth by overlapping I/O and computation. The root node is always kept in the main memory and implemented as an `std::map`. To save I/Os, the most frequently used nodes and leaves are cached in corresponding node and leaf *caches* that are implemented in a single template class. An iterator keeps the block identifier (BID) of the external block where the pointed data element is contained, the offset of the data element in the block and a pointer to the B$^+$-tree. In case of reorganizations of the data in external memory blocks (rebalancing, splitting, fusing blocks), all iterators pointing to the moved data have to be updated. For this purpose, the addresses of all instantiated iterators are kept in the iterator map object. The iterator map facilitates fast accounting of iterators, mapping BID and block offsets of iterators to its main memory addresses using an *internal* memory search tree. Therefore, the number of "alive" B$^+$-tree iterators must be kept reasonably small. The parent pointers in leaves and nodes can be useful for finger search [3] and insertions using a finger, however, that would require to store the whole B-tree path in the iterator data structure. This might make the iterator accounting very slow, therefore we do not maintain the parent links. The implementation can save I/Os when `const_iterator`s are used: no flushing of supposedly changed data is needed (e.g. when scanning or doing other read-only operations). Our implementation of B$^+$-tree supports bulk bottom-up construction from the presorted data given by an iterator range in $\mathcal{O}(n/B)$ I/Os.

We have compared the performance of our B$^+$-tree implementation with the performance of the Berkeley DB B$^+$-tree (BDB) implementation version 4.4 [OBS00], which is a *commercial* product. This implementation is known to be one of the fastest implementations available. We also measured the

---

[3]The program can help the search tree finding an element by giving some "position close by" which was determined by an earlier search.

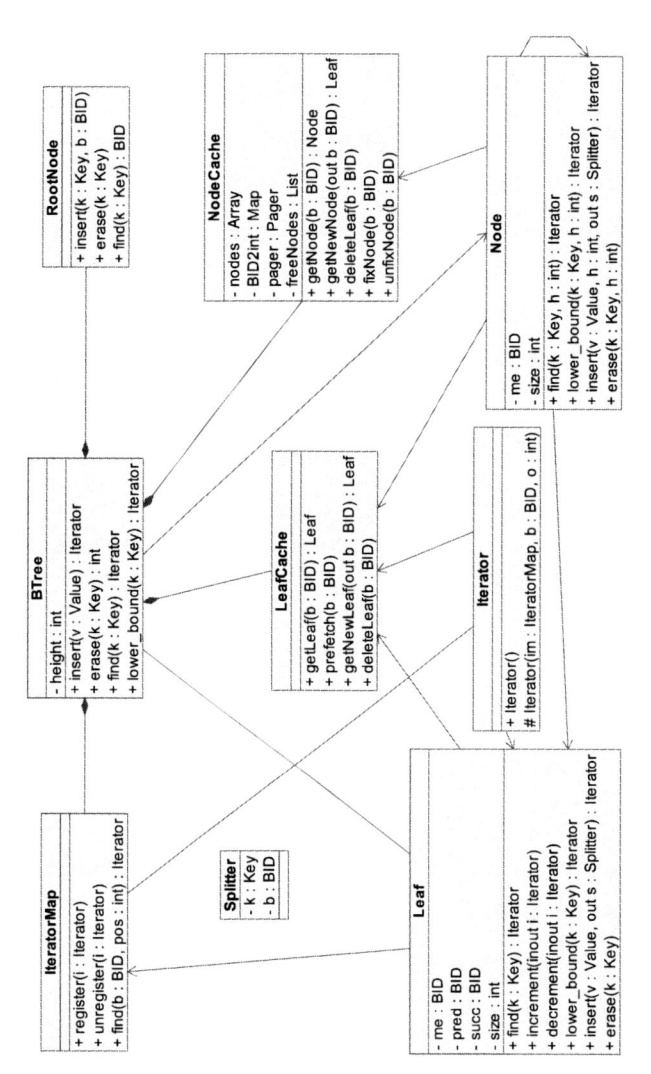

Figure 3.16: The simplified UML class diagram of the B$^+$-tree implementation.

performance of the TPIE [4] B$^+$-tree implementation, but not the LEDA-SM implementation because it does not support predecessor/successor and range queries. For the experiments we used the SATAOpteron machine (Section 2.4) using one GByte of main memory. Each implementation used a separate hard disk for storing its external memory back file. STXXL map and TPIE have used a cache of 750 MBytes and BDB's cache was slightly less because it has used more memory than the given cache size [5]. The block size was set to 32 KBytes for all implementations.

The B$^+$-trees indexed records with eight character random keys (letters 'a'-'z') and 32 bytes data field. First, B$^+$-trees have been constructed from a sorted set of n records. To make the comparison fair we configured BDB to store records with *unique* keys, since the map interface does keep multiple records with equal keys. STXXL map supports the bottom up bulk construction from a sorted range of iterators. TPIE B$^+$-tree supports the bulk construction from a pre-sorted TPIE stream of data which must reside on a hard disk (AMI_STREAM). According to the Berkeley DB support team, BDB lacks the bulk load capability, therefore we had to insert the records one by one in ascending order. This insertion pattern leads to nearly 100 % cache hits and produces a BDB B$^+$-tree with a fill factor of about 100 % in the leaves. The stxxl::map and the TPIE bulk construction were configured to achieve the 100 % fill factor, too. Figure 3.17 shows the construction time without the pre-sorting. In this test, STXXL map is about three times faster than BDB. The obvious reason for this is that BDB has to do many searches in the leaves and nodes to find an appropriate place to insert, and thus is highly CPU bound. STXXL map bulk construction performs only a small constant number of operations per input element. The TPIE bulk construction was up to 70 % slower than the construction of the stxxl::map, because, in fact, it repeatedly inserts all input elements into the leaves doing a *binary search* of the place to insert them into the last leaf over and over from the scratch. This inefficiency makes the construction more CPU-bound.

After the construction of the base element set index we generated 100,000 random records and inserted them. The running times of this experiment are shown in Figure 3.18. For large inputs one has to load up to two leaves and flush up to three leaves per insertion since the leaves are full after the construction and they need to be split. Note that the links between the leaves must be updated, too. This can explain the long 25 ms of the STXXL and TPIE B$^+$-trees since a random access to this hard disk takes up to 8 ms

---

[4]Version from 19.09.2005

[5]The BDB process has been killed by an out-of-memory exception when run with 750 MByte cache. Therefore we had to reduce the cache size.

3.4. STL-USER LAYER

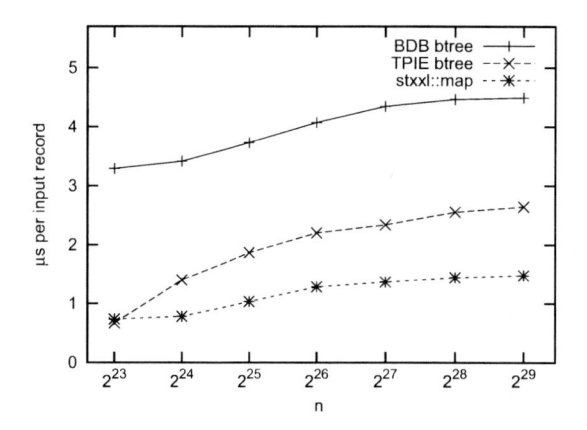

Figure 3.17: The running times of B^+-tree construction.

on average according to its specifications paper. BDB is about 30% faster for large inputs; this advantage could to some extent be due to the adaptive compression of sequences of keys with the same prefix, an optimization exploited in the recent versions of BDB. Another reason would be a highly tuned node/leaf splitting strategy of BDB [OBS00].

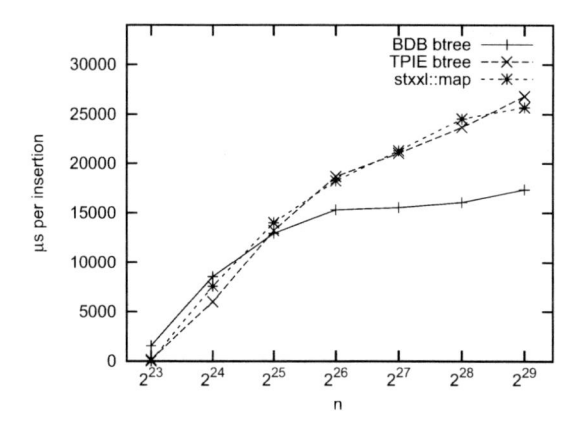

Figure 3.18: The running times of B^+-tree insertions.

The next test (Figure 3.19) is run after the insertions and performs 100,000 random *locate* queries of the smallest record that is not smaller than the given key. For large inputs, in almost every locate query, a random leaf has to be loaded. This is the reason of the observed latency of 10–13 ms. BDB is faster again, but the advantage is smaller here (below 20 %). The STXXL B$^+$-tree is slightly faster than the TPIE B$^+$-tree.

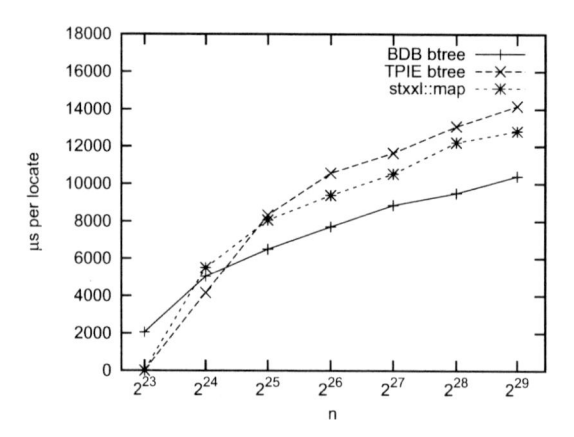

Figure 3.19: The running times of B$^+$-tree locates.

Figure 3.20 (left) shows the running time of random range queries with scanning. We sample the possible ranges uniformly at random and scan the obtained ranges until about n records are scanned after all queries. This way only 3–5 queries suffice. In order to explain the trends in the running times we have drawn Figure 3.20 (right) that shows the leaf space overuse factor computed as $\frac{\text{number of leaves} \cdot B}{(n+a) \cdot \text{size of record}}$ before this test, where $B = 32$ KBytes is the block size and $a = 100,000$ is the number of the additional records inserted. This metric shows how inefficiently the leaves are filled with data. After the bulk construction the overuse factor is very close to 1 for the STXXL and BDB implementations. We could not generate such statistic for the TPIE B$^+$-tree since it does not offer the required counters. Adding the 100,000 random elements to small inputs worsens the overuse factor: For stxxl::map, it almost reaches 2, and for BDB it is larger than 2.5. This difference plays a big role in the ratio of the records that can be kept in the memory for $n = 2^{23}$. STXXL can keep almost the whole data set, and thus the scanning time is very small. For larger inputs $n \geq 2^{24}$ only a small fraction of the input can reside in the main memory for the implementations. This increases the scanning time significantly, because many leaves have to be loaded and flushed from/to the hard disk. However, the overuse factor of STXXL is still considerably smaller for $n = 2^{24}$. This contributes to a speedup about 2 over

3.4. STL -USER LAYER

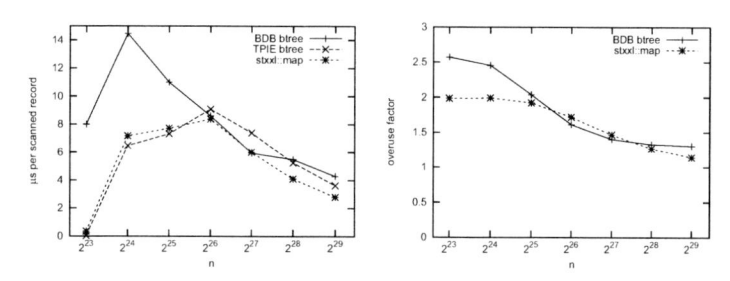

Figure 3.20: The running times of B$^+$-tree range queries with scanning (left). The space overuse factor in leaves of B$^+$-tree (right).

the BDB. In the middle region, all data structures are equally fast and the overuse factor is about the same. For the largest inputs, the STXXL map has again a small advantage of about 20 % in scanning speed due to the better leaf fill factor and perhaps due to the better overlapping of I/O and computation. The latter might also be the reason of the small advantage of the STXXL B$^+$-tree over the TPIE B$^+$-tree for $n \geq 2^{26}$.

After the tests described above we delete the 100,000 records inserted after the bulk construction from the B$^+$-trees. Here, we need to load and store one leaf for almost every delete operation. Fusing and rebalancing of leaves and nodes should not occur frequently. Again, the BDB is faster by about 18 % for large inputs (Figure 3.21). For $n \geq 2^{26}$ the delete time of the TPIE B$^+$-tree goes *down* and approaches the time of the BDB B$^+$-tree. This trend remains unexplained.

The source code of all B$^+$-tree tests described above is distributed with the STXXL library.

Discussion: The tests have shown that the STXXL map is somewhat slower than the BDB in insert, locate and delete operations. These operations have been highly tuned in *commercial* BDB implementations over the last 15 years of development [OBS00]. However, an advantage of STXXL is that it can do fast bulk construction, which is not available in BDB. The speed of scanning of the records in a range is competitive with the BDB. Just looking at the code of the benchmark above, one sees an advantage of the STXXL map that has little to do with the execution speed, but is very important in the software development: the expressiveness and compactness of the STL interface. The BDB has been implemented in C, and the C++ interface of the BDB is very similar to the original C interface: BDB methods operate on pointers to user allocated data buffers, there is no use of advanced features of

Listing 3.3: Locates with the Berkeley DB.

```
struct my_key { char keybuf[KEY_SIZE]; };
struct my_data { char databuf[DATA_SIZE]; };

Dbc *cursorp; // data base cursor
// db is the BDB B-tree object
db.cursor(NULL, &cursorp, 0); // initialize cursor

for (int64 i = 0; i < n_locates; ++i)
{
    rand_key(key_storage); // generate random key
    // initialize BDB key object for storing the result key
    Dbt keyx(key_storage.keybuf,KEY_SIZE);
    // initialize BDB key object for storing the result data
    Dbt datax(data_storage.databuf,DATA_SIZE);
    cursorp->get(&keyx, &datax,DB_SET_RANGE); // perform locate
}
```

C++ like templates. Pieces of code testing random locates are presented in Listings 3.3 and 3.4 to demonstrate the difference in interfaces. The complete code of the STXXL map test is about two times shorter than the equivalent BDB test code.

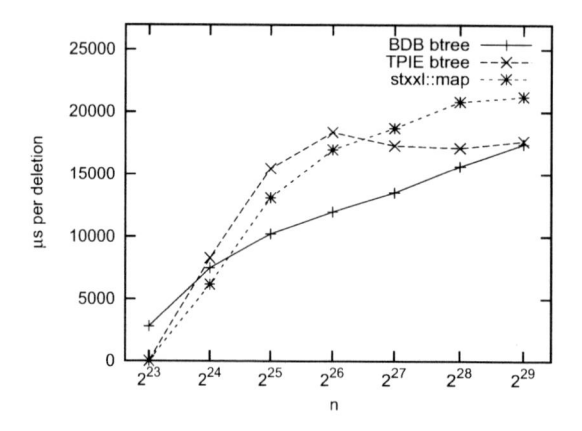

Figure 3.21: The running times of B^+-tree deletions.

3.4. STL-USER LAYER

Listing 3.4: Locates with the STXXL map.
```
struct my_key { char keybuf[KEY_SIZE]; };
struct my_data { char databuf[DATA_SIZE]; };

std::pair<my_key,my_data> element; // key-data pair

for (i = 0; i < n_locates; ++i)
{
    rand_key(i,element.first); // generate random key
    // CMap is a constant reference to a map object
    map_type::const_iterator result = // perform locate
        CMap.lower_bound(element.first);
}
```

3.4.7 General Issues Concerning STXXL Containers

Similar to other external memory algorithm libraries [CM99, ABH+03], STXXL has the restriction that the data types stored in the containers cannot have C/C++ pointers or references to other elements of external memory containers. The reason is that these pointers and references get invalidated when the blocks containing the elements they point/refer to are written to disk. To get around this problem, the links can be kept in the form of external memory iterators (e.g. `stxxl::vector::iterator`). The iterators remain valid while storing to and loading from the external memory. When dereferencing an external memory iterator, the pointed object is loaded from external memory by the library on demand (if the object is not in the cache of the data structure already).

STXXL containers differ from STL containers in treating allocation and distinguishing between uninitialized and initialized memory. STXXL containers assume that the data types they store are plain old data types (POD) [6]. The constructors and destructors of the contained data types are not called when a container changes its size. The support of constructors and destructors would imply a significant I/O cost penalty, e.g. on the deallocation of a non-empty container, one has to load all contained objects and call their destructors. This restriction sounds more severe than it is, since external memory data structures cannot cope with custom dynamic memory management anyway, which is the common use of custom constructors/destructors.

---

[6] Plain old data structures (PODs) are data structures represented only as passive collections of field values, without using aggregation of variable-size objects (as references or pointers), polymorphism, virtual calls or other object-oriented features. Most naturally they are represented as C/C++ `structs`.

3.4.8 Algorithms

The algorithms of the STL can be divided into two groups by their memory access pattern: *scanning* algorithms and *random access* algorithms.

Scanning Algorithms

Scanning algorithms work with Input, Output, Forward, and Bidirectional iterators only. Since random access operations are not allowed with these kinds of iterators, the algorithms inherently exhibit a strong spatial locality of reference. efficient. STXXL containers and their iterators are STL-compatible, therefore one can directly apply STL scanning algorithms to them, and they will run I/O-efficiently (see the use of std::generate and std::unique algorithms in the Listing 3.6). Scanning algorithms are the majority of the STL algorithms (62 out of 71). STXXL also offers specialized implementations of some scanning algorithms (stxxl::for_each, stxxl::generate, etc.), which perform better in terms of constant factors in the I/O volume and internal CPU work. These implementations benefit from accessing lower level interfaces of the BM layer instead of using iterator interfaces, resulting in a smaller CPU overhead. Being aware of the sequential access pattern of the applied algorithm, the STXXL implementations can do prefetching and use queued writing, thereby leading to the overlapping of I/O with computation.

Random Access Algorithms

Random access algorithms require random access iterators, hence may perform (many) random I/Os [7]. For such algorithms, STXXL provides specialized I/O efficient implementations that work with STL-user layer external memory containers. Currently, the library provides two implementations of sorting: an std::sort-like sorting routine – stxxl::sort, and a sorter that exploits integer keys – stxxl::ksort. Both sorters are implementations of parallel disk algorithms described in Section 3.5.

Listing 3.6 shows how to program using the STL-user layer and how STXXL containers can be used together with both STXXL algorithms and STL algorithms. The definitions of the classes edge, random_edge and edge_cmp are in Listing 3.5. The purpose of our example is to generate a huge random

---

[7] The std::nth_element algorithm is an exception. It needs $\mathcal{O}(\text{scan}(n))$ I/Os on average.

3.4. STL -USER LAYER

Listing 3.5: Definitions of classes.

```
struct edge { // edge class
    int src,dst; // nodes
    edge() {}
    edge(int src_, int dst_): src(src_), dst(dst_) {}
    bool operator == (const edge & b) const {
        return src == b.src && dst == b.dst;
    }
};
struct random_edge { // random edge generator functor
    edge operator () () const {
        edge Edge(random()-1,random()-1);
        while(Edge.dst == Edge.src)
            Edge.dst = random() - 1 ; //no self-loops
        return Edge;
    }
};
struct edge_cmp { // edge comparison functor
    edge min_value() const {
        return edge(std::numeric_limits<int>::min(),0); };
    edge max_value() const {
        return edge(std::numeric_limits<int>::max(),0); };
    bool operator () (const edge & a,
                      const edge & b) const {
        return a.src < b.src ||
            (a.src == b.src && a.dst < b.dst);
    }
};
```

Listing 3.6: Generating a random graph using the STL-user layer.
```
stxxl::vector<edge> ExtEdgeVec(10000000000ULL);
std::generate(ExtEdgeVec.begin(),ExtEdgeVec.end(),
               random_edge());
stxxl::sort(ExtEdgeVec.begin(),ExtEdgeVec.end(),edge_cmp(),
     512*1024*1024);
stxxl::vector<edge>::iterator NewEnd =
          std::unique(ExtEdgeVec.begin(),ExtEdgeVec.end());
ExtEdgeVec.resize(NewEnd - ExtEdgeVec.begin());
```

directed graph in a sorted edge array representation, i.e. the edges in the edge array must be sorted lexicographically. A straightforward procedure to do this is to: 1) generate a sequence of random edges, 2) sort the sequence, 3) remove duplicate edges from it. If we ignore definitions of helper classes the STL/STXXL code of the algorithm implementation is only five lines long: Line 1 creates an STXXL external memory vector with 10 billion edges. Line 3 fills the vector with random edges (**generate** from the STL is used). In the next line the STXXL external memory sorter sorts randomly generated edges using 512 megabytes of internal memory. The lexicographical order is defined by functor **my_cmp**, **stxxl::sort** also requires the comparison functor to provide upper and lower bounds for the elements being sorted. Line 7 deletes duplicate edges in the external memory vector with the help of the STL **unique** algorithm. The **NewEnd** vector iterator points to the right boundary of the range without duplicates. Finally (in Line 8), we chop the vector at the **NewEnd** boundary. Now we count the number of I/Os performed by this example: external vector construction takes no I/Os; filling with random values requires a scan — N/DB I/Os; sorting will take $4N/DB$ I/Os; duplicate removal needs no more than $2N/DB$ I/Os; chopping a vector is I/O-free. The total number of I/Os is $7N/DB$.

3.5 Parallel Disk Sorting

Sorting is the first component we have designed for STXXL, because it is *the* fundamental tool for I/O-efficient processing of large data sets. Chapters 4 and 5 contain numerous examples for this fact. Therefore, an efficient implementation of sorting largely defines the performance of an external memory software library as a whole. To achieve the best performance our implementation [DS03] uses parallel disks, has an optimal I/O volume $\mathcal{O}\left(\frac{N}{DB}\log_{M/B}\frac{N}{B}\right)$ (that matches the lower bound), and guarantees almost perfect overlap be-

3.5. PARALLEL DISK SORTING

tween I/O and computation.

No previous implementation has all these properties, which are needed for a good practical sorting. LEDA-SM [CM99] and TPIE [APV02] concentrate on single disk implementations. For the overlapping of I/O and computation they rely on prefetching and caching provided by the operating system, which is suboptimal since the system knows little about the application's access pattern.

Barve and Vitter implemented a parallel disk algorithm [BGV97] that can be viewed as the immediate ancestor of our algorithm. Innovations with respect to our sorting are: a different allocation strategy that enables better theoretical I/O bounds [HSV01, KV01]; a prefetching algorithm that optimizes the number of I/O steps and never evicts data previously fetched; overlapping of I/O and computation; a completely asynchronous implementation that reacts flexibly to fluctuations in disk speeds; and an implementation that sorts many GBytes and does not have to limit internal memory size artificially to obtain a nontrivial number of runs. Additionally, our implementation is not a prototype, it has a generic interface and is a part of the software library STXXL.

Algorithms in [Raj98, CC02, CCW01] have the theoretical advantage of being deterministic. However, they need three passes over data even for not too large inputs.

Prefetch buffers for disk load balancing and overlapping of I/O and computation have been intensively studied for external memory merge sort [PV92, CFKL96, AGL98, HSV01, KV01, KK00]. But we have not seen results that guarantee overlapping of I/O and computation during the parallel disk merging of arbitrary runs.

There are many good practical implementations of sorting (e.g. [NBC+94, Aga96, NKG00, Wyl99]) that address parallel disks, overlapping of I/O and computation, and have a low internal overhead. However, we are not aware of fast implementations that give theoretical performance guarantees on achieving asymptotically optimal I/O. Most practical implementations use a form of striping that requires $\Omega(\frac{N}{DB} \log_{\Theta(\frac{M}{DB})} \frac{N}{B})$ I/Os rather than the optimal $\Theta(\frac{N}{DB} \log_{\Theta(M/B)} \frac{N}{B})$. This difference is usually considered insignificant for practical purposes. However, already on our experimental system we have to go somewhat below the block sizes that give the best performance in Figure 3.31 if the input size is 128 GBytes. Another reduction of the block size by a factor of eight (we have eight disks) could increase the run time significantly. We are also not aware of high performance implementations that guarantee overlap of I/O and computation during merging for inputs such as the one described in Section 3.5.1.

On the other hand, many of the practical merits of our implementation are at least comparable with the best current implementations: We are close to the peak performance of our system.

The Sort Benchmark competition [Gra] is held yearly and includes several categories; some of them define restrictions on the cost of the hardware used for sorting. In the "Terabyte" category, the goal is to sort quickly a terabyte of data. As this benchmark type is not limited by the hardware costs, distributed memory sorting algorithms win running on expensive clusters with SAN disks. Distributed memory sorters also lead in the "Minute" category which asks to sort as much data as possible in a minute. In the "Penny" category the cost of the hardware is spread over three years. Then, it is measured how much data can be sorted in an interval of time that costs one US-cent. Competition participants are responsible for the choice of their hardware. Each category has two subcategories: Daytona (for general-purpose sorting) and Indy (sort 100-byte records with 10-byte random keys).

The most interesting category for us is the "Penny" category because it addresses the cost-efficiency aspect of sorting, and it turns out that the cheapest way to sort is to use an I/O-efficient sorting. All winners in this category since the announcement in 1998 were external memory sorters. We overview the past "Penny sort" winners [Gra]. The NTSort (won Indy in 1998) is a command line sorting utility of Windows NT implementing multi-way merge sort. The implementation adopted for the competition relied on direct unbuffered I/O, but used no overlapping between I/O and computation. PostmanSort (Daytona winner in 1998 and 2005) is a commercial sorting utility; it is a variant of the bucket sort. The recent version utilizes asynchronous I/O of Windows to overlap I/O and computation. HMSort (winner in 1999 and 2000) also exploits overlapping of I/O and computation, however, other details about the algorithm are not published. DMSort (Indy 2002) is based on the most-significant byte radix sort. The implementation works with two disks: The input data elements are read from the first disk and distributed to the bins on the second disk, explicitly overlapping I/O and computation. The second phase reads the bins from the second disk, sorts them, and writes the sorted result to the first disk in an overlapped fashion. Only few algorithmic details of THSort (Daytona 2004), Sheenksort (Indy 2004, 2005) and Byte-Split-Index Sort (Daytona 2006) are published. The authors of the THSort, SheenkSort and Byte-Split-Index have used systems with four disks. The GpuTeraSort (Indy 2006) [GGKM05] uses a graphic processing unit (GPU) for internal sorting, mapping a bitonic sorting network to GPU

3.5. PARALLEL DISK SORTING

rasterization operations and using the GPUs programmable hardware and high bandwidth memory interface. The implementation accesses the files directly and explictly overlaps I/O and computation. To achieve a higher I/O-bandwidth, a RAID-0 has been used.

We have participated in the "Penny" sort competition in 2003 with an earlier variant of the implementation presented below. We took the second place, sorting 25 GBytes in our time budget. We would have been be very close to the winner's value of 40 GBytes if we had been more lucky with the choice of hardware: Our more expensive system ran with errors at the full speed, we also have overlooked the fast (and cheap) hard disks used by our opponents, because the manufacturer did not bother to specify their characteristics. The "Penny sort" external sorters mentioned above are very impressive pieces of engineering. However, these algorithms and implementations do not give *theoretical guarantees* of the performance, including the overlapping of I/O and computation and the optimal use of parallel disks.

3.5.1 Multi-way Merge Sort with Overlapped I/Os

Perhaps the most widely used external memory sorting algorithm is k-way merge sort: During *run formation*, chunks of $\Theta(M)$ elements are read, sorted internally, and written back to the disk as sorted *runs*. The runs are then merged into larger runs until only a single run is left. $k = \mathcal{O}(M/B)$ runs can be sorted in a single pass by keeping up to B of the smallest elements of each run in internal memory. Using randomization, prediction of the order in which blocks are accessed, a prefetch buffer of $\mathcal{O}(D)$ blocks, and an optimal prefetching strategy, it is possible to implement k-way merging using D disks in a load balanced way [HSV01]. However, the rate at which new blocks are requested is more difficult to predict so that this algorithm does not guarantee overlapping of I/O and computation. In this section, we derive a parallel disk algorithm that compensates these fluctuations in the block request rate by a FIFO buffer of $k + \Theta(D)$ blocks.

Run Formation

There are many ways to overlap I/O and run formation. We start with a very simple method that treats internal sorting as a black box and therefore can use the fastest available internal sorters. Two threads cooperate to build k runs of size $M/2$:

```
post a read request for runs 1 and 2
thread A:                      | thread B:
for r:=1 to k do               | for r:=1 to k-2 do
  wait until                   |   wait until
    run r is read              |     run r is written
  sort run r                   |   post a read for run r+2
  post a write for run r       |
```

Figure 3.22 illustrates how I/O and computation is overlapped by this algorithm. Formalizing this figure, we can prove that using this approach an input of size N can be transformed into sorted runs of size $M/2 - \mathcal{O}(DB)$ in time $\max(2T_{\text{sort}}(M/2)N/M, \frac{2LN}{DB}) + \mathcal{O}\left(\frac{LM}{DB}\right)$, where $T_{\text{sort}}(x)$ denotes the time for sorting x elements internally and where L is the time needed for a parallel I/O step.

In [DS03] one can find an algorithm which generates longer runs of average length $2M$ and overlaps I/O and computation.

Multi-way Merging

We want to merge k sorted sequences comprising N' elements stored in N'/B blocks (In practical situations, where a single merging phase suffices, we will have $N' = N$). In each iteration, the merging thread chooses the smallest remaining element from the k sequences and hands it over to the I/O thread. Prediction of read operations is based on the observation that the merging thread does not need to access a block until its smallest element becomes

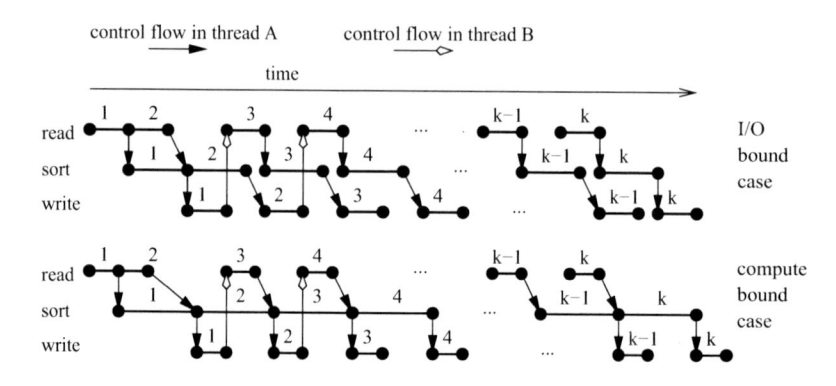

Figure 3.22: Overlapping I/O and computation during run formation.

3.5. PARALLEL DISK SORTING

the smallest unread element. We therefore record the *smallest* keys of each block during run formation. By merging the resulting k sequences of smallest elements, we can produce a sequence σ of block identifiers that indicates the exact order in which blocks are logically read by the merging thread. The overhead for producing and storing the prediction data structure is negligible because its size is a factor at least B smaller than the input.

The prediction sequence σ is used as follows. The merging thread maintains the invariant that it always buffers the k first blocks in σ that contain unselected elements, i.e., initially, the first k blocks from σ are read into these *merge buffers*. When the last element of a merge buffer block is selected, the now empty buffer frame is returned to the I/O thread and the next block in σ is read.

The keys of the smallest elements in each buffer block are kept in a tournament tree data structure [Knu98] so that the currently smallest element can be selected in time $\mathcal{O}(\log k)$. Hence, the total internal work for merging is $\mathcal{O}(N' \log k)$.

We have now defined multi-way merging from the point of view of the sorting algorithm. Our approach to merging slightly deviates from previous approaches that keep track of the run numbers of the merge blocks and pre-assign each merge block to the corresponding input sequence. In these approaches also the *last* key in the *previous* block decides about the position of a block in σ. The correctness of our approach is shown in [DS03]. With respect to performance, both approaches should be similar. Our approach is somewhat simpler, however — note that the merging thread does not need to know anything about the k input runs and how they are allocated. Its only input is the prediction sequence σ. In a sense, we are merging individual blocks and the order in σ makes sure that the overall effect is that the input runs are merged. A conceptual advantage is that data *within* a block decides about when a block is read.

Overlapping I/O and Merging

Although we can predict the order in which blocks are read, we cannot easily predict how much internal work is done between two reads. For example, consider k identical runs storing the sequence $\boxed{1^{B-1}2}\boxed{3^{B-1}4}\boxed{5^{B-1}6}\cdots$. After initializing the merge buffers, the merging thread will consume $k(B-1)$ values '1' before it posts another read. Then it will post one read after selecting each of the next k values (2). Then there will be a pause of another $k(B-1)$ steps and another k reads are following each other quickly, etc. We explain how to

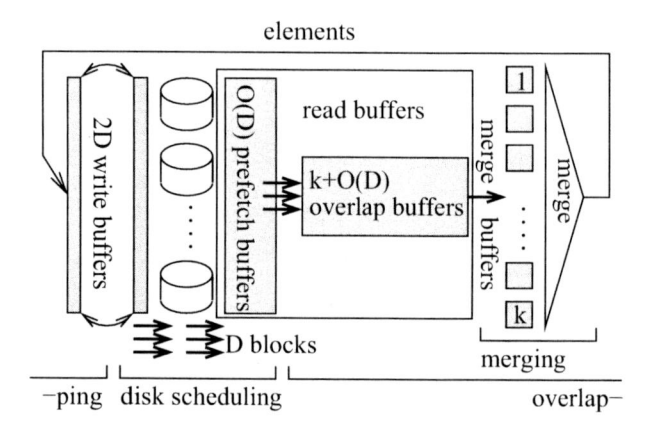

Figure 3.23: Data flow through the different kinds of buffers for overlapped parallel disk multi-way merging. Data is moved in units of blocks except between the merger and the write buffer.

overlap I/O and computation despite this irregularity using the I/O model of Aggarwal and Vitter [AV88] that allows access to D arbitrary blocks within one I/O step. To model overlapping of I/O and computation, we assume that an I/O step takes time L and can be done in parallel with internal computations. We maintain an *overlap buffer* that stores up to $k+3D$ blocks in a FIFO manner (see Figure 3.23). Whenever the overlap buffer is non-empty, a read can be served from it without blocking. Writing is implemented using a *write buffer* FIFO with $2DB$ elements capacity. An *I/O thread* inputs or outputs D blocks in time L using the following strategy: Whenever no I/O is active and at least DB elements are present in the write buffer, an output step is started. When no I/O is active, less than D output blocks are available, and at least D overlap buffers are unused, then the next D blocks from σ are fetched into the overlap buffer. This strategy guarantees that merging k sorted sequences with a total of N' elements can be implemented to run in time $\max\left(\frac{2LN'}{DB}, \ell N'\right) + \mathcal{O}\left(L\left\lceil\frac{k}{D}\right\rceil\right)$ where ℓ is the time needed by the merging thread to produce one element of output and L is the time needed to input or output D arbitrary blocks [DS03].

Disk Scheduling

The I/Os for the run formation and for the output of merging are perfectly balanced over all disks if all sequences are *striped* over the disks, i.e., sequences are stored in blocks of B elements each and the blocks numbered $i,\ldots,i+D-1$ in a sequence are stored on different disks for all i. In particular, the original input and the final output of sorting can use any kind of striping.

The merging algorithm presented above is optimal for the unrealistic model of Aggarwal and Vitter [AV88] which allows to access any D blocks in an I/O step. This facilitates good performance for fetching very irregularly placed input blocks. However, this model can be simulated using D independent disks using *randomized striping allocation* [VH01] and a prefetch buffer of size $m = \Theta(D)$ blocks: In almost every input step, $(1 - \mathcal{O}(D/m))D$ blocks from prefetch sequence σ can be fetched [DS03].

Figure 3.23 illustrates the data flow between the components of our parallel disk multi-way merging.

3.5.2 Implementation Details

Run Formation. We build runs of a size close to $M/2$ but there are some differences to the simple algorithm from Section 3.5.1. Overlapping of I/O and computation is achieved using the call-back mechanism supported by the I/O layer. Thus, the sorter remains portable over different operating systems with different interfaces to threading.

We have two implementations with respect to the internal work: stxxl::sort is a comparison based sorting using std::sort from STL to sort the runs internally; stxxl::ksort exploits integer keys and has smaller internal memory bandwidth requirements for large elements with small key fields. After reading elements using DMA (i.e. the STXXL direct access), we extract pairs (key, pointerToElement), sort these pairs, and only then move elements in sorted order to write buffers from where they are output using DMA.

Furthermore, we exploit random keys. We use two passes of MSD (most significant digit) radix sort of the key-pointer pairs. The first pass uses the m most significant bits where m is a tuning parameter depending on the size of the processor caches and of the TLB (translation look-aside buffer). This pass consists of a counting phase that determines bucket sizes and a distribution phase that moves pairs. The counting phase is fused into a single loop with pair extraction. The second pass of radix sort uses a number of bits that brings us closest to an expected bucket size of two. This two-pass algorithm is much more cache efficient than a one-pass radix sort.[8] The remaining buckets are sorted using a comparison based algorithm: Optimal straight line code for $n \leq 4$, insertion sort for $n \in \{5..16\}$, and quicksort for $n > 16$.

Multi-way Merging. We have adapted the tuned multi-way merger from [San00], i.e. a tournament tree stores pointers to the current elements of each merge buffer.

Overlapping I/O and Computation. We integrate the prefetch buffer and the overlap buffer to a *read buffer*. We distribute the buffer space between the two purposes of minimizing disk idle time and overlapping I/O and computation indirectly by computing an optimal prefetch sequence for a smaller buffer space.

Asynchronous I/O. I/O is performed without any synchronization between the disks. The prefetcher computes a sequence σ' of blocks indicating the order in which blocks should be fetched. As soon as a buffer block becomes available for prefetching, it is used to generate an asynchronous read request for the next block in σ'. The I/O layer of STXXL queues this request at the disk storing the block to be fetched. The thread for this disk serves the queued request in FIFO manner. All I/O is implemented without superfluous copying. STXXL opens files with the option O_DIRECT so that blocks are directly moved by DMA (direct memory access) to user memory. A fetched block then travels to the prefetch/overlap buffer and from there to a merge buffer simply by passing a pointer. Similarly, when an element is merged, it is directly moved from the merge buffer to the write buffer and a block of the write buffer is passed to the output queue of a disk simply by passing a pointer to the the I/O layer of STXXL that then uses `write` to output the data using DMA.

3.5.3 Experiments

Hardware. For the experiments we have used the system with two 2GHz Xeon processors, one GByte of RAM and eight IDE disks (described in Section 2.4). The maximum parallel disk bandwidth from the outermost (fastest) zones was about 375 MB/s.

---

[8]On our system we get a factor of 3.8 speedup over the one pass radix sort and a factor of 1.6 over STL's sort which in turn is faster than a hand tuned quicksort (for sorting 2^{21} pairs storing a random four byte key and a pointer).

3.5. PARALLEL DISK SORTING

Software. The system ran the Debian Linux distribution with kernel 2.4.20 and the `ext2` file system. All programs were compiled with `g++` version 3.2 and the optimization level `-O3`.

If not otherwise mentioned, we use random 32 bit integer keys to keep internal work limited. Runs of size 256 MByte[9] are built using key sorting with an initial iteration of 10 bit MSD radix sort. We choose block sizes in such a way that a single merging phase using 512 MBytes for all buffers suffices. Input sizes are powers of two between 2 GByte and 128 GByte with a default of 16 GByte[10]. When not otherwise stated, we use eight disks, 2 MByte blocks, and the input is stored on the fastest zones.

To compare our code with previous implementations, we have to run them on the same machine because technological development in recent years has been very fast. Unfortunately, the implementations we could obtain, LEDA-SM [CM00] and TPIE [APV02], are limited to inputs of size 2 GByte which, for our machine, is a rather small input. Figure 3.24 compares the single disk performance of the three libraries using the best block size for each library. The flat curves for TPIE and STXXL indicate that both codes are I/O bound even for small element sizes. This is even true for the fully comparison based version of STXXL. Still, STXXL is significantly faster than TPIE. This could be due to better overlapping of I/O and computation or due to the higher bandwidth of the file system calls we use. STXXL sustains an I/O bandwidth of 45.4 MByte/s, which is 95 % of the 48 MByte/s peak bandwidth of the disk at their outermost zone. LEDA-SM is compute-bound for small keys and has the same performance as TPIE for large keys.

To get some kind of comparison for parallel disks, we ran the other codes using Linux Software-RAID 0.9 and 8×128KBytes stripes (larger stripes did not improve performance). Here, STXXL is between two and three times faster than TPIE and sustains an I/O bandwidth of 315 MByte/s for large elements (Figure 3.25). Much of this advantage is lost when STXXL also runs on the Software-RAID. Although we view it as likely that the Software-RAID driver can be improved, this performance difference might also be an indication that treating disks as independent devices is better than striping (as predicted by theory).

Figure 3.26 shows the dependence of the performance on the element size in more detail. For element sizes ≥ 64, the merging phase starts to wait for I/Os

---

[9]This leaves space for two runs build in an overlapped way, buffers, operating system, code, and, for large inputs, the fact that the implementation of the `ext2` file system needed 1 byte of internal memory for each KBytes of disk space accessed via `O_DIRECT`.

[10]We have a few measurements with 256 GBytes but the problem with `ext2` mentioned above starts to distort the results for this input size.

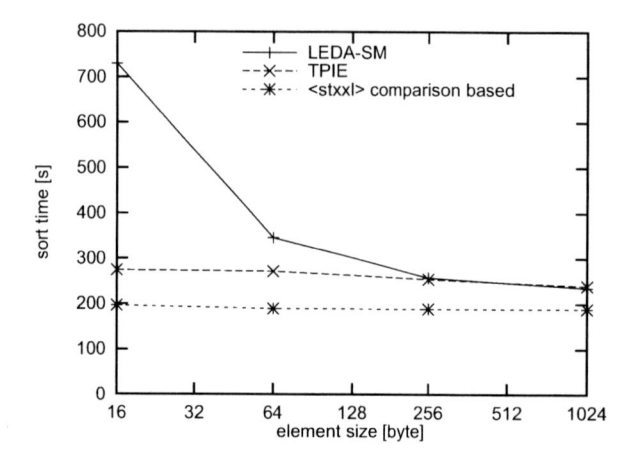

Figure 3.24: Comparison of the single disk performance of STXXL, LEDA-SM, and TPIE.

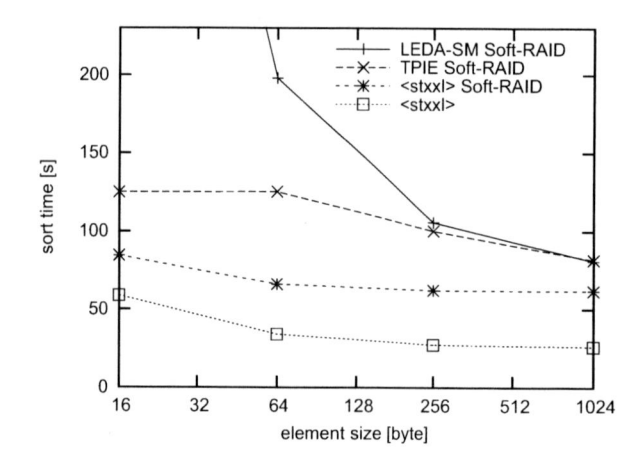

Figure 3.25: Comparison of STXXL, LEDA-SM, and TPIE for eight disks.

3.5. PARALLEL DISK SORTING

and hence is I/O-bound. The run formation phase only becomes I/O-bound for element sizes above 128. This indicates areas for further optimization. For small elements, it should be better to replace key sorting by sorters that always (or more often) move the entire elements. For example, we have observed that the very simple loop that moves elements to the write buffer when the key-pointer pairs are already sorted can take up to 45 % of the CPU time of the run formation. For small keys it also looks promising to use parallelism. Already our cheap machine supports four parallel threads.

We now turn to a more detailed analysis of prefetching and overlapping of I/O and computation. We first focus on the read buffers and hence fix the write buffer size to $4D$ blocks in Figures 3.27–3.29. Figure 3.27 compares the I/O time of the naive algorithm that tries to fetch blocks in the order specified by σ with optimal prefetching. It varies the fraction of the read buffer devoted to prefetching. The rest read buffers are used for overlapping. As one would expect from the theoretical analysis in [HSV01], the I/O time decreases as this fraction grows. However, Figure 3.28 indicates that the overall time needed for merging is best if most of the read buffer is dedicated to overlapping I/O and computation. Only for very small read buffers there is a significant difference between the naive algorithm and optimal prefetching.

In Figure 3.29 we compare the overall merging time for the naive algorithm and the following heuristics for choosing the prefetch buffer size w as a function of the read buffer size r: $w = 2D + \frac{3}{10}(r - 2D)$. We have not shown the empirically optimal choice because it is very close to this heuristics.

Based on this heuristics for the read buffer, Figure 3.30 explores the tradeoff between read buffer size and write buffer size given a total buffer size of 188 blocks. Although we see the asymmetry between read buffer size and write buffer size predicted by the theoretical analysis, it turns out that write buffers much larger than $2D$ blocks can be profitable. A likely reason is that a write buffer of size $w = aD$ blocks leads to an effective output block size of $(a - 1)B$, thereby reducing seek times and perhaps also rotational delays. Based on this observation, we use the following heuristics for the write buffer size in the subsequent figures: $w = \max(t/4, 2D)$ where the total number of buffer blocks available for read and write buffers is t. The total number of blocks available in our measurements is $t = (M - kB)/B$ where $M = 512$ MByte and $k = \lceil 2N/M \rceil$ is the number of runs.

Figure 3.31 shows the dependence of the execution time on the block size. We see that block sizes of several MBytes are needed for good performance. The main reason is the well known observation that blocks should consist of several disk tracks to amortize seeks and rotational delays over a large

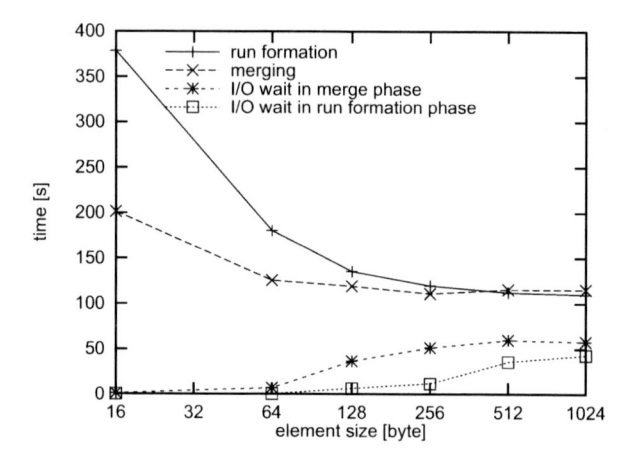

Figure 3.26: Dependence execution time and I/O wait time on the element size.

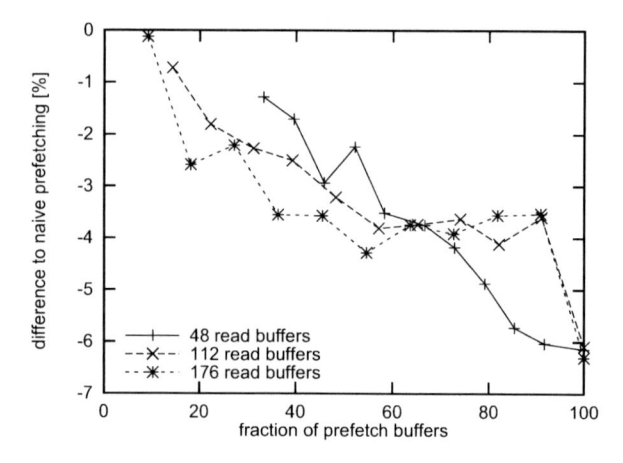

Figure 3.27: Change in input time due to optimal prefetching.

3.5. PARALLEL DISK SORTING

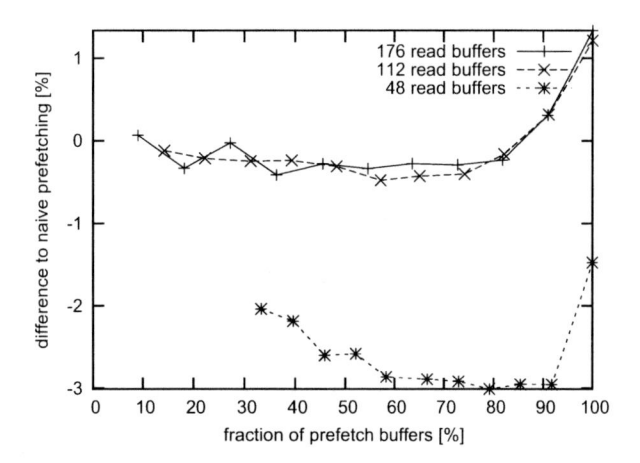

Figure 3.28: Change in total merge time due to "optimal" prefetching.

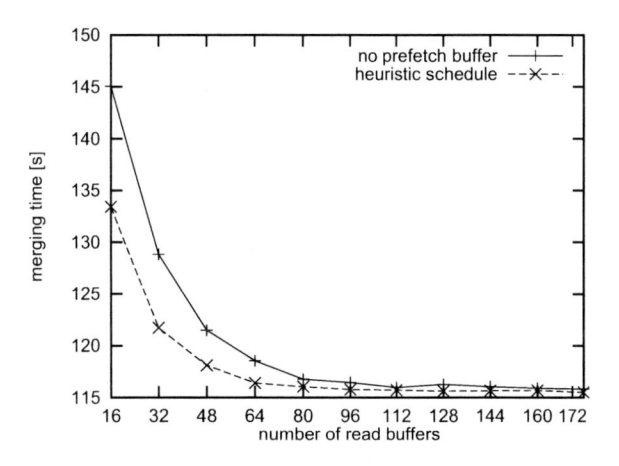

Figure 3.29: Impact of prefetch and overlap buffers on merging time.

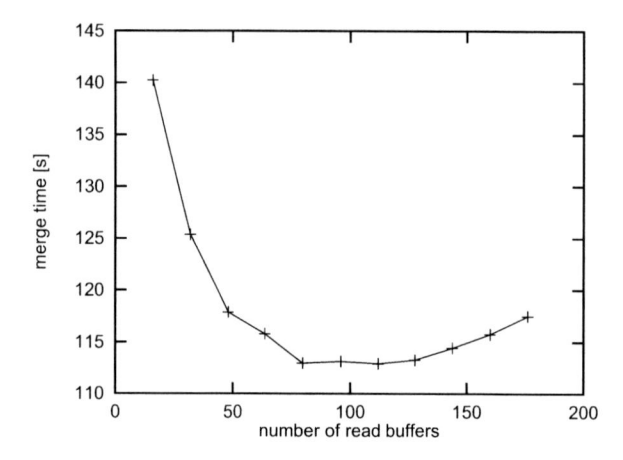

Figure 3.30: Tradeoff: write buffer size versus read buffer size.

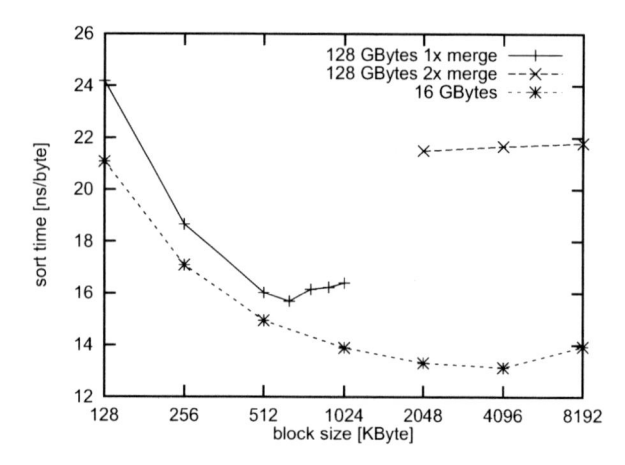

Figure 3.31: Dependence of sorting time on the block size.

3.5. PARALLEL DISK SORTING

consecutive data transfer. This value is much larger than the block sizes used in older studies because the data density on hard disks has dramatically increased in the last years. This effect is further amplified in comparison to the SCSI disks used in most other studies because modern IDE disks have even higher data densities but larger rotational delays and less opportunities for seek time optimization.

Nevertheless, the largest possible block size is not optimal because it leaves too little room for read and write buffers. Hence, in most measurements we use the heuristics to choose half the largest possible block size that is a power of two.

For very large inputs, Figure 3.31 shows that we already have to go below the "really good" block sizes because of the lack of buffer space. Still, it is not a good idea to switch to two merge passes because the overall time increases even if we are able to stick to large block sizes with more passes. The large optimal block sizes are an indicator that "asymptotically efficient" can also translate into "practically relevant" because simpler suboptimal parallel disk algorithms often use logical blocks striped over the disks. On our system, this leads to a further reduction of the possible block size by a factor of about eight.

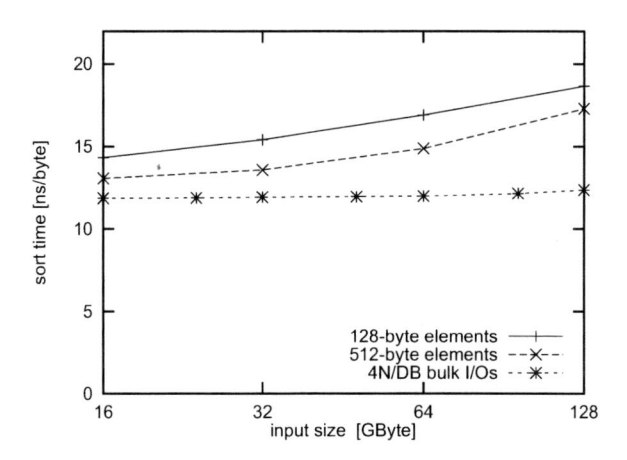

Figure 3.32: Dependence of sorting time on the input size.

Finally, Figure 3.32 shows the overall performance for different input sizes using all the heuristics introduced above. Although we can stick to two passes, the execution time per element goes up because we need to employ increasingly slow zones, because the block sizes go down, and because the seek times go during merging up.

3.5.4 Discussion

We have engineered a sorting algorithm that combines a very high performance on state of the art hardware with theoretical performance guarantees. This algorithm is compute-bound although we use small random keys and a tuned linear time algorithm for the run formation. Similar observations apply to other external memory algorithms that exhibit a good spatial locality, i.e. those dominated by scanning, sorting, and similar operations (see e.g. Chapters 4 and 5). This indicates that bandwidth is no longer a limiting factor for external memory algorithms if parallel disks are used.

On the other hand, the fact that it is challenging to sustain a peak bandwidth for eight disks on a dual processor system implies that using even more disks requires a more aggressive use of parallel processing. Using the MCSTL [Sin06] library we have parallelized the internal work in the run formation and merge phases of our implementation. On the *SCSIOpteron* system (Section 2.4) with eight fast SCSI disks we have sorted *small* 8-byte records with a speedup close to *two* using four processors. The compute bound could be raised by dividing the load onto many processors [Sin06].

Algorithmically, several promising improvements remain, even for small cheap machines: There are several ways to speed up the run formation for small elements. During merging, it would be good to reduce seek times for large inputs, either by some clever compromise between seek minimization and prefetching, or by switching to the distribution sort [VH01] that can be implemented to have an inherently low seek overhead.

3.6 Algorithm Pipelining

The pipelined processing technique is very well known in the database world [SKS01].

Usually, the interface of an external memory algorithm assumes that it reads the input from (an) external memory container(s) and writes output into (an) external memory container(s). The idea of pipelining is to equip the external memory algorithms with a new interface that allows them to feed the output as a data stream directly to the algorithm that consumes the output, rather than writing it to the external memory first. Logically, the input of an external memory algorithm does not have to reside in the external memory, rather, it could be a data stream produced by another external memory algorithm.

Many external memory algorithms can be viewed as a data flow through a directed acyclic graph G with node set $V = F \cup S \cup R$ and edge set E. The *file nodes* F represent physical data sources and data sinks, which are stored on disks (e.g. in the external memory containers of the STL-user layer). A file node writes or/and reads one stream of elements. The *streaming nodes* S read zero, one or several streams and output zero, one or several new streams. Streaming nodes are equivalent to scan operations in non-pipelined external memory algorithms. The difference is that non-pipelined conventional scanning needs a linear number of I/Os, whereas streaming nodes usually do not perform any I/O, unless a node needs to access external memory data structures (stacks, priority queues, etc.). The sorting nodes R read a stream and output it in a sorted order. Edges E in the graph G denote the directions of data flow between nodes. The question "When is a pipelined execution of the computations in a data flow graph G possible in an I/O-efficient way?" is analyzed in [DMKS05].

3.7 Streaming Layer

The streaming layer provides a framework for the *pipelined* processing of large sequences. Many external memory algorithms implemented with the STXXL streaming layer save a factor of at least two in I/Os. To the best of our knowledge we are the first who apply the pipelining method systematically in the domain of external memory algorithms. We introduce it in the context of an external memory software library.

In STXXL, all data flow node implementations have an STXXL stream interface which is similar to the STL Input iterators[11]. As an input iterator, an STXXL stream object may be dereferenced to refer to some object and may be incremented to proceed to the next object in the stream. The reference obtained by dereferencing is read-only and must be convertible to the `value_type` of the STXXL stream. The concept of the STXXL stream also defines a boolean member function `empty()` which returns `true` iff the end of the stream is reached.

Now we tabulate the valid expressions and the expression semantics of the STXXL stream concept in the style of the STL documentation.

Notation

`X, X1, ..., Xn`	A type that is a model of the STXXL stream
`T`	The value type of `X`
`s, s1, ..., sn`	Object of type `X, X1, ..., Xn`
`t`	Object of type `T`

Valid expressions

Name	Expression	Type requirements	Return type
Constructor	`X s(s1,...,sn)`	`s1, ..., sn` are convertible to `X1&, ..., Xn&`	
Dereference	`*s`		Convertible to `T`
Member access	`s->m`	`T` is a type for which `t.m` is defined	
Preincrement	`++s`		`X&`
End of stream check	`(*s).empty()`		`bool`

---

[11] Not be confused with the stream interface of the C++ `iostream` library.

Expression semantics

Name	Expression	Precondition	Semantics	Postcondition
Constructor	`X s(s1,...,sn)`	`s1, ..., sn` are the n input streams of `s`		
Dereference	`*s`	`s` is incrementable		
Member access	`s->m`	`s` is incrementable	Equivalent to `(*s).m`	
Preincrement	`++s`	`s` is incrementable		`s` is incrementable or past-the-end

The binding of a STXXL stream object to its input streams (incoming edges in a data flow graph G) happens at compile time, i.e. statically. The other approach would be to allow binding at running time using the C++ virtual function mechanism. However this would result in a severe performance penalty because most C++ compilers are not able to inline virtual functions. To avoid this disadvantage, we follow the static binding approach using C++ templates. For example, assuming that streams `s1`, ..., `sn` are already constructed, construction of stream `s` with constructor `X::X(X1& s1,..., Xn& sn)` will bind `s` to its inputs `s1`, ..., `sn`.

After creating all node objects, the computation starts in a "lazy" fashion, first trying to evaluate the result of the topologically latest node. The node reads its intermediate input nodes, element by element, using the dereference and increment operator of the STXXL stream interface. The input nodes proceed in the same way, invoking the inputs needed to produce an output element. This process terminates when the result of the topologically latest node is computed. This style of pipelined execution scheduling is I/O efficient, it allows to keep the intermediate results in-memory without needing to store them in external memory.

The Streaming layer of the STXXL library offers generic classes which implement the functionality of sorting, file, and streaming nodes:

- File nodes: Function `streamify` serves as an adaptor that converts a range of ForwardIterators into a compatible STXXL stream. Since iterators of `stxxl::vector` are RandomAccessIterators, `streamify` can be used to read external memory. The set of (overloaded) `materialize` functions implement data sink nodes, they flush the content of a STXXL stream object to an output iterator. The library also offers specializations of `streamify` and `materialize` for `stxxl::vector`, which are more efficient than the generic implementations due to the support of overlapping between I/O and computation.

- Sort nodes: The Stream layer `stream::sort` class is a generic pipelined sorter which has the interface of an STXXL stream. The input of the sorter may be an object complying to the STXXL stream interface. As the STL-user layer sorter, the pipelined sorter is an implementation of parallel disk merge sort [DS03] that overlaps I/O and computation. The implementation of `stream::sort` relies on two classes that encapsulate the two phases of the algorithm: sorted run formation (class `runs_creator`) and run merging (`runs_merger`). The separate use of these classes breaks the pipelined data flow: the `runs_creator` must read the entire input to compute the sorted runs. This facilitates an efficient implementation of loops and recursions: the input for the next iteration or recursion can be the sorted runs stored on disks [Meh04, DMKS05]. The templated class `runs_creator` has several specializations which have input interfaces different from the STXXL stream interface: a specialization where elements to be sorted are `push_back`'ed into the `runs_creator` object and a specialization that accepts a set of presorted sequences. All specializations are compatible with the `runs_merger`.

- Streaming nodes: In general, most of the implementation effort for algorithms with the streaming layer goes to the streaming nodes. The STXXL library exposes generic classes that help to accelerate coding the streaming node classes. For example `stream::transform` is similar to the `std::transform` algorithm: it reads n input streams `s1`, ..., `sn` and returns the result of a user-given n-ary function object `functor(*s1,...,*sn)` as the next element of the output stream until one of the input streams gets empty.

As mentioned above, STXXL allows streaming nodes to have more than one output. In this case, only one output of a streaming node can have the STXXL stream interface (it is an iterator). The other outputs can be passed to other nodes using a "push-item" interface. Such an interface have file nodes (e.g. the method `push_back` of `stxxl::vector`) and sorting nodes (`push_back`-specializations). Streaming nodes do not have such methods by definition,

3.7. STREAMING LAYER

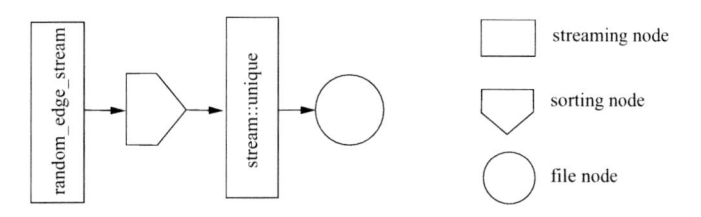

Figure 3.33: Data flow graph for the example in Listing 3.7.

however, it is always possible to reimplement all streaming nodes between sorting and/or file nodes as a single streaming node that will push_back the output elements to the corresponding sorting/file nodes.

Now we "pipeline" the random graph generation example shown in the previous chapter. The data flow graph of the algorithm is presented in Figure 3.33 in the appendix. Listing 3.7 shows the pipelined code of the algorithm, the definitions of edge, random_edge, and edge_cmp are in Listing 3.5. Since the sorter of the streaming layer accepts an STXXL stream input, we do not need to output the random edges. Rather, we generate them on the fly. The random_edge_stream object (model of STXXL stream) constructed in Line 19 supplies the sorter with a stream of random edges. In Line 21, we define the type of the sorter node; it is parameterized by the type of the input stream and the type of the comparison function object. Line 23 creates a SortedStream object attaching its input to the RandomStream. The internal memory consumption of the sorter stream object is limited to 512 MB. The UniqueStream object filters the duplicates in its input edge stream (Line 25). The generic stream::unique stream class stems from the STXXL library. Line 28 records the content of the UniqueStream into the external memory vector. As in the Listing 3.6 (Line 29), we cut the vector at the NewEnd boundary. Let us count the number of I/Os the program performs: random edge generation by RandomStream costs no I/O; sorting in SortedStream needs to store the sorted runs and read them again to merge — $2N/DB$ I/Os; UniqueStream deletes duplicates on the fly, it does not need any I/O; and materializing the final output can cost up to N/DB I/Os. All in all, the program only incurs $3N/DB$ I/Os, compared to $7N/DB$ for the nonpipelined code in Section 3.4.

Listing 3.7: Generating a random graph using the Streaming layer.

```
using namespace stxxl;
class random_edge_stream {
    int64 counter;
    edge current;
    random_edge_stream();
public:
    typedef edge value_type;
    random_edge_stream(int64 elements):
        counter(elements), current(random_edge()()){ }
    const edge & operator * () const { return current; }
    const edge * operator ->() const { return &current; }
    random_edge_stream & operator ++ () {
        --counter;
        current = random_edge()();
        return *this;
    }
    bool empty() const { return counter==0; }
};
random_edge_stream RandomStream(10000000000ULL);
typedef stream::sort<random_edge_stream, edge_cmp>
    sorted_stream;
sorted_stream SortedStream(RandomStream, edge_cmp(),
    512*1024*1024);
typedef stream::unique<sorted_stream> unique_stream_type;
unique_stream_type UniqueStream(SortedStream);
stxxl::vector<edge> ExtEdgeVec(10000000000ULL);
stxxl::vector<edge>::iterator NewEnd =
    stream::materialize(UniqueStream, ExtEdgeVec.begin());
ExtEdgeVec.resize(NewEnd - ExtEdgeVec.begin());
```

Chapter 4

Engineering Algorithms for Large Graphs

This chapter is devoted to engineering practical algorithms for large graphs not fitting into the main memory. We implement the algorithms using STXXL and show how its features, like pipelining, help to improve the performance of the implementations. The performance characteristics of the implementation are tested on several architectures and on various random and real-world data sets.

4.1 Overview

We start from the simple introductory example in Section 4.2 that computes a maximal independent set of a graph. We also implement the algorithm using the LEDA-SM library to make some conclusions about the performance. In this example the usefulness of pipelining is shown. Section 4.3 engineers a practical I/O-efficient algorithm for computing minimum spanning forests (MSF). Its performance is excellent: It is only 2–5 times slower than the best internal memory algorithms. The algorithm is modified in Section 4.4 to compute spanning forests (SF) and connected components (CC). The SF/CC implementation turns out to be 1.4–7.1 times faster than the MSF implementation. In Section 4.5 we compare STXXL-implementations of two I/O-efficient breadth first search algorithms. A simpler algorithm of Munagala and Ranade [MR99] produced bad results on difficult graphs with a large diameter. An implementation of a more involved algorithm of Mehlhorn and Meyer [MM02] has provided a better running time and I/O guarantees for these inputs. In Section 4.6 we implement an I/O-efficient algorithm for finding, counting and listing all triangles in a graph. We show the practicality of the implementation running it on a real huge web graph. I/O-efficient algorithms for coloring graphs are studied in Section 4.7. We investigate existing heuristics and develop a new fast heuristic that can 7-color planar graphs in $\mathcal{O}(\text{sort}(n))$ I/Os.

4.2 Maximal Independent Set

We demonstrate some performance characteristics of STXXL using the external memory maximal independent set (MIS) [1] algorithm from [Zeh02] as an example. The MIS problem is used, for example, for scheduling dependent parallel jobs. The algorithm [Zeh02] is based on the time-forward processing technique. As input for the MIS algorithm we use the random graph computed by the examples in the previous Sections (Listings 3.6 and 3.7). Our benchmark also includes the running time of the input generation.

Now we describe the MIS algorithm implementation in Listing 4.1 which is only nine lines long not including `typedef` declarations. The algorithm visits the graph nodes scanning lexicographically sorted input edges. When a node is visited, we add it to the maximal independent set if none of its visited neighbors is already in the MIS. The neighbor nodes of the MIS nodes are stored as events in a priority queue. In Lines 7-9, the template metaprogram [CE00] `PRIORITY_QUEUE_GENERATOR` computes the type of priority queue that will store events. The metaprogram finds the optimal values for numerous tuning parameters (the number and the maximum arity of external/internal mergers, the size of merge buffers, the external memory block size, etc.) under the constraint that the total size of the priority queue internal buffers must be limited by `PQ_MEM` bytes. The `node_greater` comparison functor defines the order of nodes of the type `node_type` and the minimum value that a node object can have, such that the `top()` method will return the smallest contained element. The last template parameter assures that the priority queue cannot contain more than the `INPUT_SIZE` elements (in 1024 units). Line 11 creates the priority queue `depend` having a prefetch buffer pool of size `PQ_PPOOL_MEM` bytes and a buffered write memory pool of size `PQ_WPOOL_MEM` bytes. The external vector `MIS` stores the nodes belonging to the maximal independent set. Ordered input edges come in the form of an STXXL stream called `edges`. If the current node `edges->src` is not a neighbor of a MIS node (the comparison with the current event `depend.top()`, Line 16), then it is included in `MIS` (if it was not there before, Line 18). All neighbor nodes `edges->dst` of a node in MIS `edges->src` are inserted in the event priority queue `depend` (Line 19). Lines 14-15 remove the events already passed through from the priority queue.

To make a comparison with other external memory libraries, we have im-

---

[1] An independent set I is a set of nodes on a (multi)graph G such that no edge in G joins two nodes in I, i.e. the nodes in I are not neighbors. A *maximal* independent set is an independent set such that adding any other node would cause the set not to be independent anymore.

Listing 4.1: Computing a Maximal Independent Set using STXXL.
```
struct node_greater: public std::greater<node_type> {
    node_type min_value() const  {
        return std::numeric_limits<node_type >::max();
    }
};
typedef
stxxl::PRIORITY_QUEUE_GENERATOR<node_type,
    node_greater,PQ_MEM, INPUT_SIZE/1024>::result pq_type;

// keeps "not in MIS" events
pq_type depend(PQ_PPOOL_MEM,PQ_WPOOL_MEM);
stxxl::vector<node_type> MIS;  // output
for(;!edges.empty();++edges)  {
    while(!depend.empty() && edges->src > depend.top())
        depend.pop();  // delete old events
    if(depend.empty() || edges->src != depend.top() ) {
        if(MIS.empty() || MIS.back() != edges->src )
            MIS.push_back(edges->src);
        depend.push(edges->dst);
    }
}
```

plemented the graph generation algorithm using the TPIE and LEDA-SM libraries. The MIS algorithm was implemented in LEDA-SM using its array heap data structure as a priority queue. The I/O efficient implementation of the MIS algorithm was not possible in TPIE, since it does not have an I/O efficient priority queue implementation. For TPIE, we only report the running time of the graph generation [2].

To make the benchmark closer to real applications, we have added two 32-bit integer fields to the **edge** data structure, which can store some additional information associated with the edge. The implementations of a priority queue of LEDA-SM always store a pair <key,info>. The info field takes at least four bytes. Therefore, to make a fair comparison with STXXL, we have changed the event data type stored in the priority queue (Listing 4.1) such that it also has a 4-byte dummy info field.

The experiments were run on the MPIXeon system described in Section 2.4 with swapping switched off. The OS was Debian with Linux kernel 2.4.20. The computer had four hard disks formatted with the XFS file system and dedicated solely for the experiments. We used the LEDA-SM version 1.3 with

---

[2]The source code of all our implementations is available under http://i10www.ira.uka.de/dementiev/stxxl/paper/index.shtml.

4.2. MAXIMAL INDEPENDENT SET

the LEDA version 4.2.1[3] and TPIE of January 21, 2005. For the compilation of the STXXL and TPIE sources the g++ compiler version 3.3 was used. LEDA-SM and LEDA were compiled with the g++ compiler version 2.95, because they could not be compiled by later g++ versions. The compiler optimization level was set to -O3. For sorting we used library sorters that use C++ comparison operators to compare elements. All programs have been tuned to achieve their maximum performance. We have tried all available file access methods and disk block sizes. In order to tune the TPIE benchmark implementation, we followed the performance tuning Section of [ABH+03]. The input size (the length of the random edge sequence, see Listing 3.6) for all tests was 2000 MB[4]. The benchmark programs were limited to use only 512 MB of main memory. The remaining 512 MB were given to the operating system kernel, daemons, shared libraries and the file system buffer cache, from which TPIE and LEDA-SM might benefit. The STXXL implementations do not use the file system cache.

Table 4.1: Running time (in seconds)/I/O bandwidth (in MB/s) of the MIS benchmark running on single disk. For TPIE, only the graph generation is shown (marked with *). The running time of the input graph generation is split into the three phases: filling, sorting and duplicate removal.

	LEDA-SM	STXXL-STL	STXXL-Pipel.	TPIE
Filling	51/41	89/24	100/20	40/52
Sorting	371/23	188/45		307/28
Dup. removal	160/26	104/40	128/26	109/39
MIS computation	513/6	153/21		–N/A–
Total	1095/16	534/33	228/24	456*/32*

Table 4.1 compares the MIS benchmark performance of the LEDA-SM implementation with the array heap priority queue, the STXXL implementation based on the STL-user level, a pipelined STXXL implementation, and a TPIE implementation with only input graph generation. The running times, averaged over three runs, and average I/O bandwidths are given for each stage of the benchmark. The running time of the different stages of the pipelined implementation cannot be measured separately. However, we show the values of time and I/O counters from the beginning of the execution till the time when the sorted runs are written to the disk(s) in the run formation phase of sorting, and from this point to the end of the MIS computation. The

---
[3] Later versions of the LEDA are not supported by the last LEDA-SM version 1.3.
[4] Algorithms and data structures of LEDA-SM are limited to inputs of size 2 GB.

total running time numbers show that the pipelined STXXL implementation is significantly faster than the other implementations. It is 2.4 times faster than the second leading implementation (STXXL-STL). The win is due to the reduced I/O volume: the STXXL-STL implementation transfers 17 GB, the pipelined implementation only needs 5.2 GB. However, the 3.25 fold I/O volume reduction does not imply equal reduction of the running time because the run formation fused with the filling/generating phase becomes compute-bound. This is indicated by the almost zero value of the STXXL I/O wait counter, which measures the time the processing thread waited for the completion of an I/O. The second reason is that the fusion of merging, duplicate removal and CPU intensive priority queue operations in the MIS computation is almost compute-bound. Comparing the running times of the total input graph generation, we conclude that the STXXL-STL implementation is about 20 % faster than TPIE and 53 % faster than LEDA-SM. This could be due to better (explicit) overlapping between I/O and computation. Another possible reason could be that TPIE uses a more expensive way of reporting run-time errors, such as I/O errors[5]. The running time of the the filling stage of the STXXL-STL implementation is much higher than that of TPIE and LEDA-SM. This is because those libraries rely on the operating system cache. The filled blocks do not go to the disk(s) immediately but remain in the main memory until other data needs to be cached by the system. An indication for this is the very high bandwidth of 52 MB/s for the TPIE implementation, which is even higher than the maximum physical disk bandwidth (48 MB/s) at its outermost zone. However, the cached blocks need to be flushed in the sorting stage and then the TPIE implementation pays the remaining due. The unsatisfactory bandwidth of 24 MB/s of the STXXL-STL filling phase could be improved by replacing the call `std::generate` by the native `stxxl::generate` call that efficiently overlaps I/O and computation. With a single disk it fills the vector in 60 seconds with a bandwidth of 33 MB/s. The STXXL STL-user sorter sustains an I/O bandwidth of about 45 MB/s which is 95 % of the disk's peak bandwidth. The high CPU load in the priority queue and the less then perfect overlapping between I/O and computation explain the low bandwidth of the MIS computation stage in all three implementations. We also run the graph generation test on 16 GByte inputs. All implementations scale with the input size almost linearly: the

---

[5]TPIE uses function return types for error codes and diagnostics, which can become quite expensive at the level of single-item interfaces (e.g. `read_item` and `write_item`) that are predominantly used in TPIEs algorithms. Instead, STXXL checks (I/O) errors on a per-block basis. We will use C++ exceptions to propagate errors to the user layer without any disadvantage for the library users. First experiments indicate that this will have an negligible impact on runtime.

4.2. MAXIMAL INDEPENDENT SET

TPIE implementation finishes in 1h 3min, the STXXL-STL in 49min, and the STXXL-Pipelined in 28min.

The MIS computation of STXXL, which is dominated by PQ operations, is 3.35 times faster than LEDA-SM. The main reason for this big speedup is likely to be the more efficient priority queue algorithm from [San00].

Table 4.2: Running time (in seconds)/I/O bandwidth (in MB/s) of the MIS benchmark running on multiple disk.

		STXXL-STL		STXXL-Pipelined	
Disks		2	4	2	4
Input graph generation	Filling	72/28	64/31	98/20	98/20
	Sorting	104/77	80/100	—	—
	Dup. removal	58/69	34/118	112/30	110/31
MIS computation		127/25	114/28		
Total		360/50	291/61	210/26	208/27

Table 4.2 shows the parallel disk performance of the STXXL implementations. The STXXL-STL implementation achieves a speedup of about 1.5 using two disks and 1.8 using four disks. The reason for this low speedup is that many parts of the code become compute-bound: priority queue operations in the MIS computation stage, the run formation in the sorting stage, and the generating random edges in the filling stage. The STXXL-pipelined implementation was almost compute-bound in the single disk case, and, with two disks the first phase shows no speedup as expected. However the second phase has a small improvement in speed due to faster I/O. A close to zero I/O wait time indicates that the STXXL-pipelined implementation is fully compute-bound when running with two or four disks. We had run the STXXL-pipelined implementation on very large graphs that require the entire space of four hard disks (360 GBytes). The results of this experiment, using the faster *SCSIOpteron* system (Section 2.4), are shown in Table 4.3.

Table 4.3: Running time of the STXXL-pipelined implementation on very large random graphs (*SCSIOpteron* system).

Input volume	N/M	n	m	m/n	D	Running time
100 GB	200	$2.1 \cdot 10^9$	$13.4 \cdot 10^9$	6.25	4	2h 34min
100 GB	200	$4.3 \cdot 10^9$	$13.4 \cdot 10^9$	3.13	4	2h 44min

4.3 Minimum Spanning Trees

The results presented in this section were partially published in [DSSS04] and in the bachelor thesis [Sch03a].

4.3.1 Definitions

A spanning tree of a connected undirected graph $G = (V, E)$ is a connected acyclic subgraph $T = (V, E'), E' \subseteq E$ that contains all nodes of G. Given a weight function $w : E \to \mathbb{N}_0$, the weight of a spanning tree is the sum of the weights of all edges belonging to it: $w(T) = \sum_{e \in E'} w(e)$. A *minimum spanning tree* (MST) is a spanning tree with the smallest weight over all possible spanning trees. Graphs having *several* connected components cannot have a single spanning tree, but a spanning forest, which consists of trees spanning the connected components. Analogously, a minimum spanning forest (MSF) has the smallest weight over all spanning forests.

4.3.2 Related Work and Motivation

The problem of finding an MST (or MSF) has already been mentioned in 1926 by Boruvka [Bor26]. His goal was to find an efficient electrical coverage of Bohemia. MST can be used to model many other kinds of minimum cost network coverage problems. Many graph algorithms need an MST computation as a subroutine.

The MST problem can be solved in internal memory very efficiently. Recently, Pettie and Ramachandran [PR00] have found a provably *optimal* deterministic MST algorithm. However, the running time complexity of this algorithm is unknown, it is a long standing open problem. Like the algorithm of Chazelle [Cha00], the algorithm of Pettie and Ramachandran has complexity $\mathcal{O}(m\alpha(m, n))$, where α is the inverse Ackermann function. The function α grows extremely slowly, so that for all practical purposes it may be considered a constant no greater than 4. Thus these algorithms can be considered to run in time very close to linear. Randomized MST algorithms are known that run in linear expected time.

MST is one of the rare graph problems that can be solved I/O-efficiently. Using a randomized algorithm a MST can be found in $\mathcal{O}(\text{sort}(m))$ expected I/Os [ABW02]. The best known deterministic algorithm finds a MST using $\mathcal{O}(\text{sort}(m) \cdot \max\{1, \log \log(nBD/m)\})$ I/Os [MR99]. The deterministic lower bound for the number of I/Os is unknown, too.

4.3. MINIMUM SPANNING TREES

Despite the fact that a number of I/O-efficient MST algorithms exist, none of them has ever been implemented. A reason for that may be that even the simplest algorithms turned out to be difficult to implement. The authors of [DSSS04] developed a *simple* I/O-efficient algorithm for computing MSTs of very large graphs. In the following we describe this algorithm as well as its two STXXL implementations.

The algorithm consists of two phases. The first phase (Section 4.3.4) reduces the node set of the input graphs until the number of nodes reaches $n' = \mathcal{O}(M)$, simultaneously outputting some MST edges. For this phase one has two implementations: an implementation for graphs with arbitrary node degrees, based on `stxxl::priority_queue`, and a faster *bucket* implementation that works if the node degree is limited by $\mathcal{O}(M)$. In the second phase (Section 4.3.3) the main memory can hold a constant size per-node information, thus the algorithm can operate in semi-external mode [6]. The rest of the MST edges is then output. Section 4.3.5 presents the performance characteristics of the algorithm implementation on various families of sparse random graphs.

4.3.3 Semi-External Algorithm

This algorithm is a variant of Kruskal's algorithm [Kru56]. It processes the edges in order of increasing weight. To sort the edges by weight, `stxxl::ksort` is used (Section 3.5). This sorter version is faster than `stxxl::sort` because it can take advantage of the integer weights with respect to the internal work. During processing, the algorithm maintains a minimum spanning forest F of the edges seen so far. If an edge (u, v) joins two spanning trees in F then it is output as MST edge, otherwise it is discarded. The necessary operations can be implemented very efficiently using a union-find data structure [Tar75] if nodes are numbered $0..n-1$. This data structure has been implemented using an array of integer tree links and an array of merging ranks, both having n entries. The paper [DSSS04] shows how to dispense with the merging rank array.

4.3.4 Node Reduction

The node reduction algorithm is based on edge contraction. In each step a random node v is chosen from the graph, and the lightest edge (v, w)

---

[6]Semi-external graph algorithms are the algorithms which operate I/O-efficiently for graphs with $n = \mathcal{O}(M)$.

incident to v is found. Edge (v,w) is output as an MST edge. Node v is removed from the graph and all its incident edges (v,u) are replaced with edges (w,u) (relinking), i.e. nodes v and w are contracted. Since the nodes are renamed during the processing, one keeps the original edge id in the edge data structure to obtain the original ids in the MST output.

The expected number of edges inspected till the number of nodes is reduced to n' by this abstract algorithm is bounded by $2m \ln \frac{n}{n'}$ (see [DSSS04] for details of the proof). Instead of choosing the node to delete at random the I/O-efficient implementation fixes the order of nodes in advance. If the nodes are numbered $0..n-1$ one renames the node ids using a random permutation $\pi : 0..n-1 \to 0..n-1$. Then the nodes are removed in the order $n-1, n-2, \ldots, n'$. One can prove that this approach is equivalent to random sampling [DSSS04].

Priority Queue Implementation

The above mentioned algorithm easily can be implemented using an I/O-efficient priority queue. Our implementation uses `stxxl::priority_queue` from Section 3.4.5. Edges are stored in the form $((u,v), c, e_{old})$, where (u,v) is the edge in the current graph, c is the weight of the edge and e_{old} is the original id of the edge. The queue stores edges (u,v) with $u > v$ with the order defined as $((u,v), c, e_{old}) < ((u',v'), c', e'_{old})$ iff $u > u'$ or $u = u'$ and $c < c'$. Using these conventions the algorithm shown in Figure 4.1 reduces the node set to n' nodes and outputs the MST edges performing $\mathcal{O}(\text{sort}(m) \ln \frac{n}{n'})$ I/Os [DSSS04]. The real code [Sch03a] that implements the pseudocode using STXXL is very short and simple: the reduction is programmed using only 12 lines of C++ code (see Listing 4.2).

Bucket Implementation

The priority queue implementation has a substantional internal CPU work overhead since it unnecessarily sorts the edges within the adjacency list of a node. However, one should assure that the lightest edge comes first. The authors of the paper [DSSS04] propose an implementation of the reduction phase that has linear work in the total I/O volume.

As in the PQ implementation, in iteration i node i is removed by outputting the lightest edge incident to it and relinking all the other edges. The edges (u,v), $v < u \wedge n' < u \leq n-1$ are stored in k equal sized external memory *buckets*, where $k = \mathcal{O}(M/B)$. The remaining edges (u,v), $v < u$, $u \in [0, n')$ are stored in a special external memory bucket. This bucket is implemented

4.3. MINIMUM SPANNING TREES

Listing 4.2: C++ code for reduction with STXXL priority queue.

```
// get shortest edge incident to the last node
RelabeledEdge minWeightEdge( _pqueue.top() );
_pqueue.pop();
_result.add( minWeightEdge );
// Process all edges in the priority queue
while ( ! _pqueue.empty() ) {
    // get current edge
    RelabeledEdge currentEdge( _pqueue.top() );
    _pqueue.pop();
    // check whether the current edge has the same
    // source vertex as the predecessor
    if( minWeightEdge.source() == currentEdge.source() ) {
        // throw the old source vertex away
        RelabeledEdgeWithoutSource
            curEdgeWithoutSource(currentEdge);
        // add the relabeled edge to the first external
        // bucket resp. to the priority queue
        add(RelabeledEdge(curEdgeWithoutSource,
            minWeightEdge.target()));
    }
    else {
        // the current edge is the shortest one incident
        // to the currently last node
        minWeightEdge = currentEdge;
        _result.add( minWeightEdge );
    }
}
```

```
ExternalPriorityQueue: Q
foreach (e = (u, v), c) ∈ E do Q.insert(((π(u), π(v)), c, e))     // rename
currentNode := −1                          // node currently being removed
i := n                                     // number of remaining nodes
while i > n' do
   ((u, v), c, e_old) := Q.deleteMin()
   if u ≠ currentNode then                 // lightest edge out of a new node
      currentNode := u                     // node u is removed
      i--
      relinkTo := v
      output e_old                         // MST edge
   elsif v ≠ relinkTo then
      Q.insert((v, relinkTo), c, e_old)    // relink non-self-loops
```

Figure 4.1: An I/O-efficient implementation of the node reduction algorithm using a priority queue.

as an `stxxl::vector`. It is assumed that the current bucket completely fits into the internal memory. The other external buckets are implemented as `stxxl::stacks`. We have tried both the basic implementation `normal_stack` (Section 3.4.2) that keeps a single private write block with the recently re-linked edges and the advanced stack implementation `grow_shrink_stack2` that owns a private write block and can overlap I/O and computation using a common pool of additional output buffers. Preliminary tests have shown that the `grow_shrink_stack2` version of the node reduction is faster by 40-50 % even if the block size is reduced to make space for the overlap buffers.

When i reaches a new external memory bucket, it is distributed to *internal buckets* — one for each node in the external memory bucket. Before reading the edges from the external memory bucket its `grow_shrink_stack2` is switched to *prefetch* mode such that it can use additional buffers to read ahead the data, overlapping I/O and computation. The internal bucket for node i is scanned twice: Once for finding the lightest edge and once for re-linking. Relinked edges belonging to the current external memory bucket are immediately inserted to the corresponding internal memory bucket. The remaining edges are put into their external memory buckets.

When n' nodes are left, the special bucket is used directly as input for the semi-external algorithm (Section 4.3.3).

Note that the bucket implementation can fail if internal memory buckets must

4.3. MINIMUM SPANNING TREES

hold adjacency list of nodes with very a high degree. [DSSS04] proposes solutions for this problem, namely, it is possible to move the high-degree nodes from the internal bucket to the special bucket and even if the average size external bucket does not fit into the internal memory then one can apply a multi-level distribution scheme. As an option for problem buckets one could also temporarily switch to the priority queue implementation.

Parallel Edges and Sparse Graphs

The node reduction algorithm described earlier can produce parallel edges during relinking. Moreover, these edges also remain in the graph after subsequent relinking operations. However, they can be removed relatively easily. While scanning the internal buckets the edges (u, v) are put into an intermediate hash table before before moving them to the appropriate buckets. Note that this hash table only keeps the lightest edge between the nodes u and v seen so far. When the capacity of the hash table is reached or all nodes in the current external bucket are scanned, the edges accumulated in the hash table are flushed to the buckets.

[DSSS04] proves that this simple treatment reduces the I/O complexity of the algorithm to $\mathcal{O}(\text{sort}(n))$ I/Os for planar graphs, graphs with a bounded tree-width and other families of graphs that remain sparse under edge contraction.

Implementation Details

The implementation of the internal buckets is very efficient both in running time and space consumption. They are represented as linked lists of small blocks that can hold several edges each. An edge structure stored in an internal bucket does not keep the source node id because this information is redundant. In the external memory part, the edge data structure is stored as a 5-tuple of 32-bit integers and stores the original edge id directly as two end points. This saves the additional sort/scan phase at the end for the restoring of the original ids of MST edges. Another advantage is that it allows to give ids to more than 2^{32} edges in a straightforward way without needing any special coding scheme for ids greater than 2^{32}. More details about the implementation can be found in [Sch03a].

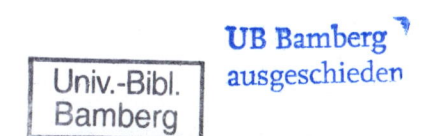

4.3.5 Experiments

In this section we present the most important subset of the experimental results reported in [Sch03a, DSSS04]. For the detailed data see the original sources.

The performance of the STXXL implementations of the MST algorithm was evaluated on several graph families:

- random graphs with given n and m and random edge weights,

- random geometric graphs where random points in the unit square are connected to their d closest neighbors.

- planar graphs — grid graphs with random edge weights and nodes connected with (up to four) direct neighbors.

The number of edges m was chosen between $2m$ and $8m$. The dense graph families were not considered since they can be easily solved by the semiexternal algorithm.

Experiments were conducted on the $MPIXeon$ computer described in Section 2.4, but only up to four disks have been in use for external memory implementations, which were given about 800 MB of main memory. Swapping was switched off to avoid paging effects. Programs were compiled with the GNU C++ compiler version 3.2 with an the optimization level -O3. The time spent for the experiments was about 25 days producing a total volume of several dozens TBytes.

Figure 4.2 compares the bucket implementation with the internal memory MST implementations by Irit Katriel [KST03]. The curves for internal memory implementations show the running times on random graph instances, since the behavior of these algorithms is very similar to other graph classes. Given the 1 GByte of main memory, the internal memory Kruskal implementations can handle graphs with up to 20 million edges. Prim's algorithm implementation requires more internal memory for the same graph such that it could process graphs with up to 10 million edges. For very sparse graphs ($m \leq 4n$) Kruskal's algorithm performs better than Prim's algorithm, while for denser graphs Prim's is slightly faster. For $n \leq 160,000,000$, the bucket implementation runs semiexternally, such that it is about *two* times slower than the internal memory implementations. The internal and semiexternal implementations leave some room for improvements: e.g. using a specialized integer sorting, the semiexternal Kruskal's implementation can benefit from

4.3. MINIMUM SPANNING TREES

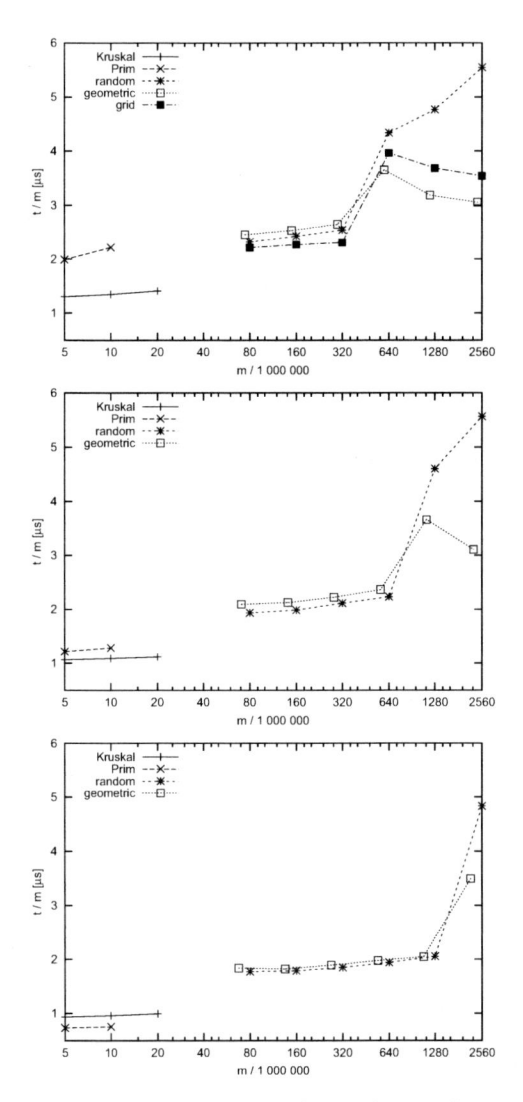

Figure 4.2: Execution time per edge of the *bucket* implementation for $m \approx 2 \cdot n$ (top), $m \approx 4 \cdot n$ (center), $m \approx 8 \cdot n$ (bottom).

merging the sort and the scan part in a pipeline saving I/Os (Section 3.7). Beyond 160,000,000 nodes the full bucket implementation is needed. The running time almost doubles because of the additional costs of the node renaming, node reduction, and a blowup of the size of the edge data structure from 12 to 20 bytes. As the complexity of the reduction is superlinear (Section 4.3.4), the running time keeps growing with n/M for random graphs.

The running time on grid graphs and geometric graphs is much better than one could expect. The time per edge even decreases with m. An explanation for this is that for these types of graphs, many parallel edges are produced and eliminated during relinking. For denser graphs less edges survive during the node reduction, such that the semiexternal Kruskal's implementation processes unproportionally small number of edges.

The largest graph that has been tried out was a grid graph with about 2^{32} nodes taking 96 GBytes just to represent the input (12 bytes per edge). This graph was processed in a record time of about 8h 40min transferring 830 GBytes of data.

The bucket implementation has been compared with the implementation based on the `stxxl::priority_queue`. The following small table shows the running time in μs per edge for random graphs with $n = 320 \cdot 10^6$ and $m = 640 \cdot 10^6$, where we varied the number of disks:

	1 disk	4 disks
bucket implementation	6.7	4.3
priority queue implementation	11.0	8.9

Since the speedup for the bucket algorithm after quadrupling the number of disks is only 1.56, one can conclude that even with a single disk and the internally efficient bucket algorithm, the computation is rather CPU-bound. Since the bucket implementation requires less CPU work, it performs considerably better than the the PQ implementation. However, the PQ implementation is still interesting because it is simple, can process graphs on which the bucket implementation might fail, and also achieves a reasonable performance for a single disk.

4.3.6 Conclusions

It has been demonstrated that massive minimum spanning trees filling several disks can be solved "overnight" on a cheap hardware. In particular, this became possible due to the simple and efficient implementations that profit from the STXXL library.

4.4 Connected Components and Spanning Trees

In this section we show how the external memory implementations of MST algorithms from Section 4.3 can be modified to compute spanning forests (SF) and connected components (CC). This material is based on the extension [Sch03b] of the bachelor thesis of Schultes [Sch03a].

4.4.1 Introduction

The connected component problem on an undirected graph $G = (V, E)$ is the problem of finding a mapping $c : V \to \mathbb{N}$, such that $c(v) = c(u)$ for $v, u \in V$ iff v and u belong to the same connected component.

In the internal memory the connected component problem and the spanning forest problem can be solved in linear time $\mathcal{O}(m + n)$ using the Breadth- or Depth-First-Search algorithms. However, in the external memory setting these problems can be solved only within the same asymptotic bounds as the MST problem (Section 4.3.2 and [MR99, ABW02]). No better bounds are known.

4.4.2 Spanning Forest

The node reduction algorithm (Section 4.3) coupled with the semiexternal algorithm already produces a spanning forest. One can speedup this algorithm by simplifying and removing some steps of the algorithm since the output does not have to be a minimum forest. The I/O volume of the node reduction can be reduced since the *weight* component of the edge tuples is not needed anymore. This also leads to some saving of internal memory space of the internal buckets. Thus, the block size of the external memory buckets can be increased, which can affect the overall performance positively. The base case (semiexternal Kruskal's algorithm) can be simplified as the sorting step can be skipped. In the node reduction phase, while removing node i, instead of choosing the *lightest* adjacent edge to contract, one chooses an adjacent edge (i, v) with the smallest id v. By intuition, this is a good decision, because the work is postponed to *later* iterations and the number of nodes to process in the future reduces faster (e.g. compared to the random choice) [Sib97].

The improvements concerning the node reduction phase can be applied to both bucket and priority queue versions. In [Sch03b] only the reduction with buckets has been implemented since the priority queue version would have had a similar speedup.

4.4.3 Connected Components

Schultes [Sch03b] modifies and extends the bucket version of the algorithm to perform accordingly with the algorithm described in [Sib04, SM02]. As in the spanning forest algorithm, the input is an unweighted graph represented as a list of edges. The output of the algorithm is a list of entries $(v, c), v \in V$, where c is the connected component id of node v, at the same time c is the id of a node belonging to the connected component. This special node c is sometimes called the *representative* node of a component. The algorithm makes two passes over adjacency lists of nodes (left-to-right pass $v = n-1..0$ and right-to-left $v = 0..n-1$, $v \in V$), relinking the edges such that they connect node v with the representative node of its connected component.

Schultes integrates the algorithm [Sib04, SM02] into the bucket implementation of the spanning forests algorithm. If there are $k = \mathcal{O}(M/B)$ external memory buckets then bucket $i \in \{0..k-1\}$ contains the adjacent edges $(u,v), u > v$ of nodes $u_{i-1} < u \leq u_i$, where u_i is the upper (lower) bound of node ids in bucket i ($i+1$). Additionally, there are k *question* buckets and k *answer* buckets with the same bounds. A *question* is a tuple $(v, r(v))$ that represents the assignment of node v to a *preliminary* representative node $r(v)$. An answer is a tuple $(v, r(v))$ that represents the assignment of node v to an *ultimate* representative node. Function $b : V \to \{0..k-1\}$ maps a node id to the coresponding bucket id according to the bucket bounds.

The bucket implementation is complemented with the following steps. During the processing of node v, the algorithm assigns $r(v)$ tentatively the id of its neighbor with the smallest id. If no neighbor exists then $r(v) := v$. After processing the bucket i we post the preliminary assignments $(v, r(v))$ of nodes v, $u_{i-1} < v \leq u_i$ to question bucket $b(r(v))$ if $r(v)$ does not belong to bucket i. Otherwise we can update $r(v)$ with $r(r(v))$. If the new $r(v)$ belongs to bucket i than it is the ultimate representative node of v and $(v, r(v))$ can be written to the answer bucket $b(v)$, otherwise we post question $(v, r(v))$ to the appropriate question bucket. Note that the first answer bucket is handled differently as it is implemented as the union-find data structure in the base case. For v in the union-data structure $r(v)$ is the id of the leader node of the union where v belongs to. The connected component algorithm needs an additional right-to-left scan to determine the ultimate representatives which have not been determined in the previous left-to-right scan. The buckets are read in the order $0..k-1$. For each $(v, r(v))$ in question bucket i we update $r(v)$ with the ultimate representative $r(r(v))$ looking up values in answer bucket i. The final value $(v, r(v))$ is appended to answer bucket $b(v)$. After answering all questions in bucket i, the content of answer bucket i is added to the output of the connected component algorithm.

If one only needs to compute the component ids and no spanning tree edges then the implementation does not keep the original edge id in the edge data structure. It is sufficient to invert randomization for the node ids in the output, which can be done with the chosen randomization scheme [DSSS04, Sch03a] without additional I/Os. Due to this measure the total I/O volume and the memory requirements of the internal buckets are reduced such that the block size of the external memory buckets can be made larger. All this leads to an overall performance improvement.

4.4.4 Experiments

The experiment setup including the computer system and input instances was the same as in the MST algorithm evaluation (Section 4.3).

Since the connected component and spanning tree algorithms are modifications of the MST algorithm they show a similar development of running time with the change in problem size and in density of the graphs. Thus we only show the relative speedup of the algorithms over the MST algorithm for the semi-external and the external case in Table 4.4. For the detailed data see [Sch03b]. Computing connected components and/or spanning forests is at least 1.4 times faster than computing MST. The most important reason for that is that the I/O volume is decreased: the weight field in the edge tuple is not needed and the edges are not sorted like in Kruskal's algorithm. The computation of connected components takes more time than the computation of a spanning forest mainly because it needs an additional pass through the nodes. Nethertheless SF&CC is still faster than the MST implementation.

type	$n/10^6$	$m/10^6$	SF	CC	SF&CC
grid	80	160	7.1	5.8	5.8
grid	1280	2560	1.8	1.8	1.5
random	80	160	2.1	2.0	2.0
random	1280	2560	2.1	2.3	1.9
random	40	320	2.5	2.4	2.4
random	320	2560	2.1	2.5	2.0
geometric	80	149	2.8	2.4	2.4
geometric	640	1190	1.7	1.6	1.4
geometric	40	270	3.6	3.4	3.5
geometric	160	1080	3.3	3.2	3.2

Table 4.4: Speedup of the connected component and/or the spanning forest algorithm over the MST algorithm.

4.5 Breadth First Search

Some of the material of this section has been published in [ADM06] and in the master's thesis [Ajw05].

4.5.1 Introduction

Many combinatorial problems need to traverse a graph in a structured way. Breadth First Search (BFS) is one of the most useful traversal strategies. For an undirected graph $G = (V, E)$ and a source node $s \in V$, BFS decomposes nodes of the graph into at most $n = |V|$ levels, where each level i contains the nodes that can be reached from s via a path of i edges, but can not be reached using less than i edges.

In the internal memory setting, the problem of finding the BFS decomposition can be solved by a simple linear time algorithm [CLR90]. In the external memory setting, i.e. when the input graph is too big to be processed in the main memory, this algorithm incurs $\Theta(n+m)$ I/Os. Until recently it was not clear if the exact BFS computation for such large graphs is feasible at all. Therefore heuristics (exploiting some graph properties), and special precomputations producing approximate solutions have been developed. However, two promising I/O-efficient BFS algorithms with small constant factors both in I/O volume and CPU-time complexity exist: the MR-BFS [MR99] and MM-BFS [MM02] algorithms.

In the remaining part of this section we show that MR-BFS and MM-BFS algorithms implemented with STXXL are able to compute the *exact* BFS-level decomposition for huge synthetic and real graphs in a *few hours*. Thanks to the STXXL pipelining the implementations save at least a factor two in I/O-volume.

4.5.2 Internal Memory BFS

The internal memory BFS (IM-BFS) algorithm [CLR90] visits the nodes of the graph sequentially, starting from the source node s. The algorithm keeps the candidate nodes to visit in a FIFO queue Q. When a node v is extracted from Q, the adjacency list of v is examined and unvisited neighbors are added to Q. This simple algorithm is not I/O-efficient due to two reasons: (1) remembering the visited nodes costs $\Theta(m)$ I/Os in the worst case; (2) unstructured accesses to the adjacency lists need up to $\Theta(n)$ I/Os.

4.5.3 MR-BFS

The MR-BFS algorithm [MR99] addresses the first problem reducing the worst case I/O-complexity to $\mathcal{O}(n + \text{sort}(n+m))$. The algorithm computes the BFS levels incrementally. Let $L(t)$ be the set of the nodes in level t, $N(S)$ be the multi-set of the neighbors of the nodes in set S and let $A(t) := N(L(t-1))$. The current level $L(t)$ is constructed as follows: $A(t)$ is created by $|L(t-1)|$ accesses to the adjacency lists. This incurs $\mathcal{O}(|L(t-1)| + \text{scan}(|A(t)|))$ I/Os. Then the duplicate nodes are removed from the multi-set $A(t)$ obtaining set $A'(t)$ using a sorting and a scanning step. This needs $\mathcal{O}(\text{sort}(|A(t)|))$ I/Os. $L(t)$ can be computed now as $A'(t) - \{L(t-1) \cup L(t-2)\}$. Filtering out the nodes contained in the sorted sets $L(t-1)$ and $L(t-2)$ is possible by parallel scanning in $\mathcal{O}(\text{scan}(|A(t)| + |L(t-1)| + |L(t-2)|))$ I/Os. Since $\sum_t |A(t)| = 2m$ [7] and $\sum_t |L(t)| = n$, the algorithm requires the $\mathcal{O}(n + \text{sort}(n+m))$ I/Os. The unstructured access to the adjacency lists of $L(t-1)$ is responsible for the $\mathcal{O}(n)$ term.

Figure 4.3 shows the scheme of the pipelined and nonpipelined implementations of one MR-BFS iteration. In the pipelined version the whole algorithm complexity can be implemented in one scanner that reads the nodes in $L(t-1)$ and $L(t-1)$ and the adjacency lists $E(t)$ of nodes in $L(t)$ from the corresponding `stxxl::vector`s and scans through the stream of $A'(t)$ and in just one pass outputs the nodes in the current level $L(t)$ and the multi-set $A(t+1)$, which is passed directly to the sorter. The output of the sorter is scanned once to delete duplicates and output as the set $A'(t+1)$ used in the next iteration.

Analyzing the schemes we conclude [8] that pipelining reduces the worst case number of I/Os from

$\sum_t \text{scan}(|L(t-1)| + |L(t-2)| + |A(t)|) +$
$\sum_t 2\,\text{scan}(|L(t)|) +$
$\sum_t (|L(t)| + \text{scan}(|N(L(t))|)) +$
$\sum_t 2\,\text{scan}(|A(t+1)|) +$
$\sum_t (\text{sort}(|A(t+1)|) + 3\,\text{scan}(|A(t+1)|)) = n + \text{scan}(4n + 14m) + \text{sort}(2m)$

to

$\sum_t \text{scan}(|L(t-1)| + |L(t-2)|) +$
$\sum_t (|L(t)| + \text{scan}(|N(L(t))|)) +$

---
[7] Note that graph is undirected and each edge is stored twice.
[8] To simplify the analysis the record size is assumed to be equal in all data streams.

4.5. BREADTH FIRST SEARCH 107

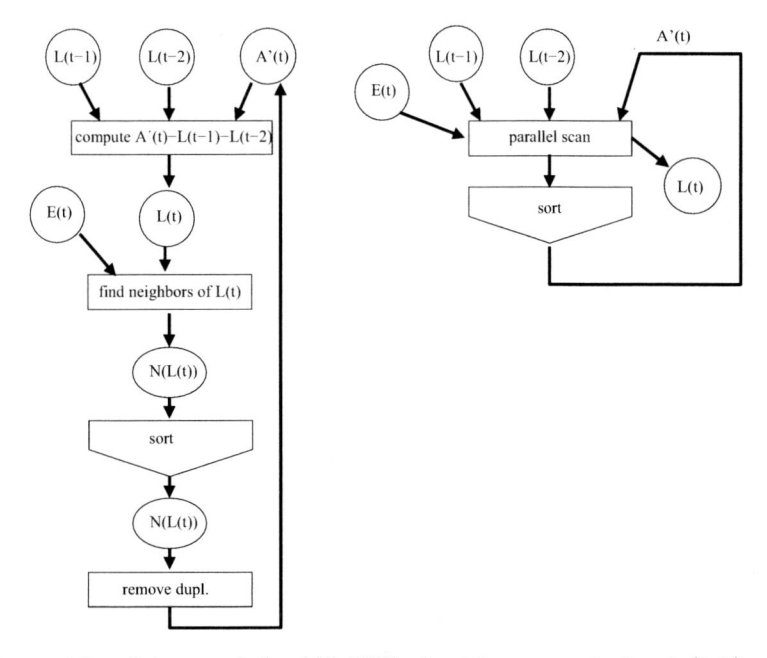

Figure 4.3: Scheme of the MR-BFS algorithm: nonpipelined (left) and pipelined (right).

$\sum_t \text{scan}(|L(t)|) +$
$\sum_t \text{sort}(|A(t+1)|) = n + \text{scan}(3n + 2m) + \text{sort}(2m).$

Assuming that $\text{sort}(x) = 2 \cdot \text{scan}(x)$ with a careful choice of block size B we conclude that pipelining can save at least half of the required I/O volume (ignoring the worst case n term).

4.5.4 MM-BFS

The MM-BFS algorithm [MM02] is a refinement of the MR-BFS algorithm that trades in the unstructured I/O for the increase of the number of iterations in which an edge may be involved. On sparse graphs the total amount of the unstructured I/O can be reduced by a factor of up to $\sqrt{B}$. MM-BFS runs in two phases: a preprocessing phase that partitions the graph into disjoint clusters and the BFS phase itself. In [MM02], deterministic and nondeterministic variants of preprocessing have been proposed. [ADM06, Ajw05] implements the simpler randomized version.

In order to efficiently store the graph partition the following graph representation has been designed. The adjacency array is implemented as two `stxxl::vectors` $\overline{V}$ and E. Vector E contains all edges of the graph twice – once in the adjacency array of each adjacent node. Vector $\overline{V}$ contains the iterators pointing to locations in E where a new adjacency array starts. An `stxxl::vector` F stores the iterators to locations in $\overline{V}$ marking the first node of clusters, i.e. nodes pointed by $F[i], F[i] + 1, \ldots, F[i+1] - 1$ build cluster F_i. Edges and nodes in $\overline{V}$ and E are kept sorted according to the cluster indices they belong to. Using this representation an arbitrary cluster can be accessed in $\mathcal{O}(1) + \text{scan}(F[i+1] - F[i])$ I/Os.

The preprocessing step partitions the graph into disjoint connected subgraphs $S_i, 0 \leq i \leq K$, with a small expected diameter [MM02]. It also partitions the adjacency arrays accordingly, i.e. it constructs vector F and reorganizes $\overline{V}$ and E accordingly, such that cluster F_i contains the adjacency arrays of all nodes in S_i. We assume that S_0 contains the source node s. The partition is built by choosing *master* nodes independently and uniformly at random with a probability $\mu = \sqrt{\frac{(n+m)\log n}{nDB}}$ and running a local BFS from all master nodes "in parallel": in each round, each master node s_i tries to capture all unvisited neighbors of its current subgraph S_i; this is done by first sorting the nodes of the active fringes of all S_i, and then scanning the dynamically shrinking adjacency-array representation of the yet unexplored graph. If several master nodes want to include a certain node, an arbitrary master nodes wins.

After choosing master nodes, the partitioning can run in pipelined mode as shown in Figure 4.3 (left). The top scanner takes the sorted sequence of the nodes on the fringe, updates their cluster ids in the external vector $\overline{V}$, adding them to the corresponding cluster. In the same scanner, adjacency lists of the fringe nodes are read and a new sequence of fringe nodes is determined. The sequence is sent then to the sorter. After partitioning, we generate the graph data structure described above. For this purpose, each edge in E is supplemented with source and destination node cluster ids. Sorted with respect to cluster ids, E and $\overline{V}$ are scanned to produce the appropriate node and cluster iterator values. According to the analysis in [MM02] the diameter of any cluster (the number of iterations) is less than $\frac{\log n}{\mu}$ with high probability. Thus the total number of I/Os for the partitioning is $\frac{\log n}{\mu}(\text{scan}(2m) + \text{sort}(2n)) + \text{scan}(4n + \mu n + 4m) + \text{sort}(4m + n)$.

In the BFS phase the algorithm performs similarly to the MR-BFS with one difference: the adjacency arrays are not accessed directly, but cached in a special pool H ("hot" adjacency arrays). The hot pool contains parts of the cluster adjacency arrays F_i if F_i has a node in level $L(t-1)$. Pool H initially

4.5. BREADTH FIRST SEARCH

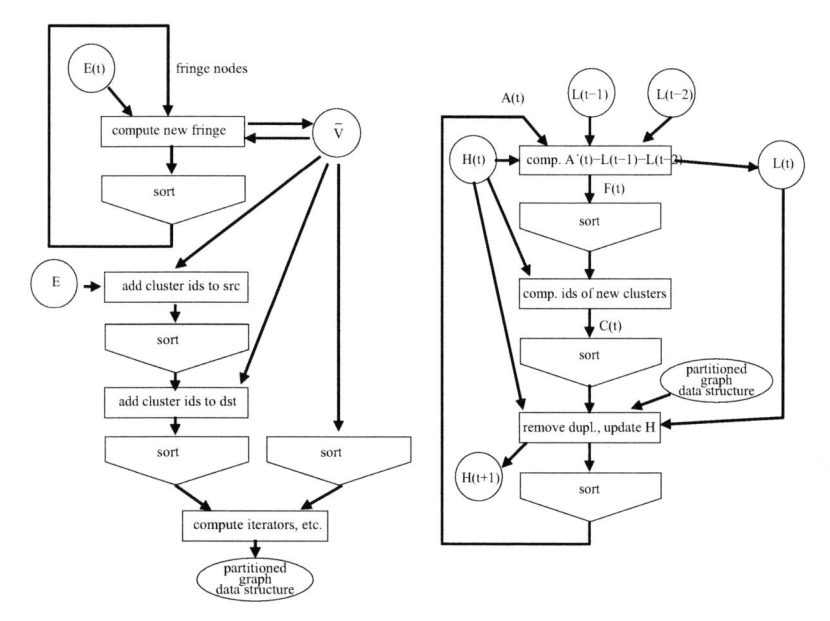

Figure 4.4: Pipelined scheme of the MM-BFS algorithm: partitioning phase (left) and BFS phase (right).

contains cluster F_0 with the adjacency lists of the source node s. To create level $L(t)$ based on $L(t-1)$ and $L(t-2)$, MM-BFS does not access single adjacency arrays like MM-BFS. Instead it scans H to extract $N(L(t-1))$. In order to maintain the invariant that H contains the adjacency arrays of all nodes on the current level $L(t)$, the cluster adjacency arrays F_i of the nodes whose adjacency arrays are not yet included in H will be merged in H. The adjacency arrays of nodes in $L(t)$ are removed completely from H at the end of the iteration t. Each cluster F_i is added to H at most once. After an adjacency array was copied to H, it will only be used for $\frac{\log n}{\mu}$ expected iterations; afterwards it will be discarded from H.

The pipelined execution plan of the BFS phase is shown in Figure 4.4 (right). The first scanner receives the sorted sequence $A(t)$ of neighbors of $L(t-1)$ from the previous iteration, reads $L(t-1)$ and $L(t-2)$ from the external vectors and adjacency arrays of nodes in $L(t-1)$ from H in one scan. Sequence $F(t)$ is computed – the multi-set of cluster ids of nodes in $L(t)$. In parallel, $L(t)$ is written to disk. The second scanner takes the sorted $F(t)$ and the hot pool H to compute the multi-set $C(t)$ of cluster ids that need to be merged into H. The third scanner reads the sorted sequence of $C(t)$, eliminates duplicate cluster ids (we denote the set of unique ids as $C'(t)$), computes $A(t)$ – the neighbor multi-set of $L(t)$ – and updates H:

$$H_{new} := H_{old} + \bigcup_{i \in C'(t)} F_i - \mathrm{Adj}(L(t))$$

where $\mathrm{Adj}(S)$ represents the adjacency arrays of nodes in S. The total number of I/Os for this phase is bounded by

$$\mu n + \mathrm{scan}(2m + 4n + \frac{8m \log n}{\mu}) + \mathrm{sort}(2m + 2n)$$

w.h.p.

4.5.5 Experiments

In this experimental section we present some of the computational results obtained in [ADM06].

Configuration. The implementations were compiled with the `g++` version 3.32 with the optimization level `-O3` on a Linux Debian system with a 2.4 kernel and STXXL version 0.77. The computer had two 2 GHz Intel Xeon processors (only one was used by the computations), one GByte of main memory, and four 250 GByte Seagate Barracuda hard disks. The average seek time for read and write is 8 and 9 msec, respectively, while the maximum sustained bandwidth is 65 MByte/s.

Figure 4.5 shows the total running time of the presented algorithms on random graphs of varying sizes (keeping $m = 4n$). An important point to note here is that even when half of the graph fits in the internal memory, the performance of IM-BFS is much worse than that of external BFS algorithms. For this case (2^{22} nodes and 2^{24} nodes) the I/O wait time of IM-BFS (8.09 hours) dominates the total running time (8.11 hours), thereby explaining the worse results of IM-BFS. On the other hand, MR-BFS and MM-BFS have much less I/O wait time (1.55 and 4.93 minutes) and consequently, the total running time (2.57 and 10.6 minutes) is small also. This clearly establishes the need for efficient implementations of external memory BFS algorithms.

Running the experiments on single disk on other random graph instances it was observed that MR-BFS is faster than the MM-BFS algorithm by a

4.5. BREADTH FIRST SEARCH

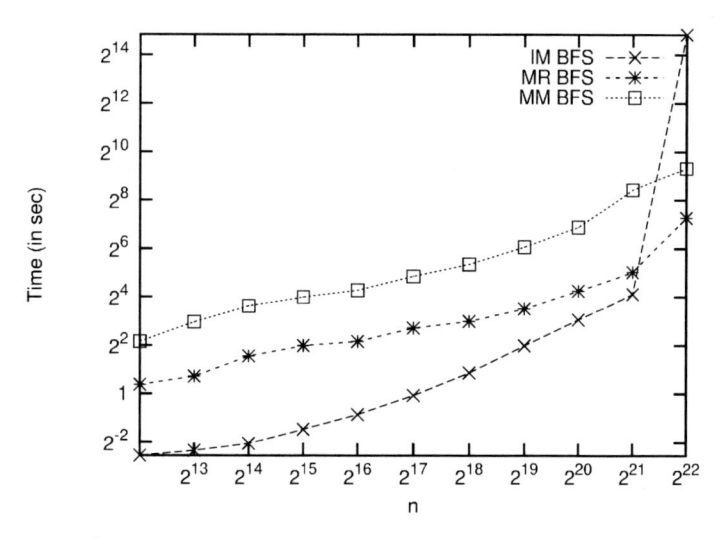

Figure 4.5: Running times of IM-BFS, MR-BFS and MM-BFS with graph size ($D = 1$).

factor of 3.8. This result is expected, since random graphs have a small diameter of size $\mathcal{O}(\log n)$, and edges can remain in the hot pool for quite a long time in MM-BFS. On high diameter graphs like grid graphs $\sqrt{n} \times \sqrt{n}$, MM-BFS outperforms MR-BFS by a factor of 87.9 in total running time. Since the difference in running time for small diameter graphs is moderate, the overhead of MM-BFS can be considered as an acceptable investment, because it provides much stronger running time guarantees for really difficult inputs.

The experiments in [ADM06] have shown that a bad initial layout of the graph on the disk(s) can destroy the performance of the MR-BFS algorithm. On the contrary, MM-BFS is not sensitive to the layout, because it neutralizes the impact of bad layouts in the preprocessing phase giving a better worst case guarantee. Thus, losing some time for MM-BFS preprocessing (days), much time can be saved for adverse layouts (months).

When using all four disks the I/O-efficient implementations become more CPU-bound; a speedup of about two can be obtained. The MM-BFS algorithm gains more from the parallel I/O: It reduces the I/O wait time by a factor of three, whereas for the MR-BFS algorithm the reduction is only two-fold. However, the total running time of the MM-BFS is relatively far above from the I/O wait time, such that further STXXL optimizations including better overlapping between I/O and computation and usage of multiple CPUs for sorting can bring an improvement in performance.

As an instance of a real world graph, we considered an actual WWW crawl from the WebBase project[9], where an edge represents a hyperlink between two nodes. For the BFS experiments the direction of edges was ignored. The graph has around 130 million nodes and 1.4 billion edges. For this graph, the total I/O volume of the BFS algorithm (with the data structure described earlier) is around 25 GB. The bulk of the nodes is contained in the core of this graph spread across 10-12 BFS levels (similar to random graphs). The remaining nodes are spread out over thousands of levels with 2-3 nodes per level. However, the I/O wait time as well as the total running time for the BFS traversal is dominated by the core of this graph, hence the results are similar to the ones for random graphs. The graph can be processed in a *few* hours using a PC with four cheap disks. MR-BFS (2.3 hours) beats MM-BFS (4.5 hours).

---

[9] http://www-diglib.stanford.edu/~testbed/doc2/WebBase/

4.6 Listing All Triangles in Huge Graphs

Recently, there is an increasing interest in analyzing huge networks like the Internet, the WWW [BLMP06, DLMT05, HL04, BYBC06, Leo04], or social networks. The number of triangles in a graph is a very important metric in (social) network analysis [HK79]. It is used to compute the clustering coefficient [WS98] — the measure of concentration of clusters in graphs with regard to its tendency to decompose into communities.

The problem of finding, counting and listing all triangles in a graph has been studied theoretically and, only recently, in practice. In [SW05a, SW05b] the authors extensively study various internal memory algorithms for the problem. They investigate the performance of the algorithms running them on random and real world graphs. However, the presented implementations, due to the I/O-bottleneck, can not cope with very large graphs that do not fit into the main memory (like the WWW graph [DLL$^+$06]).

In the following we design an I/O-efficient STXXL implementation of the *node-iterator* algorithm [SW05b], and show that it can list all triangles in a huge web crawl graph in a few hours.

4.6.1 I/O-Efficient Node-Iterator Algorithm

We denote $deg(v)$ as the degree of node v and Δ as the maximum node degree in the undirected graph $G = (V, E)$ with n nodes and m edges.

The node-iterator algorithm [SW05a, SW05b] iterates over all nodes and tests each pair of neighbors of a node if they are connected by an edge. In the worst case there can be up to $\sum_{v \in V} \binom{deg(v)}{2} = \mathcal{O}(n\Delta^2)$ pairs. This results in $\mathcal{O}(n\Delta^2)$ I/Os accessing the adjacency lists.

We can reduce the number of edge queries heuristically if the nodes are processed in the order of increasing degrees. While examining the neighbors of node v an edge query is made only for neighbors u and w if $v < u < w$. The traversal of the graph in the increasing degree order can be implemented I/O-efficiently by renaming the nodes with new ids: nodes with smaller degree get smaller ids. This can be done using a constant number of sorting and scanning steps. To achieve I/O-efficiency the queries are not answered immediately, but collected in batches of size $\Theta(m)$. A sorted query batch is answered in a parallel scan with a lexicographically sorted array of all edges in E.

4.6.2 Pipelined Implementation

Figure 4.6 shows the pipelined data flow graph of the I/O-efficient algorithm [10]. The implementation assumes that the input is an array E of edges sorted lexicographically, where each edge is stored twice: as (u,v) and (v,u). Any other graph representation can be easily converted to this format in $\mathcal{O}(\text{sort}(n+m))$ I/Os. In the first scanner, the graph array is scanned computing the degree of nodes: a stream K of pairs $(v, deg(v))$, $v \in V$ is output. K is sorted by the degree component and fed to the second scanner which computes new ids: a stream of maps $(newID, oldID)$ is produced. This stream is sorted by $oldID$ and stored in an external vector R. The stream is read in parallel by the third scanner which also scans E and adds the $newID$ for the source node v in the edge tuples. The fourth scanner adds the $newID$ for the destination node w and feeds edge tuples with $newID(v) < newID(w)$ into the sorter. Edge tuples, sorted lexicographically by new IDs, are read by the fifth scanner and are stored in an external vector E' in parallel. The scanner scans the adjacency lists of nodes v and for each neighbor pair u and w such that $newID(u) < newID(w)$ a query $(newID(u), newID(w), v)$ is added to array Q. If array Q gets longer than $k \cdot m$, where k is a constant, then the scanner suspends and the accumulated queries are answered. For answering queries, Q is sorted and scanned with E'. The old node IDs of the triangles can be output directly, since they have been kept in the edge tuple. After answering, the content of Q is emptied. The choice of parameter k trades in the external space consumption of the algorithm (query storage) for the number of scans of E'.

In Figure 4.6 the arrows denoting the streams between the nodes are labeled with the I/O-volume in 32-bit words transfered through the links (italic font face). The total number of queries is denoted as t', the number of triangles in the graph is denoted as t. Using the diagram we can easily figure out the precise I/O volume of the implementation:

$$\text{scan}(m(10 + 2\lceil \tfrac{t'}{km} \rceil) + 4n + 3t) + \text{sort}(4n + 6m + 3t').$$

In the fifth scanner, the implementation copies previous neighbors of the current node into an internal array assuming they fit in the internal memory. Otherwise, an external storage can be used, causing an additional $\text{scan}(m+t')$ I/Os in the worst case.

---

[10] The source code is available at
http://algo2.iti.uka.de/dementiev/tria/algorithm.shtml.

4.6. LISTING ALL TRIANGLES IN HUGE GRAPHS

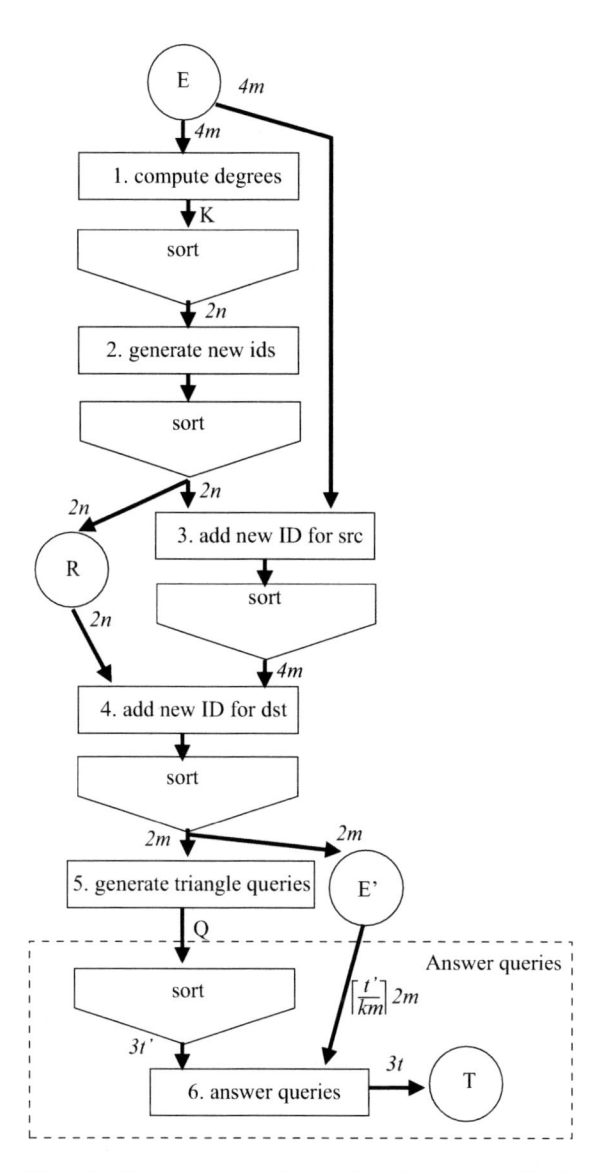

Figure 4.6: The pipelined scheme of the triangle counting/listing algorithm.

4.6.3 Experiments

Using our STXXL implementation we have counted the number of triangles in a web crawl graph from the WebBase project [11]. In this graph the nodes are web pages and the edges are hyperlinks between them. For the computation we ignored the direction of the links. Our crawl graph had 135 million nodes and 1.2 billion edges. The machine we have used is described in Section 2.4 as SCSIOpteron. The difference is that we have used seven hards disks and one GByte of main memory. During the computation which took only 4h 46min we have detected 10.6 billion triangles. A total volume of 851 GB was transferred between the main memory and the hard disks.

---

[11] http://www-diglib.stanford.edu/~testbed/doc2/WebBase/

4.7 Graph Coloring

4.7.1 Introduction

Coloring a graph using as few colors as possible is an important problem having many diverse applications, such as solving sparse linear systems of equations, resource allocation, scheduling, and the construction and testing of VLSI circuits. Finding the smallest possible number of colors is known to be an NP-complete problem. Therefore it makes more sense to concentrate on fast algorithms that give good non-optimal colorings. A class of such algorithms are heuristics, they do not give guarantees on the quality of the produced coloring, however, they give colorings with a small number of colors on real-world instances and are very fast. Highest-degree-first [WP67] and smallest-degree-last [MMI72] are the classical heuristics.

A special case of the problem is coloring *planar* graphs. Finding the minimum number of colors for this type of graphs is also NP-complete [GJS76]. However, it is known that the nodes of every planar graph can be colored with at most *four* colors. The best known internal memory $\mathcal{O}(n^2)$ algorithm [RSST96] for finding such a color assignment has very large constants and is considered impractical. Coloring planar graphs with *five* colors can be done faster, in linear time [Fre84].

The problem of coloring has been studied theoretically and experimentally in the standard RAM model (see links in [Cul]). Solving the problem of coloring in more advanced models of computation has attracted much attention. Many parallel and distributed coloring algorithms have been published, however, much less has been done to evaluate these algorithms experimentally. Parallel variants of the highest-degree-first and smallest-degree-last heuristics are implemented in [ABC+95]. In the paper [JP93] the authors devise a heuristic for distributed memory computers that generates colorings of a quality comparable with sequential greedy heuristics. Finnocchi *et al.* [FPS05] provides a very detailed experimental study of fast randomized distributed memory heuristics.

Many efficient parallel algorithms have been devised for finding a color assignment with 8,7,6 and 5 colors [GPS87, Nao87, BK87, HCD89, Dik86, BJ85] for planar graphs. The main idea behind most of these algorithms is to remove a constant fraction of small degree nodes and proceed with computing the coloring of the (modified) rest of the graph recursively. Then, the set of the removed nodes is colored based on the colors of the remaining nodes.

Parallel algorithms for coloring planar algorithms with only seven colors (7-

coloring) can be considered folklore. In at least two papers [GPS87, Nao87] the authors propose a simple graph reduction, which leads to an optimal external memory coloring algorithms. The reduction allows to remove at least 1/6 nodes of the graph keeping it planar. The authors of [Nao87, BK87] came up with somewhat complicated (R)NC parallel algorithms for the 5-color version of the problem. The algorithms run in $\Omega\left(\log^3 n\right)$ suboptimal worst-case parallel time and use the computation of connected components as a subroutine. Diks [Dik86] presented a very complicated parallel 6-coloring algorithm, which requires an efficient BFS algorithm as a subroutine. There is an *optimal* parallel algorithm that can 5-color planar graphs [HCD89]. Its externalization can give an I/O-efficient algorithm with sorting time complexity. The algorithm is far from being practical: its reduction procedure is very expensive and it can only reduce a tiny number of nodes ($< n/196$) in a recursion in the worst case. A similar 5-coloring algorithm in [GPS87] reduces the node set in the recursion by an even smaller fraction in the worst case.

Although parallel (coloring) algorithms can often be reformulated as external algorithms, the external memory model gives us additional opportunities. In particular, the technique of *time forward processing* is I/O-efficient yet inherently sequential. The only coloring algorithm explicitly developed for the I/O model we are aware of is the greedy algorithm by Zeh [Zeh02]. Although this algorithm is based on time forward processing, it can be viewed as a particularly efficient externalization of the parallel algorithm from [JP93]. A particular application of an external memory coloring algorithm would be computing a schedule for executing *many* parallel jobs if only a single processor is available for computing the schedule. Each color gives a subset of jobs that can be processed in parallel.

Our contributions. We propose a fast I/O-efficient implementation of the Highest-Degree-First graph coloring heuristic, a new external memory variant of the Smallest-Degree-First heuristic, and its implementation, develop new simple I/O-efficient algorithms for computing 6- and 7-colorings of *planar* graphs, provide a practical implementation of the 7-coloring algorithm, and show how to implement the 2-coloring algorithm I/O-efficiently. We implement the algorithms using the STXXL library and compare the performance of the devised implementations experimentally, running them on huge random and real-world graph instances. To the best of our knowledge, no algorithm for finding *good* colorings of graphs exceeding the size of the main memory has been published so far. Our experimental study of I/O-efficient coloring algorithms is the first of that kind.

4.7. GRAPH COLORING

Definitions and Theoretical Background. A coloring of graph $G = (V, E)$ with m edges and n nodes is an assignment of colors to the nodes of G such that adjacent nodes receive distinct colors, i.e., a function $c \colon V \to \mathbb{N}_0$ that has the property that $c(u) \neq c(v)$ for all edges $(u, v) \in E$. A k-coloring is a coloring that uses at most k colors. We say G is k-colorable if there is a k-coloring of G.

We denote V_i as the subset of V that includes all nodes with degree i. Then $V_{i..j} = \bigcup_{h=i}^{j} V_h$ for $0 \leq i \leq j$. Let n_i be the number of nodes with degree i, i.e. $n_i = |V_i|$.

Lemma 1. *Let U_d be a set of nodes whose degree is at most d. The size of every maximal independent set in the induced subgraph defined by U_d is at least $\frac{1}{d+1}|U_d|$.*

Proof. The lemma follows from the fact that a node in a maximal independent set can be incident to at most d other nodes in U_d. □

Lemma 2. *Let U_d be a set of nodes whose degree is at most d. The size of every maximal matching in the induced subgraph defined by U_d is at least $\frac{k}{2d-1}$, where k is the number of edges in the induced subgraph.*

Proof. The lemma follows from the fact that an edge in a maximal matching can be incident to at most $2(d-1)$ other edges in the subgraph induced by U_d. □

4.7.2 Greedy Coloring

Zeh [Zeh02] gives a greedy I/O-efficient algorithm for graph coloring. The nodes are processed in arbitrary order. When a node v is visited, it is assigned the smallest color, which has not been assigned to any of the already visited neighbors of v. Figure 4.7 shows the pseudocode of an implementation of the greedy algorithm. The algorithm accepts a lexicographically sorted list of edges $(src, dst) \in E$, $src < dst$. Priority queue Q stores pairs $(node, color)$ ordered by $node$, signaling that $node$ has a neighbor colored with $color$. It is assumed that $E = \emptyset \Leftrightarrow E.front().src = \infty$ and $Q = \emptyset \Leftrightarrow Q.min().node = \infty$. Line (2) determines the node to be visited. In Line (4) the colors of already visited neighbors of v are accumulated in array U. Line (6) colors node v with the smallest available color C. Line (7) sends the color signal (u, C) to each neighbor u of v via the priority queue.

Theorem 3 ([Zeh02]). *In the worst case the greedy coloring algorithm performs $\mathcal{O}(\operatorname{sort}(m))$ I/Os on an undirected graph with m edges.*

Function *GreedyColoring(E)*
    ExternalPriorityQueue: Q //stores neighbor colors
    while $E \neq \emptyset \vee Q \neq \emptyset$ **do**   (1)
        $v := \min\{E.front().src, Q.min().node\}$ (2)
        $U := \emptyset$ //used colors   (3)
        while $v = Q.min().node$ **do** $U.append(Q.delMin().color)$ **od**   (4)
        sort U (5)
        scan U and assign node v color $C := \min_{c \notin U}\{c\}$ (6)
        while $v = E.front().src$ **do** $Q.insert((E.popFront().dst, C))$ **od**   (7)

Figure 4.7: The implementation of the greedy algorithm.

Proof. The algorithm performs m insertions in the priority queue, each taking $(1/B)\log_{M/B}(m/M)$ amortized I/Os [San00]. Sorting and scanning in Lines (5–6) take $\sum_{v \in V} \text{sort}(deg(v)) + \text{scan}(deg(v)) \leq \text{sort}(2m) + \text{scan}(2m)$ I/Os. For each visited node v, there is a color in $[0, \ldots, d]$ which has not been assigned to a neighbor of v. Therefore, at most $d+1$ colors are used. □

4.7.3   Highest-Degree-First Heuristic

HDF heuristic is a variant of the greedy algorithm that visits and colors the nodes in the order of their degree, starting from highest degree nodes. A high level pseudocode of the I/O-efficient HDF heuristic is shown in Figure 4.8. The algorithm accepts a lexicographically sorted list of edges $(src, dst) \in E$, $src < dst$.

(1) Rename nodes in E such that
    $deg(v) > deg(u) \Rightarrow newName(v) < newName(u)$.

(2) Call *GreedyColoring(E)* computing a coloring.

(3) Restore the old names in the coloring.

Figure 4.8: The I/O-efficient HDF algorithm.

Corollary 4. *The I/O-efficient HDF heuristic colors an undirected graph with m edges in $\mathcal{O}(\text{sort}(m))$ I/Os.*

4.7. GRAPH COLORING

The pipelined scheme of our STXXL HDF heuristic implementation is presented in Figure 4.9. Renaming of the nodes according to their degree is implemented using a constant number of scan/sort passes in blocks from (a) to (k). Calling greedy coloring in block (l) colors the graph with new node ids. The old ids are restored in blocks (m)–(n).

Now we treat the diagram in detail. The algorithm duplicates each incoming each edge producing two edges: (u,v) and (v,u) for $(u,v) \in E$ (a). While processing (b) the sorted adjacency lists, stream of pairs $J = \{(v, deg(v)) : v \in V\}$ is computed (c). Stream J is sorted by $deg(v)$ in descending order (d). The nodes are numbered in (e): node v obtains a new ID that is equal to the position of pair (v,d) in the sorted stream J; pair $(v, newID)$ is output; v is appended to external array O. The name maps $(oldID, newID)$ are sorted in (f) and stored in external array R. Blocks (g)–(i) rename the nodes in edges E. Block (j) exchanges src and dst in edges with $src > dst$. Edges ordered by src are fed to the greedy coloring algorithm (l). The nodes in the result of (l) receive their old names in (m).

We can precisely compute the worst case I/O volume of the implementation considering the data flow between the nodes in the diagram. Assuming that the pipelined sorters need only one merge pass and with proper settings the priority queue performs only $(64m/DB)$ I/Os [San00], and node and color ids are represented with 4-byte C++ `int`s, then the pipelined HDF heuristic has I/O volume at most $112m + 72n$ bytes. A non-pipelined implementation would transfer $224m + 120n$ bytes.

4.7.4 Batched Smallest-Degree-Last Heuristic

The Smallest-Degree-Last (SDL) heuristic [MMI72] algorithm operates in two phases. In the first phase, it removes a node with smallest degree from the graph (reducing the degrees of its neighbors). The procedure is applied recursively to the graph that remains. Denote the node removed in recursion i as v_i. The second phase of the algorithm greedily colors the nodes of the graph in the *backward* order $v_n, v_{n-1}, \ldots, v_1$.

A direct implementation of the SDL heuristic needs to do random accesses to the adjacency lists of v_i and its neighbors in each recursion, therefore the implementation might require $\Omega(m)$ I/Os. We propose the Batched Smallest-Degree-Last heuristic (BSDL), where a *set* of small degree nodes (batch) is removed in a recursion. The recursion step gets more expensive with respect to the number of I/Os and internal work, but the total number of recursions is reduced. Nodes with degrees at most $\delta(V, E)$ are

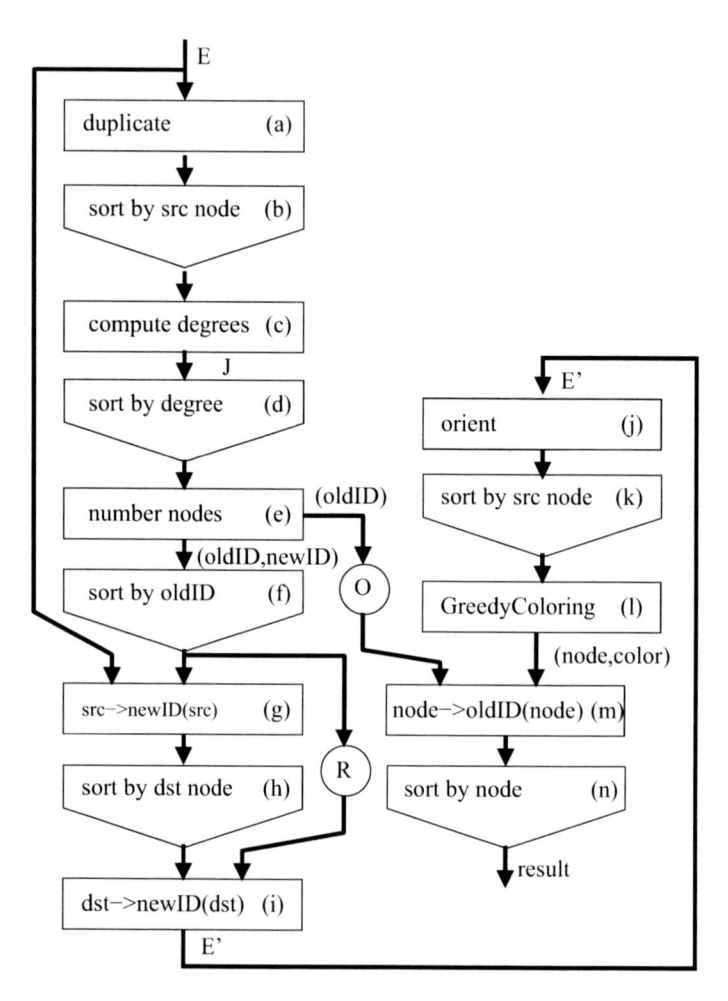

Figure 4.9: The pipelined scheme of the I/O-efficient HDF algorithm.

4.7. GRAPH COLORING

taken in a batch, where function δ maps a graph to an integer in the range $[\min_{v \in V} \{deg(v)\}, \infty)$. We will refer to function δ as the maximum batch degree function. The choice of this function balances the quality of the coloring and the running time of the heuristic: the smaller the value of $\delta(V, E)$, the fewer color classes are used, and the slower the graph is reduced. Ideally, the computation of the value of $\delta(V, E)$ should not cause much computational and I/O overhead. In this book, we experimentally investigate an obvious maximum batch degree function: the rounded up average degree $\delta(V, E) = \lceil 2|E|/|V| \rceil$. Other possible functions one might consider are the median degree, node c-quantile $\delta(V, E) = \min \{k : |V_{1..k}| \geq cn\}$, edge c-quantile $\delta(V, E) = \min \{k : \sum_{v \in V_{1..k}} deg(v) \geq 2mc\}$. However, the values of those functions are more expensive to compute.

The I/O-efficient BSDL procedure is shown in Figure 4.10.

(1) Compute the value of $\delta(V, E)$.

(2) Find the set of nodes $R = \{v : v \in V, deg(v) \leq \delta(V, E)\}$.

(3) Delete the nodes in R from the graph G reducing it to graph $G' = (V', E')$, where $V' = V - R$ and $E' = \{(u, v) \in E \mid u, v \in V'\}$.

(4) Color G' recursively.

(5) Color the nodes in R calling *GreedyColoring* on the subgraph of G induced by R. Before running the algorithm the priority queue is filled with entries signaling the existence of already colored neighbors of nodes in R, i.e. values $\{(v, color(u)) \mid (u, v) \in E, v \in R, u \notin R\}$ are inserted.

Figure 4.10: I/O-efficient implementation of the Batched Smallest-Degree-Last coloring heuristic.

Figure 4.11 depicts an STXXL pipelined implementation of the recursion of the I/O-efficient BSDL heuristic. The nodes to remove R, the edges incident to R and the input graph G' for the recursion call are computed in a constant number of scan/sort passes in blocks from (a) to (g). After the recursion the nodes in set R are colored using the greedy coloring algorithm and a few scan/sort passes (blocks (j)–(l)).

Now we consider the processing that goes on in the implementation in detail: In each recursion, the algorithm receives a stream of edges E sorted by the source node, which is fed into the duplicate algorithm (a). For each incoming edge (v, w) the duplicate algorithm outputs two edges (v, w) and (w, v) to the output stream, which is consumed by the sorter (b). The output of sorter is a sequence of adjacency lists, which is fed to the algorithm (c), computing the degrees of the nodes. In algorithm (d) the value of function $\delta(V, E)$ is computed. The stream of triples in the form $(src, dst, deg(src))$ is analyzed, passing the triples (src, dst, B), $src < dst$ with binary bit $B = (deg(src) \leq \delta(V, E))$ to sorter (e) and pushing the nodes $src \in R$ to an external vector. To save I/O volume, field B is coded as the most significant bit of the src field. In our implementation, algorithms (c) and (d) are combined into one algorithm to reduce the computational overhead. Algorithm (f) passes the incoming edge (src, dst) from sorter (e) to the next recursion (f) if $src, dst \notin R$. Edges in $E^C = \{(src, dst) \mid src, dst \in R\}$ are fed to sorter (i), and edges in $E^{IN} = \{(dst, src) \mid src \notin R, dst \in R\} \cup \{(src, dst) \mid src \in R, dst \notin R\}$ go to sorter (h). Let $V_0'(i)$ be the set of nodes $v \in V'$ having degree zero in graph G' in the current recursion i, i.e., the nodes that become isolated after removal of edges E^{IN}, and let $V_0^* = \bigcup_{j=i}^{\infty} V_0'(j)$. Then the stream of color assignments $(v', color(v'))$, $v' \in V' - V_0^*$ sorted by v' comes from the recursion call (g). Algorithm (j) initializes the priority queue used in the *GreedyColoring* with entries $(v, color(u))$, $v \in R, u \in V'$, indicating that node v has a neighbor colored with $color(u)$. For nodes $u \in V_0^*$ algorithm (j) assumes that they have color 0. This way the nodes in V_0^* are *implicitly* colored with zeros. Nodes in R are colored calling *GreedyColoring* on graph (V, E^C) (k). Algorithm (l) merges the color assignment stream from algorithm (k) with the color assignments of nodes in G' stored in external array C. The array C is rewritten with the output of algorithm (l), such that it finally contains the color assignments for all nodes in $G - V_0^*$.

4.7.5 7-Coloring of Planar Graphs

In this section we show that the BSDL heuristic with maximum batch degree function $\delta(V, E) = 6$ computes a 7-coloring of a planar graph I/O in $\mathcal{O}(\text{sort}(m))$ I/Os. In contrast to the parallel algorithm of Naor [Nao87] our 7-coloring algorithm does not filter adjacent nodes computing a maximal independent set of R. Using the time-forward-processing technique we are able to reduce by more nodes per iteration.

Lemma 5 ([Nao87]). *In planar graphs, the number of nodes with a degree less than seven is at least* $n/6$.

4.7. GRAPH COLORING

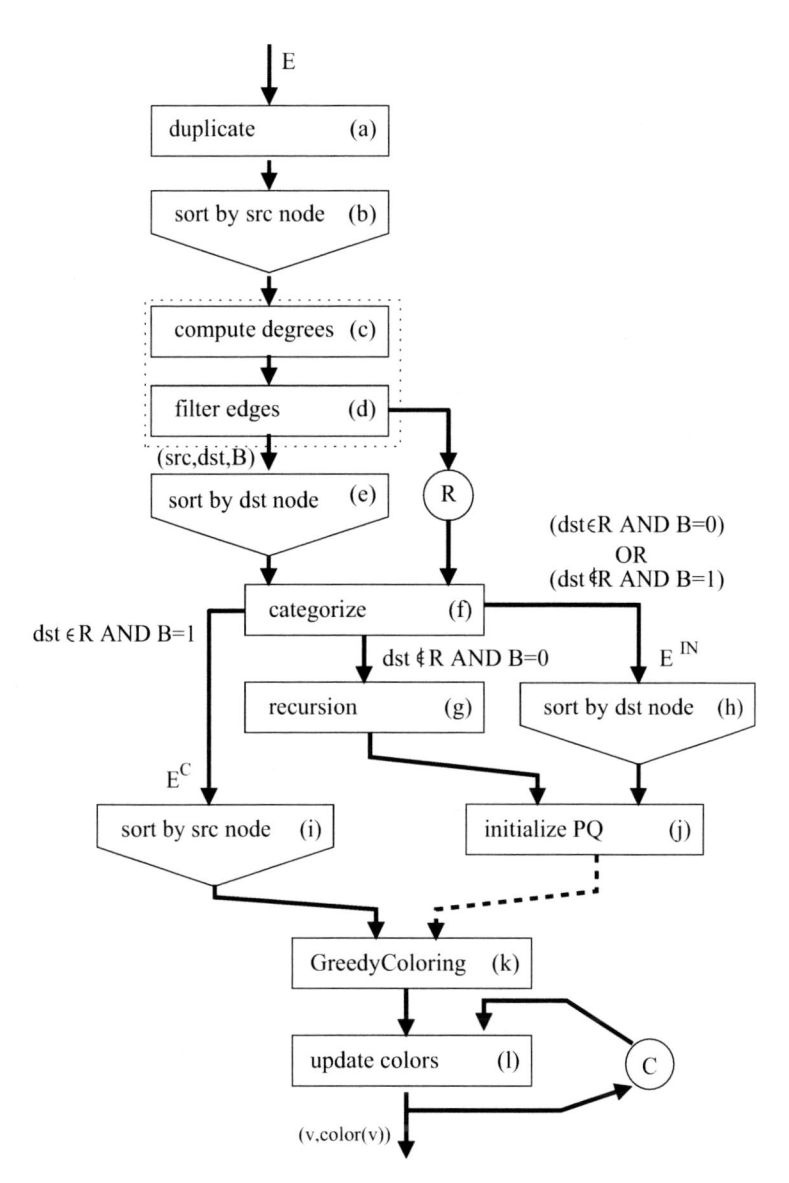

Figure 4.11: The pipelined scheme of the Batched Smallest-Degree-Last coloring heuristic.

Proof. According to Euler's formula for planar graphs [Har69]:

$$2m < 6n \qquad (4.1)$$

or

$$\sum_{i=1}^{\infty} i\, n_i < 6 \sum_{i=1}^{\infty} n_i$$

We have $\sum_{i=1}^{\infty} i\, n_i = \sum_{i=1}^{6} i\, n_i + \sum_{i=7}^{\infty} i\, n_i \geq \sum_{i=1}^{6} n_i + 7\sum_{i=7}^{\infty} n_i$. On the other hand $6 \sum_{i=1}^{\infty} n_i = 6\sum_{i=1}^{6} n_i + 6\sum_{i=7}^{\infty} n_i$. Then $\sum_{i=1}^{6} n_i + 7\sum_{i=7}^{\infty} n_i < 6\sum_{i=1}^{6} n_i + 6\sum_{i=7}^{\infty} n_i$. Subtracting $6\sum_{i=7}^{\infty} n_i$ on both sides we get $\sum_{i=1}^{6} n_i + \sum_{i=7}^{\infty} n_i < 6\sum_{i=1}^{6} n_i \Leftrightarrow n < 6\sum_{i=1}^{6} n_i$. □

Theorem 6. *The BSDL heuristic with maximum batch degree function $\delta(V, E) = 6$ computes a 7-coloring of a planar graph in $\mathcal{O}(\text{sort}(m))$ I/Os.*

Proof. The pipelined implementation implies that steps (1)–(3) run in $\mathcal{O}(\text{sort}(m))$ I/Os. Step (5) needs $\mathcal{O}(\text{sort}(m))$ I/Os by Theorem 3. Lemma 5 states that $|R| \geq \frac{n}{6}$, then by Euler's formula (Equation 4.1): $|R| > \frac{m}{18}$. Since every node in R has at least one edge, the edge set E' has at most a constant fraction of edges in E: $|E'| < \frac{17}{18}m$. Therefore the I/O complexity of the algorithm can be expressed as:

$$T(m) < \mathcal{O}(\text{sort}(m)) + T\left(\frac{17}{18}m\right)$$

The recurrence has the solution $T(m) = \mathcal{O}(\text{sort}(m))$.

Since the maximum degree of nodes R in graph $(V, E^C \cup E^{IN})$ is at most 6, then by Theorem 3 the number of colors used by the heuristic is at most 7. □

Analyzing the data flow between and inside the blocks in the diagram shown in Figure 4.11, we can obtain the worst case I/O volume of the 7-coloring algorithm. With the same assumptions about the I/O volume of the pipelined sorters and priority queue as in Section 4.7.3, the I/O volume of the 7-coloring algorithm is $1168m + 144n$ bytes in the worst case. Without pipelining it would be $3192m + 336n$ bytes.

4.7.6 6-Coloring of Planar Graphs

In this section, we present an I/O-efficient algorithm that 6-colors planar graphs. As in the 7-coloring algorithm we try to find a set of low degree nodes R whose size is at least a constant fraction of the total number of nodes. This set contains the candidates for removal. In our 6-coloring algorithm, in contrast to 7-coloring, not all nodes with degree six are taken into R, one takes only those having at least *two* neighbors that can be merged into one node efficiently, thus reducing the maximum possible number of neighbor colors to *five*. In candidate set R we include two categories of nodes:

(1) nodes with a degree at most five, $V_{1..5}$.

(2) nodes with degree six having at most two *large* neighbors. We denote this set as $V'_6 \subseteq V_6$, and the cardinality of this set we denote as n'_6.

Lemma 7 proves that there is a sufficient number of nodes of that kind. Amazingly, the worst case ratio between the size of the candidate set R and n is the same as in the 7-coloring algorithm (Lemma 5), i.e. the number of degree-six nodes rejected in condition (2) is small.

Definition: A node is *small* if it has at most K neighbors, *large* otherwise. $deg(v)$ denotes the degree of node v.

Lemma 7. *There exists a constant K such that the number of nodes in set R is at least $n/6$.*

Proof. First let us bound the number of nodes with degree six having at least three large neighbors ($n_6 - n'_6$). Consider the worst case when the large nodes are incident only to the degree-six nodes. Moreover, each node of degree six has exactly three edges connecting it to the large degree nodes. Then:

$$n_6 - n'_6 \leq \frac{\sum_{i=K+1}^{\infty} i\, n_i}{3}$$

or

$$3n'_6 \geq 3n_6 - \sum_{i=K+1}^{\infty} i\, n_i \qquad (4.2)$$

According to Euler's formula

$$2m < 6n$$

$$\Rightarrow \sum_{i=1}^{\infty} i\, n_i < 6 \sum_{i=1}^{\infty} n_i$$

$$\Rightarrow \sum_{i=1}^{5} i\, n_i + 6n_6 + \sum_{i=7}^{\infty} i\, n_i < 6 \sum_{i=1}^{5} n_i + 6n_6 + 6 \sum_{i=7}^{\infty} n_i$$

$$\Rightarrow \sum_{i=7}^{\infty} (i-6)n_i + \sum_{i=1}^{5} i\, n_i - 6 \sum_{i=1}^{5} n_i < 0$$

$$\Rightarrow \sum_{i=7}^{\infty} (i-6)n_i + \sum_{i=1}^{5} n_i - 6 \sum_{i=1}^{5} n_i < 0$$

$$\Rightarrow 0 > \sum_{i=7}^{\infty} (i-6)n_i - 5 \sum_{i=1}^{5} n_i \qquad (4.3)$$

We add α times Inequality (4.3) to Inequality (4.2):

$$3n'_6 > 3n_6 + \alpha \sum_{i=7}^{\infty} (i-6)n_i - \sum_{i=K+1}^{\infty} i\, n_i - 5\alpha \sum_{i=1}^{5} n_i$$

$$\Rightarrow 5\alpha \sum_{i=1}^{5} n_i + 3n'_6 > 3n_6 + \alpha \sum_{i=7}^{K} (i-6)n_i + \sum_{i=K+1}^{\infty} ((\alpha-1)i - 6\alpha)n_i$$

$$\Rightarrow 5\alpha \sum_{i=1}^{5} n_i + 3n'_6 > 3n_6 + \alpha \sum_{i=7}^{K} n_i + \sum_{i=K+1}^{\infty} ((\alpha-1)(K+1) - 6\alpha)n_i$$

For all $K \geq 10$ the ratio $\frac{5\alpha}{\min\{3\cdot\alpha, (\alpha-1)(K+1)-6\alpha\}}$ is minimal with $\alpha = 3$. Plugging in the values of α and $K = 10$ we obtain:

4.7. GRAPH COLORING

$$15\sum_{i=1}^{5} n_i + 3n_6' > 3n_6 + 3\sum_{i=7}^{K} n_i + 4\sum_{i=K+1}^{\infty} n_i$$

$$\Rightarrow \quad 15\sum_{i=1}^{5} n_i + 3n_6' > 3\sum_{i=6}^{\infty} n_i$$

$$\Rightarrow \quad 5\sum_{i=1}^{5} n_i + n_6' > \sum_{i=6}^{\infty} n_i$$

Adding $\sum_{i=1}^{5} n_i$ to both sides of the inequality we arrive at:

$$6\sum_{i=1}^{5} n_i + n_6' > \sum_{i=1}^{\infty} n_i$$

Finally:

$$6(\sum_{i=1}^{5} n_i + n_6') > \sum_{i=1}^{\infty} n_i = n$$

$$\Rightarrow \quad |R| > \frac{n}{6}$$

□

The algorithms for 5-coloring planar graphs in [HCD89, GPS87] have similar constructions of candidate sets. However, they guarantee only a very small ratios $|R|/n$ (1/196 and 1/301 accordingly), which may lead to huge constants in the overall running times. Our construction is more practical: the reduction step is simpler and it can find more nodes in the worst case.

Now we present the algorithmical procedure of the reduction step. Let R' be a maximal independent set of R. The nodes in R' having a degree less than six ($V_{1..5} \cap R'$) are deleted from the graph as in the 7-coloring algorithm. We delete every node in $V_6' \cap R'$ from G and merge two non-adjacent *small* neighbors in a single node concatenating their adjacency lists. Such two nodes always exist, since otherwise there is a clique on five nodes (the degree-six

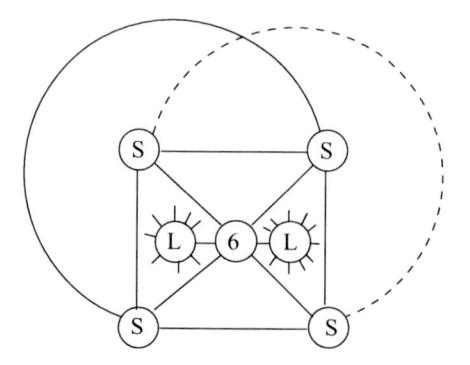

Figure 4.12: The clique between the degree-six node (center) and the four small neighbors (corner nodes).

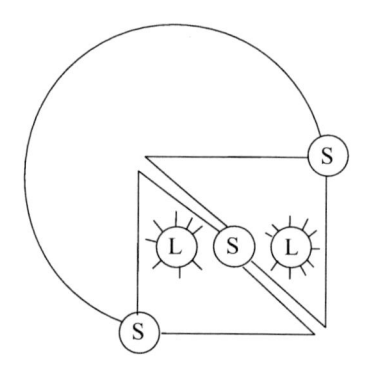

Figure 4.13: The only non-neighbor small nodes from Figure 4.12 are merged (the top-left and bottom-right nodes).

4.7. GRAPH COLORING

node and its four small neighbors, see Figure 4.12). It is easy to see that after the described reduction, the graph remains planar (see Figure 4.13).

In general, two or more nodes in V'_6 can cause the merging of the same node: $v_1 \in V'_6$ merges node w_1 with w_2 and $v_2 \in V'_6$ merges node w_1 with w_3. To resolve these conflicts we propose two solutions. The first approach computes the *connected components* in graph G_c with a node set V_c consisting of nodes that have to be merged and the edge set E_c, which models the merge operations: edge (w_1, w_2) is in E_c if w_1 has to be merged with w_2. Then we compute the connected components of the planar graph G_c, using the algorithm in [CGG+95] in $\mathcal{O}(\text{sort}(n))$ I/Os. Each connected component includes the set of nodes that have to be merged together in one node. The merging is then done by renaming the nodes to the node id of the representative node of the respective connected component. This can be performed in a constant number of sort and scan operations.

Our second solution does not require calling the connected components subprocedure. We compute a maximal matching M_c of the (multi)graph G_c using a simple algorithm from [Zeh02] running in $\mathcal{O}(\text{sort}(n))$ I/Os. We perform only those merge operations that are present in M_c. We also have to remove the nodes from R' which contributed to G_c, but their merge operations were filtered out from M_c. Since all nodes in G_c are small, this can be implemented using $\mathcal{O}(\text{sort}(n))$ I/Os. The degree of a node $v \in G_c$ can be at most K, since for each edge $(v, u) \in E$, $u \in V'_6 \cap R'$, there is exactly one edge $(v, w) \in G_c$ and node v is *small* in G. Therefore by Lemma 2 set R' might be reduced in size by a factor at most $1/(2K-1)$.

It is not clear which solution is faster: connected components is a more expensive procedure in the external memory, but the approach does not reduce set R'; the second solution is cheaper but might reduce set R' by factor $1/(2K-1)$ in the worst case, i.e. postponing the computation to later recursions.

Summing all up we present a high-level scheme of the algorithm in Figure 4.14

Theorem 8. *The I/O-efficient algorithm for computing 6-coloring of a planar graph runs in $\mathcal{O}(\text{sort}(m))$ I/Os.*

Proof. Steps (1)–(5) and (7)–(8) can be implemented in a constant number of sort and scan steps. From Lemma 7, Lemma 1 and Lemma 2 it follows that $|V'| \leq \left(1 - \frac{1}{6 \cdot 7 \cdot (2K-1)}\right) n$. Then, by the Euler's formula (Equation 4.1) there exists a constant q, such that $|E'| \leq q \cdot m$, $0 \leq q < 1$. Hence the I/O complexity of the algorithm can be expressed as:

$$T(m) \leq \mathcal{O}(\text{sort}(m)) + T(q \cdot m)$$

(1) Find sets $V_{1..5}$ and V'_6, $R = V_{1..5} \cup V'_6$.

(2) Compute a maximal independent set R' of R using the I/O-efficient algorithm from [Zeh02].

(3) Construct G_c: for each $v \in V'_6 \cap R'$ add edge (w_1, w_2), where w_1 and w_2 are two *non-adjacent small* neighbors of v, label (w_1, w_2) with v.

(4) Do (a) or (b):

  (a) Compute the connected components of G_c. In graph G merge all nodes belonging to the same connected component of G_c into one node. We denote this graph with merged nodes as $G_m = (V_m, E_m)$.

  (b) Find a maximal matching M_c in G_c. Keep a node $v \in V'_6 \cap R'$ in R' if $\exists (w_1, w_2) \in M_c$ with the label v, otherwise exclude v from R'. In graph G merge nodes w_1 with w_2 for all $(w_1, w_2) \in M_c$, obtaining graph G_m.

(5) Delete the nodes in R' from the graph G_m reducing it to graph $G' = (V', E')$, where $V' = V_m - R'$ and $E' = \{(u, v) \in E_m \mid u, v \in V'\}$.

(6) Color G' recursively.

(7) Each node in R' chooses a color different from its neighbors in G_m. It has at most five neighbors, so that a vacant color always exists.

(8) Color the nodes in G that were deleted during the merging with the colors of the nodes they were represented by in G_m.

Figure 4.14: I/O-efficient 6-coloring algorithm for planar graphs.

4.7. GRAPH COLORING

The recurrence is solved by $T(m) = \mathcal{O}(\text{sort}(m))$.

□

4.7.7 2-Coloring

The well known linear time algorithm for finding a 2-coloring of a graph (or proving that no 2-coloring exists)[12] can be implemented I/O-efficiently. The algorithm computes a spanning forest of the graph in $\mathcal{O}(\text{sort}(m)(1 + \log\log(B \cdot n/m)))$ I/Os using the deterministic algorithm [MR99] or in $\mathcal{O}(\text{sort}(m))$ I/Os using the randomized algorithm [ABW02]. Around each tree of the spanning forest, an Euler tour [CGG+95] is computed using a constant number of sort and scan steps. When the algorithm traverses the Euler tours using list ranking [CGG+95], the color ($d(v)$ mod 2) is assigned to node v, where $d(v)$ is a tree distance from the root of node v. Then, the edge list is scanned: if there is an edge $(u, v) \in E$ such that colors of u and v match, then the graph has an odd-length cycle and is not 2-colorable. Otherwise, the obtained coloring is valid.

Theorem 9. *A graph can be 2-colored in* $\mathcal{O}(\text{sort}(m)(1 + \log\log(B \cdot n/m)))$ *I/Os deterministically or in* $\mathcal{O}(\text{sort}(m))$ *expected I/Os.*

4.7.8 Experiments

In this section, we experimentally evaluate the performance of the STXXL external memory implementations of the HDF heuristic, the BSDL heuristic with $\delta(V, E) = \lceil 2|E|/|V| \rceil$, the 7-coloring algorithm for planar graphs (EM7), a *tuned* SDL implementation from the Boost library (www.boost.org) and an implementation of a 7-coloring algorithm for planar graphs that uses the LEDA library version 5.1 [MN99] (IM7 algorithm) [13]. The Boost SDL implementation uses the adjacency list graph representation with `std::vectors` storing the set of vertices and the adjacency structure. This choice reduces the internal memory consumption and guarantees constant time operations for the SDL algorithm. The implementation itself does not modify the input graph during the node removal, instead, it maintains an auxiliary array with the current node degrees. Finding the smallest degree node is implemented with a bucket priority queue. The IM7 implementation follows the algorithm from Figure 4.10 using data type `leda::graph` to represent graphs.

---

[12]2-colorability is equivalent to the bipartiteness test.

[13]The source code of the implementations and random graph generators is available at http://algo2.iti.uka.de/dementiev/files/coloring.tgz.

Node and edge removal have been implemented via *hiding*, using the method `leda::graph::hide_node`.

In the experimental evaluation we have run the implementations on random and real graph instances:

- $G(n,m)$-random graphs where edges are generated picking the end points uniformly at random from $[0,n)$. Self-loops has been discarded.

- a web crawl graph from the WebBase project[14]. In this graph the nodes are web pages and edges are hyperlinks between them (the direction was ignored).

- maximal random planar graphs with $m \approx 3n$, which were obtained using the `leda::maximal_planar_map` function, and more sparse planar graphs with $m = 2n$ generated by the `leda::random_planar_map` function. We could not generate graphs with more than 2^{23} nodes because of the 4 GBytes limit of the address space.

- instances of Delaunay triangulations of real-world point sets (Neuse River Basin of North Carolina) obtained in [AAY05].

In our experiments we have used three systems running Linux SUSE 9.3 or 10.0, their configurations are described in Tables 4.5 and 4.6. The Opteron machines correspond to the systems described in Section 2.4. The STREAM value is the average of the copy, scale, add, and triad memory bandwidths obtained by the popular STREAM benchmark [Str]. Our programs were compiled with the GNU C++ compiler version 3.4 and 4.0 with options `-O3 -DNDEBUG -DLEDA_CHECKING_OFF`. For experiments with external memory implementations, we used up to 660 MBytes of the available main memory and block sizes 512 KBytes or 1 MByte, if not stated otherwise. During all experiments, the swap file was switched off to avoid paging. The values of the running time and the number of used colors for (general and planar) random graphs are averaged over runs with 20 random instances.

Figure 4.15 compares the performance of the SDL, BSDL and HDF heuristics on random graphs with a fixed edge probability $p = 0.2$ [15]. The smaller instances fit into the internal memory, for $n \geq 2^{15}$ the inputs need to be processed in external memory. With respect to the running time, the *internal memory* SDL shows to be up to 1.6 times faster than the *external memory*

---

[14]http://www-diglib.stanford.edu/~testbed/doc2/WebBase/

[15]We consider all possible edges in an undirected graph with n nodes and choose each edge with probability p. This is another method to generate $G(n,m)$-random graphs.

Table 4.5: Parameters of experimental systems.

Name	Main mem.	CPU	STREAM
Opteron-IDE	4 GBytes	DualCore 2.0 GHz	2.9 GByte/s
Opteron-SCSI	8 GBytes	4-way 1.8 GHz	2.0 GByte/s
Pentium-4	1 GByte	3.2 GHz HT	3.1 GByte/s

Table 4.6: Disk parameters.

Name	Type	Read/write seek time	Measured read/write bandwidth (MByte/s) 1 disk	4 disks
Opteron-IDE	SATA 7200RPM	9/9 ms	60/80	240/320
Opteron-SCSI	SCSI 15000RPM	3.6/4 ms	75/63	284/244
Pentium-4	PATA 5400RPM	8.9/8.9 ms	37/31	

implementations. However, for $n > 2^{13}$ the SDL implementation needs more memory than the physical main memory of the system and aborts if the swap file is switched off. With working virtual memory, SDL already needs $57\mu s$ per edge for $n = 2^{14}$ and $180\mu s$ per edge for $n = 2^{15}$. For larger inputs it did not finish even in one day due to many unstructured accesses to the swap file; the experiments have been interrupted manually. For large inputs, we only show the performance of the BSDL and HDF heuristics, since we are not aware of any other I/O-efficient coloring heuristics. One recursion of the BSDL heuristic is *cheaper* than the whole procedure of HDF with respect to the I/O volume. However, BSDL is slower than HDF on random graphs, since there are not many nodes with a degree that is less than average, and the algorithm has to perform many recursions only discarding about 50 % of the graph in most of them. The right part of the figure shows the difference in the quality of the obtained colorings. Note that this difference is very small and below 1.2% for all input sizes and heuristics. At least for random graphs, BSDL achieves near the same quality of coloring as SDL, though BSDL colorings can be worse than SDL colorings theoretically.

Figure 4.16 compares the performance of the heuristics on random graphs with varying density and fixed size. The graphs have about five million edges such that the space consumption of SDL does not exceed the size of the main memory. Changing the density of graphs does not change the order of the heuristics with respect to the running time. As before, the difference in the number of used colors is very small (below 1.3%). BSDL and SDL achieve

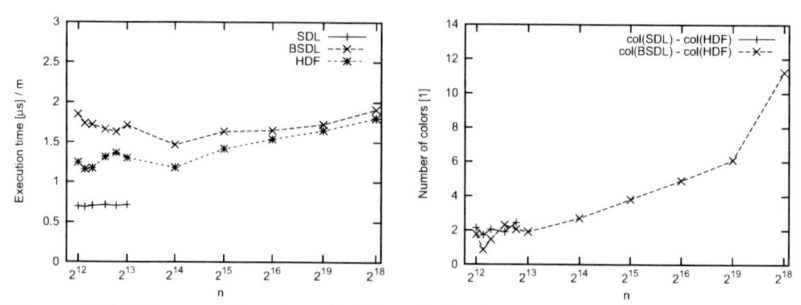

Figure 4.15: The running time (left) and the difference in the average number of colors (right) of the heuristics on random graphs with edge probability 0.2. (Opteron-IDE, 4 disks, $M = 660$ MB, $B = 2$ MB for $n > 2^{15}$, otherwise $B = 128$ KB).

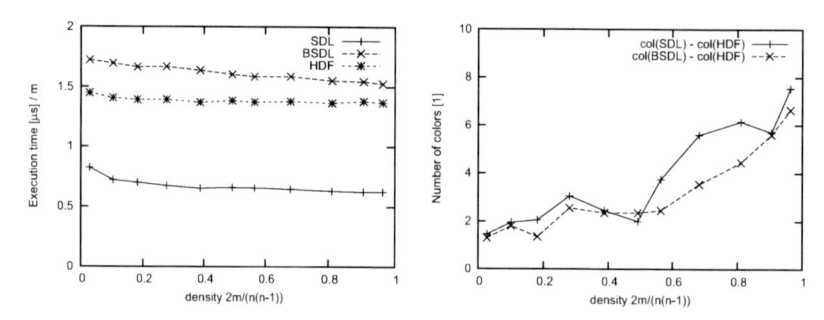

Figure 4.16: The running time (left) and the difference in the number of used colors (right) of the heuristics on random graphs with about five million edges. (Opteron-IDE, 4 disks, $M = 200$ MB, $B = 128$ KB).

almost the same quality of coloring. Figure 4.17 shows similar behavior of the HDF and BSDL heuristics on *larger* random graphs with varying density. SDL could not cope with these inputs. The curves in Figures 4.16 and 4.17 go slightly down as the graph density increases. We explain it by the presence of an $\Theta(n)$ term in the complexity of the algorithms.

The absolute number of colors obtained in the experiments above is shown in Figure 4.18. The difference between the heuristics is indistinguishable.

Table 4.7 shows the performance of the HDF and BSDL heuristics on planar graphs and the webgraph. Note that the *delaunay1* instance and random planar graphs[16] can fit into the main memory. However, the sorters work in

---

[16]These are the largest graphs we could generate with LEDA.

4.7. GRAPH COLORING

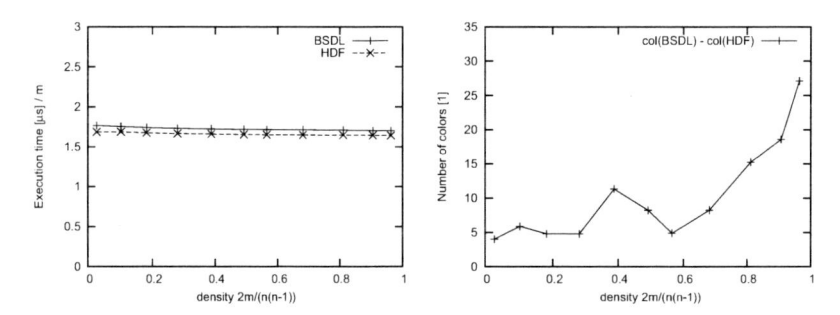

Figure 4.17: The running time (left) and the difference in the number of used colors (right) of the heuristics on random graphs with about $2 \cdot 10^9$ edges. (Opteron-IDE, 4 disks).

Table 4.7: The running times/I/O wait time/the number of obtained colors for the HDF and BSDL heuristics. The running times are given in minutes. (Opteron-IDE, 4 disks)

Instance	$n/10^6$	$m/10^6$	HDF	BSDL
rand.planar1	8.4	16.8	0.55/0.07/6.0	0.57/0.10/5.1
rand.planar2	8.4	25.2	0.72/0.07/7.0	0.77/0.11/6.1
delaunay1	8.5	25.5	0.69/0.13/7	0.67/0.10/7
delaunay2	84.7	254.0	6.95/0.96/7	6.57/0.87/7
delaunay3	503.0	1509.0	49.87/10.41/7	43.19/5.68/7
webgraph	135.0	1079.9	**35.86**/8.72/246	43.57/5.89/246

the external memory even in this setting, because they *share* the main memory. We have run the implementations with reduced $M = 200$ MBytes also, but the running time has remained almost the same. The BSDL heuristic is slightly faster than the HDF heuristic on all measured Delaunay triangulations. The reason for this is that the number of nodes with a degree that it at most average (rounded up) is large in the Delaunay graphs (about 88 %), therefore the BSDL heuristic can reduce many nodes in the first recursion already. The webgraph could be colored by HDF in 35.86 minutes using 246 colors. The last recursions of the BSDL heuristic have identified a very dense subgraph of the webgraph, which explains the relatively large number of colors used in the obtained colorings. Note that the average degree of the entire webgraph is less than 16.

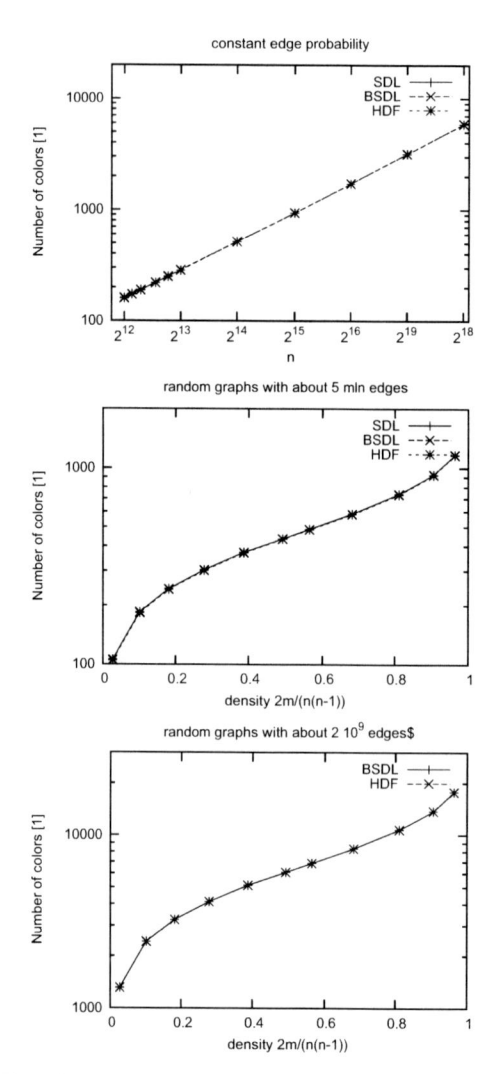

Figure 4.18: The absolute number of colors obtained by the heuristics on random graphs with constant edge probability 0.2, on random graphs with about five million edges and about $2 \cdot 10^9$ edges.

4.7. GRAPH COLORING 139

Figure 4.19 shows the execution times of the internal memory implementation IM7 and the EM7 implementation running on the instances of the random planar graphs. The linear time IM7 implementation is faster than the EM7 implementation for $n \leq 2^{22}$ because of the smaller CPU work and the use of the efficient internal memory data structures from LEDA. For larger inputs, the IM7 implementation needs more memory than the system physically holds.

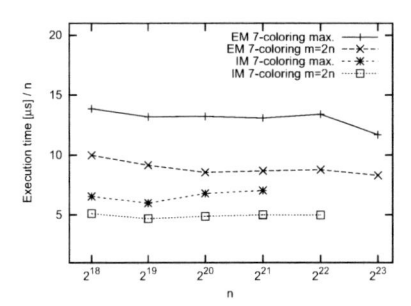

Figure 4.19: Performance of 7-coloring algorithms on random planar graphs (Pentium-4, $M = 200$ MB, $B = 128$ KB).

For each recursion the second column ($|R|/|V|$) in Table 4.8 presents the real node reduction factors in the EM7 implementation on a maximal random planar graph with 2^{23} nodes. We present numbers for this instance size only, since they are very similar to the numbers for other instances from this graph family. The obtained node factors $|R|/|V|$ are much larger than the theoretical worst case $1/6$. The algorithm could reduce about 80 % of nodes and edges in each recursion. It required only 10 recursions to complete. The real I/O volume of the algorithm is 11–14 times smaller than the bound mentioned in Section 4.7.5. This holds true for other planar graph instances also (Table 4.9). We conclude that for real graphs the performance of the EM7 algorithm is much better than the worst case. The measured I/O volume of the HDF heuristic does not deviate much from its worst case bound (only 7–15 % less).

The running times of the EM7 algorithm on instances of Delaunay triangulations are presented in Table 4.9. The bottom line of this experiment is that a real planar graph with $1.5 \cdot 10^9$ edges can be 7-colored in about 42 min by an external memory algorithm. Running with four disks, the EM7 algorithm is close to being compute-bound: the processing thread is waiting for I/O only about 10 % of the total running time. The algorithm is faster (20–30 %) on

Table 4.8: Reduction factors in the EM7 algorithm implementation on a maximal random planar graph instance with 2^{23} nodes.

recursion	$|R|/|V|$ (%)	$|V_0|/|V|$ (%)	$|E - E'|/|E|$ (%)
1	78.58	0	79.07
2	79.2	0	79.59
3	79.67	0	79.78
4	79.84	0.01	79.89
5	79.57	0.02	79.52
6	79.7	0	79.68
7	78.58	0	79.16
8	80.15	0	81.53
9	81.48	0	87.14
10	100	0	100

the Opteron-IDE system perhaps because of a faster CPU and a faster internal memory subsystem. Comparing the running times of the instances, one concludes that the EM7 algorithm almost linearly scales with the input size. In running time, the EM7 algorithm has a small advantage over the HDF and BSDL heuristics (Table 4.7) on planar graph instances because it can reduce many nodes in a recursion, leading to less recursions. In particular, it can be faster than BSDL when the average degree is less than six. We have observed that Delaunay inputs need much less recursions: *delaunay1* and *delaunay3* are processed in only *four* recursions, note also that the latter instance is 60 times larger than the first one. This fact indicates that the Delaunay triangulations have a nature different from that of maximal random planar graphs. Starting from the second recursion, the graph begins to shrink very quickly, such that only a tiny ratio of the input edges and nodes is passed to the next recursion. A reason for this is that from this point many nodes become isolated after the removal of nodes R and their incident edges E^{IN} (see $|V_0|/|V|$ ratio in Table 4.10 and Table 4.8). The described behavior is not observed for the maximal random planar instances. The colorings of the BSDL heuristic and EM7 algorithm are better than the colorings of the HDF heuristic for random planar graphs (Tables 4.7 and 4.9). Perhaps smallest-degree-last approaches are more successful for planar graphs, in particular, because the pure SDL heuristic can always *6-color* planar graphs. Moreover, in our experiments SDL produced colorings with four colors for the largest random planar graphs it could cope with.

4.7. GRAPH COLORING

Table 4.9: Running time/I/O wait time in minutes and number of colors (column 'C') of the EM7 algorithm.

Instance	$n/10^6$	$m/10^6$	C	D = 4	
				Opt.-IDE	Opt.-SCSI
delaunay1	8.5	25.5	7	0.62/0.09	0.82/0.12
delaunay2	84.7	254	7	5.80/0.24	7.43/0.49
delaunay3	503	1509	7	**42.1**/5.58	49.7/4.62
rand.planar1	8.4	16.8	5.5	0.49/0.05	
rand.planar2	8.4	25.2	6.05	0.71/0.05	

	$n/10^6$	$m/10^6$	C	D = 1		
				Pentium-4	Opt.-IDE	Opt.-SCSI
delaunay1	8.5	25.5	7	1.39/0.74	0.78/0.25	0.90/0.24
delaunay2	84.7	254	7	13.29/6.53	7.06/1.48	8.56/1.60
delaunay3	503	1509	7	*no space*	48.7/12.2	58.3/12.5

Table 4.10: Reduction factors in EM7 algorithm implementation on the *delaunay1* instance.

recursion	$|R|/|V|$ (%)	$|V_0|/|V|$ (%)	$|E - E'|/|E|$ (%)
1	71.22	0	87.89
2	99.96	3.05	99.98
3	97.21	41.03	94.65
4	100	0	100

The same experiments (Table 4.9) being run using a single disk shows the differences in the performance characteristics of the disks on the test systems. Due to a slow IDE disk with a low bandwidth, the Pentium-4 system waits for I/Os during half of the total running time. On systems with faster disks (Opteron-IDE and -SCSI) this ratio is only 18–25 %.

4.7.9 Conclusion and Future Work

We have presented I/O-efficient heuristics for graph coloring that can handle huge graphs on cheap machines. This is significant since so far only few external graph algorithms have implementations of comparable practicability. We have also presented a new I/O-efficient 6-coloring algorithm for planar graphs and shown how to externalize a 2-coloring algorithm for general graphs.

The BSDL algorithm is a particularly flexible and efficient algorithm, for example, it can be instantiated to yield 7-colorings of planar graphs. Several interesting questions arise here. Can we reduce the large constant factor gap between its guaranteed I/O-volume and its real performance using a more careful analysis? Will a more clever δ function yield colorings with less than 7 colors in practice (similar to the pure SDL algorithm)? Another approach is to combine the idea of the HDF heuristic with the BSDL heuristic, coloring the batches R in highest-degree-first order.

Acknowledgments. Kevin Yi has kindly provided some input instances.

Chapter 5

Engineering Large Suffix Array Construction

The results that presented in this section were partially published in [DKMS06] and in the master's thesis [Meh04].

5.1 Introduction

The suffix array [MM93, GBYS92], a lexicographically sorted array of the suffixes of a string, has numerous applications, e.g., in string matching [MM93, GBYS92], genome analysis [AKO02] and text compression [BW94]. For example, one can use it as a full text index: To find all occurrences of a pattern P in a text T, do a binary search in the suffix array of T, i.e., look for the interval of suffixes that have P as a prefix. A lot of effort has been devoted to the efficient construction of suffix arrays, culminating recently in three direct linear time algorithms [KSB06, KSPP03, KA03]. One of the linear time algorithms [KSB06] is very simple and can also be adapted to obtain an optimal algorithm for the external memory: The DC3-algorithm [KSB06] constructs a suffix array of a text T of length n using $\mathcal{O}(\text{sort}(n))$ I/Os.

However, suffix arrays are still rarely used for processing huge inputs. Less powerful techniques like an index of all words appearing in a text are very simple, since they have favorable constant factors and can be implemented to work well with the external memory for practical inputs. In contrast, the only previous external memory implementations of the suffix array construction [CF02] are not only asymptotically suboptimal but also so slow that measurements could only be done for small inputs and an artificially reduced internal memory size.

5.1.1 Basic Concepts

We use the shorthands $[i, j] = \{i, \ldots, j\}$ and $[i, j) = [i, j-1]$ for ranges of integers and extend to substrings as seen below. The input of the discussed algorithms is an n character string $T = T[0] \cdots T[n-1] = T[0, n)$ of characters in the alphabet $\Sigma = [1, n]$. The restriction to the alphabet $[1, n]$ is not a serious one. For a string T over any alphabet, we can first sort the characters of T, remove duplicates, assign a rank to each character, and construct a new string T' over the alphabet $[1, n]$ by renaming the characters of T with their ranks. Since the renaming is order preserving, the order of the suffixes does not change. A similar technique called *lexicographic naming* will play an important role in all of these algorithms where a string (e.g., a substring of T) is replaced by its rank in some set of strings.

Let $ be a special character that is smaller than any character in the alphabet. We use the convention that $T[i] = \$$ if $i \geq n$. $T_i = T[i, n)$ denotes the i-th suffix of T. The *suffix array* SA of T is a permutation of $[0, n)$ such that $T_{\text{SA}[i]} < T_{\text{SA}[j]}$ whenever $0 \leq i < j < n$. Let $\text{lcp}(i, j)$ denote the longest common prefix length of SA[i] and SA[j] ($\text{lcp}(i, j) = 0$ if $i < 0$ or $j \geq n$). Then $\text{dps}(i) := 1 + \max\{\text{lcp}(i-1, i), \text{lcp}(i, i+1)\}$ is the distinguishing prefix size of T_i. We get the following derived quantities that can be used to characterize the "difficulty" of an input or that will turn out to play such a role in the following analysis.

$$\text{maxlcp} := \max_{0 \leq i < n} \text{lcp}(i, i+1) \tag{5.1}$$

$$\overline{\text{lcp}} := \frac{1}{n} \sum_{0 \leq i < n} \text{lcp}(i, i+1) \tag{5.2}$$

$$\overline{\log \text{dps}} := \frac{1}{n} \sum_{0 \leq i < n} \log(\text{dps}(i)) \tag{5.3}$$

We extend the set notation to sequences in the obvious way. For example $\langle i : i \text{ is prime} \rangle = \langle 2, 3, 5, 7, 11, 13, \ldots \rangle$ in that order.

5.1.2 Overview

In Section 5.2 we present the *doubling algorithm* [AFGV97, CF02] for a suffix array construction that has I/O complexity $\mathcal{O}(\text{sort}(n \log \text{maxlcp}))$. This algorithm sorts strings of size 2^k in the k-th iteration. This variant already yields some small optimization opportunities.

Section 5.3 gives a simple and efficient way to *discard* suffixes from further iterations of the doubling algorithm when their position in the suffix array is already known. This leads to an algorithm with I/O complexity $\mathcal{O}(\text{sort}(n \log \text{dps}))$, improving on a previous discarding algorithm with I/O complexity $\mathcal{O}(\text{sort}(n \log \text{dps}) + \text{scan}(n \log \text{maxlcp}))$ [CF02]. A further constant factor is gained in Section 5.4 by considering a generalization of the doubling technique that sorts strings of size a^k in iteration k. The best multiplication factor is four (*quadrupling*) or five. A pipelined optimal algorithm with I/O complexity $\mathcal{O}(\text{sort}(n))$ in Section 5.5 and its generalization in Section 5.6 conclude our sequence of suffix array construction algorithms.

A useful tool for testing our implementations was a fast and simple external memory checker for suffix arrays described in Section 5.7.

In Section 5.8 we report on extensive experiments using synthetic difficult inputs, the human genome, English books, web-pages, and program source code using inputs of up to 4 GByte on a low cost machine and a faster high-end system. The theoretically optimal algorithm turns out to be the winner closely followed by quadrupling with discarding.

Section 5.10 summarizes the overall results and discusses how even larger suffix arrays could be build.

5.2 Doubling Algorithm

Figure 5.1 shows a pseudocode for the doubling algorithm [AFGV97, CF02]. The basic idea is to replace characters $T[i]$ of the input by *lexicographic names* that respect the lexicographic order of the length 2^k substring $T[i, i+2^k)$ in the k-th iteration. In contrast to previous variants of this algorithm, this formulation never actually builds the resulting string of names. Rather, it manipulates a sequence P of pairs (c, i) where each name c is tagged with its position i in the input. To obtain names for the next iteration $k+1$, the names for $T[i, i+2^k)$ and $T[i+2^k, i+2^{k+1})$ together with the position i are stored in a sequence S and sorted. The new names can now be obtained by scanning this sequence and comparing adjacent tuples. Sequence S can be build using consecutive elements of P if we sort P using the pair $(i \bmod 2^k, i \bdiv 2^k)$. Previous formulations of the algorithm use i as a sorting criterion and therefore have to access elements that are 2^k characters apart. Our approach saves I/Os and simplifies the pipelined implementation.

Function *doubling(T)*
 $S := \langle ((T[i], T[i+1]), i) : i \in [0, n) \rangle$ (0)
 for $k := 1$ **to** $\lceil \log n \rceil$ **do**
  sort S (1)
  $P := name(S)$ (2)
  invariant $\forall (c, i) \in P : c$ is a lexicographic name for $T[i, i + 2^k]$
  if the names in P are unique **then return** $\langle i : (c, i) \in P \rangle$ (3)
  sort P by $(i \bmod 2^k, i \text{ div } 2^k)$ (4)
  $S := \langle ((c, c'), i) : j \in [0, n), (c, i) = P[j], (c', i + 2^k) = P[j+1] \rangle$ (5)
Function *name(S : Sequence of Pair)*
 $q := r := 0;\ (\ell, \ell') := (\$, \$)$
 $result := \langle \rangle$
 foreach $((c, c'), i) \in S$ **do**
  q++
  if $(c, c') \neq (\ell, \ell')$ **then** $r := q;\ (\ell, \ell') := (c, c')$
  append (r, i) to *result*
 return *result*

Figure 5.1: The doubling algorithm.

5.3. DISCARDING

The algorithm performs a constant number of sorting and scanning operations for sequences of size n in each iteration. The number of iterations is determined by the logarithm of the longest common prefix.

Theorem 10 ([DKMS06]). *The doubling algorithm from Figure 5.1 can be implemented to run using* $\text{sort}(5n) \lceil \log(1 + \text{maxlcp}) \rceil + \mathcal{O}(\text{sort}(n))$ *I/Os.*

Proof. The following pipelined data flow graph shows that each iteration can be implemented using $\text{sort}(2n) + \text{sort}(3n) \leq \text{sort}(5n)$ I/Os. The numbers refer to the line numbers in Figure 5.1.

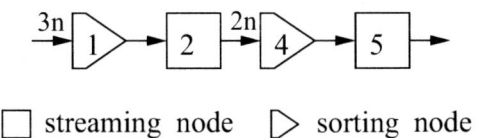

$$\xrightarrow{3n} \triangleright \boxed{1} \to \boxed{2} \xrightarrow{2n} \triangleright \boxed{4} \to \boxed{5} \to$$

$\square$ streaming node $\quad \triangleright$ sorting node

After $\lceil \log(1 + \text{maxlcp}) \rceil$ iterations, the algorithm finishes. The $\mathcal{O}(\text{sort}(n))$ term accounts for the I/Os needed in Line 0 and for computing the final result. Note that there is a small technicality here: Although naming can find out "for free" whether all names are unique, the result is known only when naming finishes. However, at this time, the first phase of the sorting step in Line 4 has also finished and has already incurred some I/Os. Moreover, the convenient arrangement of the pairs in P is destroyed now. However, we can then abort the sorting process, undo the wrong sorting, and compute the correct output. $\square$

5.3 Discarding

The paper [DKMS06] present a new discarding algorithm for computing suffix arrays. With the help of STXXL pipelining the algorithm can be implemented with very small constant factors in I/O volume.

Let c_i^k be the lexicographic name of $T[i, i+2^k)$, i.e., the value paired with i at iteration k in Figure 5.1. Since c_i^k is the number of strictly smaller substrings of length 2^k, it is a non-decreasing function of k. More precisely, $c_i^{k+1} - c_i^k$ is the number of positions j such that $c_j^k = c_i^k$ but $c_{j+2^k}^k < c_{i+2^k}^k$. This provides an alternative way of computing the names given in Figure 5.3.

Another consequence of the above observation is that if c_i^k is unique, i.e., $c_j^k \neq c_i^k$ for all $j \neq i$, then $c_i^h = c_i^k$ for all $h > k$. The idea of the discarding algorithm is to take advantage of this, i.e., discard pair (c, i) from further

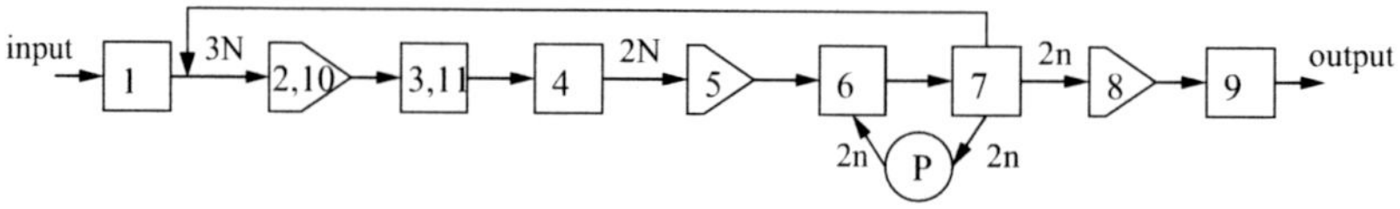

Figure 5.2: Data flow graph for the *doubling + discarding*. The numbers refer to line numbers in Figure 5.4. The edge weights are sums over the whole execution with $N = n \log dps$.

Function *name2(S : Sequence* **of** *Pair)*
    $q := q' := 0;\quad (\ell, \ell') := (\$, \$)$
    $result := \langle\rangle$
    foreach $((c, c'), i) \in S$ **do**
        if $c \neq \ell$ **then** $q := q' := 0;\ (\ell, \ell') := (c, c')$
        else if $c' \neq \ell'$ **then** $q' := q;\quad \ell' := c'$
        append $(c + q', i)$ to *result*
        $q{+}{+}$
    return *result*

Figure 5.3: The alternative naming procedure.

5.3. DISCARDING

Function $doubling + discarding(T)$
$S := \langle ((T[i], T[i+1]), i) : i \in [0, n) \rangle$ (1)
sort S (2)
$U := name(S)$ //undiscarded   (3)
$P := \langle \rangle$ //partially discarded
$F := \langle \rangle$ //fully discarded
for $k := 1$ **to** $\lceil \log n \rceil$ **do**
    mark unique names in U (4)
    sort U by $(i \bmod 2^k, i \operatorname{div} 2^k)$ (5)
    merge P into U; $P := \langle \rangle$ (6)
    $S := \langle \rangle$; $count := 0$
    foreach $(c, i) \in U$ **do**   (7)
        if c is unique **then**
            if $count < 2$ **then** append (c, i) to F
            else append (c, i) to P
            $count := 0$
        else
            let (c', i') be the next pair in U
            append $((c, c'), i)$ to S
            $count{+}{+}$
    if $S = \emptyset$ **then**
        sort F by first component   (8)
        return $\langle i : (c, i) \in F \rangle$ (9)
    sort S (10)
    $U := name2(S)$ (11)

Figure 5.4: The doubling with discarding algorithm.

Table 5.1: I/O requirements for different variants of the a-tupling algorithm. The entries specify the variable x defined in the column headings. $+\mathcal{O}(\mathrm{sort}(n))$ terms are omitted.

a	2	3	4	5	6	7
$(a+3)/\log a$	5.00	3.78	3.50	**3.45**	3.48	3.56

iterations once c is unique. A key to this is the new naming procedure shown in Figure 5.3, because it works correctly even if we exclude from S all tuples $((c, c'), i)$, where c is unique. Note, however, that we cannot exclude $((c, c'), i)$ if c' is unique but c is not. Therefore, we will *partially* discard (c, i) when c is unique. We will *fully* discard $(c, i) = (c_i^k, i)$ when also either $c_{i-2^k}^k$ or $c_{i-2^{k+1}}^k$ is unique, because then in any iteration $h > k$, the first component of the tuple $((c_{i-2^h}^h, c_i^h), i - 2^h)$ must be unique. The final algorithm is given in Figure 5.4.

Theorem 11 ([DKMS06])**.** *Doubling with discarding can be implemented to run using* $\mathrm{sort}(5n \log \mathrm{dps}) + \mathcal{O}(\mathrm{sort}(n))$ *I/Os.*

Proof. We prove the theorem by showing that the total amount of data in the different steps of the algorithm over the whole execution is as in the pipelined data flow graph in Figure 5.2. The nontrivial points are that at most $N = n \log \mathrm{dps}$ tuples are processed in each sorting step over the whole execution and that at most n tuples are written to P. The former follows from the fact that a suffix i is involved in the sorting steps as long as it has a non-unique rank, which happens in exactly $\lceil \log(1 + \mathrm{dps}(i)) \rceil$ iterations. To show the latter, we note that a tuple (c, i) is written to P in iteration k only if the previous tuple $(c', i-2^k)$ was not unique. That previous tuple will become unique in the next iteration, because it is represented by $((c', c), i - 2^k)$ in S. Since each tuple turns unique only once, the total number of tuples written to P is at most n. □

5.4 From Doubling to a-Tupling

It is straightforward to generalize the doubling algorithms from Figures 5.1 and 5.4 so that it maintains the invariant that in iteration k, lexicographic names represent strings of length a^k: just gather a names from the last iteration that are a^{k-1} characters apart. Sort and name as before.

5.5. I/O-OPTIMAL PIPELINED DC3 ALGORITHM

The pseudocode of the generalized doubling algorithm without discarding is presented in Figure 5.5.

Theorem 12 ([DKMS06]). *The a-tupling algorithm can be implemented to run using*

$$\text{sort}(\frac{a+3}{\log a}n) \log \text{maxlcp} + \mathcal{O}(\text{sort}(n)) \quad \text{or}$$

$$\text{sort}(\frac{a+3}{\log a}n) \log \text{dps} + \mathcal{O}(\text{sort}(n))$$

I/Os without or with discarding respectively.

We get a tradeoff between higher cost for each iteration and a smaller number of iterations that is determined by the ratio $\frac{a+3}{\log a}$. Evaluating this expression we get the optimum for $a = 5$ (Table 5.1). But the value for $a = 4$ is only 1.5 % worse, needs less memory, and calculations are much easier because four is a power two. Hence, we choose $a = 4$ for our implementation of the a-tupling algorithm. This *quadrupling* algorithm needs 30 % less I/Os than doubling.

Function $atupling(T)$
    $S := \langle ((T[i], T[i+1], \ldots, T[i+a-1]), i) : i \in [0, n) \rangle$
    for $k := 1$ **to** $\lceil \log_a n \rceil$ **do**
        sort S
        $P := name(S)$
        invariant $\forall (c, i) \in P : c$ is a lexicographic name for $T[i, i + a^k)$
        if the names in P are unique **then return** $\langle i : (c, i) \in P \rangle$
        sort P by $(i \bmod a^k, i \text{ div } a^k))$
        $S := \langle ((c_0, \ldots, c_q, \ldots, c_{a-1}), i) : j \in [0, n),$
            $(c_q, i + q \cdot a^k) = P[j + q], q \in [0, a) \rangle$

Figure 5.5: The a-tupling algorithm.

5.5 I/O-Optimal Pipelined DC3 Algorithm

The following three-step algorithm outlines a linear time algorithm for suffix array construction [KSB06]:

1. Construct the suffix array of the suffixes starting at positions $i \bmod 3 \neq 0$. This is done by reduction to the suffix array construction of a string of two thirds the length, which is solved recursively.

2. Construct the suffix array of the remaining suffixes using the result of the first step.

3. Merge the two suffix arrays into one.

Figure 5.6 gives a pseudocode for an external implementation of this algorithm and Figure 5.7 gives a data flow graph that allows pipelined execution. Step 1 is implemented by Lines (1)–(6) and starts out quite similar to the tripling (3-tupling) algorithm described in Section 5.4. The main difference is that triples are only obtained for two thirds of the suffixes and that we use recursion to find lexicographic names that characterize the relative order of these *sample suffixes exactly*. As a preparation for the Steps 2 and 3, in lines (7)–(10) these sample names are used to annotate each suffix position i with enough information to determine its global rank. More precisely, at most two sample names and the first one or two characters suffice to completely determine the rank of a suffix. This information can be obtained I/O efficiently by simultaneously scanning the input and the names of the sample suffixes sorted by their position in the input. With this information, Step 2 reduces to sorting suffixes T_i with $i \bmod 3 = 0$ by their first character and the name for T_{i+1} in the sample (Line 11). Line (12) reconstructs the order of the mod-2 suffixes and mod-3 suffixes. Line (13) implements Step 3 by ordinary comparison based merging. The slight complication is the comparison function. There are three cases:

- A mod-0 suffix T_i can be compared with a mod-1 suffix T_j by looking at the first characters and the names for T_{i+1} and T_{j+1} in the sample, respectively.

- For a comparison between a mod-0 suffix T_i and a mod-2 suffix T_j the above technique does not work since T_{j+1} is not in the sample. However, both T_{i+2} and T_{j+2} are in the sample so that it suffices to look at the first two characters and the names of T_{i+2} and T_{j+2} respectively.

- Mod-1 suffixes and Mod-2 suffixes can be compared by looking at their names in the sample.

The resulting pipelined data flow graph is large but fairly straightforward except for the file node which stores a copy of input stream T. The problem is that the input is needed twice. First, Line 2 uses it for generating the sample

5.5. I/O-OPTIMAL PIPELINED DC3 ALGORITHM

and later, the node implementing Lines (8)–(10) scans it simultaneously with the names of the sample suffixes. It is not possible to pipeline both scans, however, this problem can be solved by writing a temporary copy of the input stream. Note that this is still cheaper than using a file representation for the input since this would mean that this file is read twice. We are now ready to analyze the I/O complexity of the algorithm.

Function $DC3(T)$
$\quad S := \langle ((T[i, i+2]), i) : i \in [0, n), i \bmod 3 \neq 0 \rangle$ // mod12 suffixes   (1)
$\quad$ sort S by the first component   // sort triples   (2)
$\quad P := name(S)$ // name triples   (3)
$\quad$ **if** the names in P are not unique **then**
$\quad \quad$ sort the $(i, r) \in P$ by $(i \bmod 3, i \dv 3)$ // build rec. input   (4)
$\quad \quad SA^{12} := DC3(\langle c : (c, i) \in P \rangle)$ // recurse   (5)
$\quad \quad P := \langle (j+1, SA^{12}[j]) : j \in [0, 2n/3) \rangle$ (6)
$\quad$ sort P by the second component   // inv. SA of sample (7)
$\quad S_0 := \langle (T[i], T[i+1], c', c'', i) : i \bmod 3 = 0, (c', i+1), (c'', i+2) \in P \rangle$ (8)
$\quad S_1 := \langle (c, T[i], c', i) : i \bmod 3 = 1, (c, i), (c', i+1) \in P \rangle$ (9)
$\quad S_2 := \langle (c, T[i], T[i+1], c'', i) : i \bmod 3 = 2, (c, i), (c'', i+2) \in P \rangle$ (10)
$\quad$ sort S_0 by components 1,3   // sort mod0 suff. (11)
$\quad$ sort S_1 and S_2 by component 1   // resort mod12 suff.   (12)
$\quad S := merge(S_0, S_1, S_2)$ using comparison function: (13)
$\quad \quad (t, t', c', c'', i) \in S_0 \leq (d, u, d', j) \in S_1 \quad \Leftrightarrow (t, c') \leq (u, d')$
$\quad \quad (t, t', c', c'', i) \in S_0 \leq (d, u, u', d'', j) \in S_2 \quad \Leftrightarrow (t, t', c'') \leq (u, u', d'')$
$\quad \quad (c, t, c', i) \in S_1 \leq (d, u, u', d'', j) \in S_2 \quad \Leftrightarrow c \leq d$
$\quad$ **return** $\langle$last component of $s : s \in S\rangle$ (14)

Figure 5.6: The DC3-algorithm.

Theorem 13 ([DKMS06]). *The DC3 algorithm from Figure 5.6 can be implemented to run using* $\text{sort}(30n) + \text{scan}(6n)$ *I/Os.*

Proof. Let $V(n)$ denote the number of I/Os for the external DC3 algorithm. Using the pipelined data flow diagram from Figure 5.7 we can conclude that

$$V(n) \leq \text{sort}((\tfrac{8}{3} + \tfrac{4}{3} + \tfrac{4}{3} + \tfrac{5}{3} + \tfrac{4}{3} + \tfrac{5}{3})n) + \text{scan}(2n) + V(\tfrac{2}{3}n)$$
$$= \text{sort}(10n) + \text{scan}(2n) + V(\tfrac{2}{3}n)$$

This recurrence has the solution $V(n) \leq 3(\text{sort}(10n) + \text{scan}(2n)) \leq \text{sort}(30n) + \text{scan}(6n)$. Note that the data flow diagram assumes that the

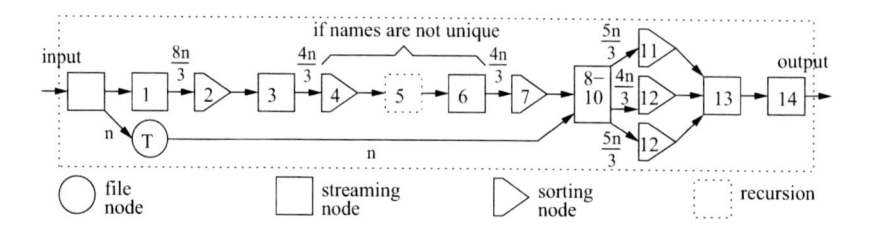

CHAPTER 5. ENGINEERING LARGE SUFFIX ARRAY CONSTRUCTION

Figure 5.7: Data flow graphs for the DC3 algorithm. The numbers refer to line numbers in Figure 5.6.

input is a data stream into the procedure call. However, we get the same complexity if the original input is a file. In that case, we have to read the input once but we save writing it to the local file node T. □

5.6 Generalized Difference Cover Algorithm

DC3 computes the suffix array of the two-thirds of the suffixes in its recursion. In the generalized algorithm DCX [KSB06] one tries to reduce the number of sample suffixes, which might decrease the cost of the recursion.

The algorithm DCX chooses the sample of suffixes starting at indexes $I_X = \{i \mid i \bmod X \in C_X\}$ (for DC3 $X = 3$ and $C_3 = \{1, 2\}$). For any given X the set C_X must be chosen such that $|C_X|$ is minimal and the order of the remaining suffixes can be reconstructed using the sample suffixes. To fulfill these requirements one uses the *minimum difference covers* [Haa04] of $\mathbb{Z}_X$ ($\mathbb{Z}_X$ is the set of integers modulo X). For a subset C' of a finite Abelian group G, we define $d(C') = \{a - b \mid a, b \in C'\}$. If $d(C') = G$, we call C' a difference cover of G. [Haa04] contains minimum difference covers C'_X of $\mathbb{Z}_X$ for primes X up to 133 (see also Table 5.2). The algorithm DCX sets $C_X = \{j \mid X - j - 1 \in C'_X\}$.

Now we find the number of I/Os needed by a recursion of the DCX algorithm: sorting S by $T[i, i + X - 1]$ (Line (2) in Figure 5.6) costs $\text{sort}((X + 1)n \cdot \frac{|C_X|}{X})$ I/Os, writing and reading T takes $\text{scan}(2n)$ I/Os, building the input for the recursion (Line (4)) needs $\text{sort}(2n \cdot \frac{|C_X|}{X})$ I/Os, permuting in Line (7) incurs $\text{sort}(2n \cdot \frac{|C_X|}{X})$ I/Os, sorting the merge tuples (Lines (11)–(12)) needs $\text{sort}(\delta_X n)$ I/Os, where δ_X is the average merge tuple size (e.g. $\delta_3 = \frac{5+4+5}{3}$).

5.6. GENERALIZED DIFFERENCE COVER ALGORITHM

Table 5.2: Minimum difference covers.

X	C'_X
3	$\{0, 1\}$
7	$\{0, 1, 3\}$
13	$\{0, 1, 3, 9\}$
21	$\{0, 1, 6, 8, 18\}$
31	$\{0, 1, 3, 8, 12, 18\}$
39	$\{0, 1, 16, 20, 22, 27, 30\}$
57	$\{0, 1, 9, 11, 14, 35, 39, 51\}$
73	$\{0, 1, 3, 7, 15, 31, 36, 54, 63\}$
91	$\{0, 1, 7, 16, 27, 56, 60, 68, 70, 73\}$
95	$\{0, 1, 5, 8, 18, 20, 29, 31, 45, 61, 67\}$
133	$\{0, 1, 32, 42, 44, 48, 51, 59, 72, 77, 97, 111\}$

Let $V_X(n)$ be the number of I/Os for the DCX algorithm.

$$V_X(n) \leq \text{sort}(((X+5)\tfrac{|C_X|}{X} + \delta_X)n) + \text{scan}(2n) + V_X(\tfrac{|C_X|}{X}n)$$

This recurrence has the solution

$$V_X(n) \leq \text{sort}(n\frac{(X+5)|C_X| + X\delta_X}{X - |C_X|}) + \text{scan}(2n\frac{X}{X - |C_X|})$$

To analyse $V_X(n)$ one needs to know the values of δ_X for given X. Unfortunately, a simple formula does not exist. Instead, we compute upperbounds for δ_X using a simple algorithm. Let

$$d_{max}(i) = \max\{k \mid i + k \mod X \in C_X \wedge k < X\}$$

be the maximal distance from starting position i to the right to the next sample, i.e. the maximum number of characters needed in a merge tuple. Then the merge tuple size for positions j such that $i \equiv j \mod X$ is $d_{max}(i) + 1 + |C_X|$, because one might need the ranks of all the $|C_X|$ samples to compare two arbitrary merge tuples and one component takes the index value. Hence the average merge tuple size is:

$$\delta_X = 1 + |C_X| + \frac{1}{X} \sum_{0 \leq i < X} d_{max}(i)$$

Table 5.3: I/O volume of DCX

X	3	7	13	21	31	39	57
$\|C_X\|$	2	3	4	5	6	7	8
sort[N]	30	24.75	30.11	38.56	50.12	60.65	79.02
scan[N]	6	3.50	2.89	2.63	2.48	2.39	2.33
Total	66	53	63.11	79.75	102.72	123.75	160.37

Table 5.4: I/O volume of DCX with the small alphabet optimization

X	3	7	13	21	31	39	57
$\|C_X\|$	2	3	4	5	6	7	8
sort[N]	28	20.43	17.08	16.48	16.16	17.51	18.18
scan[N]	4.13	2.70	1.97	1.55	1.29	1.20	0.97
Total	60.13	43.55	36.13	34.51	33.61	36.23	37.32

Table 5.3 presents the computed I/O volume for DCX algorithm with $X \in \{3, 7, 13, 21, 31, 39, 57\}$. The algorithm with the smallest I/O volume is DC7.

Each tuple component of the DCX algorithm is represented as a 32-bit word, which is wasteful for small alphabets. For the genome data with a four character alphabet one can put up to 16 characters needed for a naming tuple in one word. The merge tuple can be compressed similarly. Table 5.4 shows the computed I/O volume of the DCX algorithm that uses this bit optimization in its first recursion and calls DC3 in the further recursions.

5.7 Checker

To ensure the correctness of our algorithms we have designed and implemented a simple and fast suffix array checker. It is given in Figure 5.8 and is based on the following result.

Lemma 14 ([BK03]). *An array $SA[0, n)$ is the suffix array of a text T iff the following conditions are satisfied:*

1. *SA contains a permutation of $[0, n)$.*

2. $\forall i,j : r_i \leq r_j \Leftrightarrow (T[i], r_{i+1}) \leq (T[j], r_{j+1})$ where r_i denotes the rank of the suffix S_i according to the suffix array.

Function *Checker(SA, T)*
$\quad P := \langle (SA[i], i+1) : i \in [0,n) \rangle$ \hfill (1)
$\quad$ sort P by the first component \hfill (2)
$\quad$ **if** $\langle i : (i,r) \in P \rangle \neq [0,n)$ **then return** false
$\quad S := [(r, (T[i], r')) : i \in [0,n),$ \hfill (3)
$\quad\quad (i,r) = P[i], (i+1, r') = P[i+1]]$
$\quad$ sort S by the first component \hfill (4)
$\quad$ **if** $\langle (c, r') : (r, (c, r')) \in S \rangle$ is sorted \hfill (5)
$\quad$ **then return** true **else return** false

Figure 5.8: The suffix array checker.

Theorem 15. *The suffix array checker from Figure 5.8 can be implemented to run using* $\text{sort}(5n) + \text{scan}(2n)$ *I/Os.*

5.8 Experiments

We have implemented the algorithms (except DCX) in C++ using the g++ 3.2.3 compiler (optimization level -O2 -fomit-frame-pointer)[1] and the external memory library STXXL Version 0.52 [Dem, DKS05a]. We have run the experiments on two platforms. The first system has two 2.0 GHz Intel Xeon processors (our implementations only use one processor), one GByte of RAM and eight 80 GByte ATA IBM 120GXP disks. Refer to [DS03] for a performance evaluation of this machine whose cost was 2500 Euro in July 2002. The second platform is a high-end SMP system with four 64-bit AMD Opteron 1.8 GHz processors, 8 GByte of RAM (we use only one GByte) and eight 73 GByte SCSI Seagate 15000 RPM ST373453LC disks. In our experiments we used four disks if not specified otherwise.

Table 5.5 shows the considered input instances. We have collected some of these instances at http://algo2.iti.uka.de/dementiev/esuffix/instances.shtml and ftp://www.mpi-sb.mpg.de/pub/outgoing/sanders/. For a nonsynthetic

---
[1] The sources are available under
http://algo2.iti.uka.de/dementiev/esuffix/docu/index.html.

Name	Description
Random2	Two concatenated copies of a Random string of length $n/2$. This is a difficult instance that is hard to beat using simple heuristics.
Gutenberg	Freely available English texts from http://promo.net/pg/list.html.
Genome	The known pieces of the human genome from http://genome.ucsc.edu/downloads.html (status May, 2004). We have normalized this input to ignore the distinction between upper case and lower case letters. The result are characters in an alphabet of size 5 (ACGT and sometimes long sequences of "unknown" characters).
HTML	Pages from a web crawl containing only pages from .gov domains. These pages are filtered so that only text and html code is contained but no pictures and no binary files.
Source	Source code (mostly C++) containing coreutils, gcc, gimp, kde, xfree, emacs, gdb, Linux kernel and Open Office).

Table 5.5: Input instances.

Table 5.6: Statistics of the instances used in the experiments.

T	$n = \lvert T \rvert$	$\lvert \Sigma \rvert$	maxlcp	$\overline{\text{lcp}}$	log dps
Random2	2^{32}	128	2^{31}	$\approx 2^{29}$	≈ 29.56
Gutenberg	3 277 099 765	128	4 819 356	45 617	10.34
Genome	3 070 128 194	5	21 999 999	454 111	6.53
HTML	4 214 295 245	128	102 356	1 108	6.99
Source	547 505 710	128	173 317	431	5.80

instance T of length n, our experiments use T itself and its prefixes of the form $T[0, 2^i)$. Table 5.6 and Figure 5.9 show statistics of the properties of these instances.

Figure 5.10 shows the execution time and the I/O volume side by side, for each of our instance families and for the algorithms nonpipelined doubling, pipelined doubling, pipelined doubling with discarding, pipelined quadru-

5.8. EXPERIMENTS

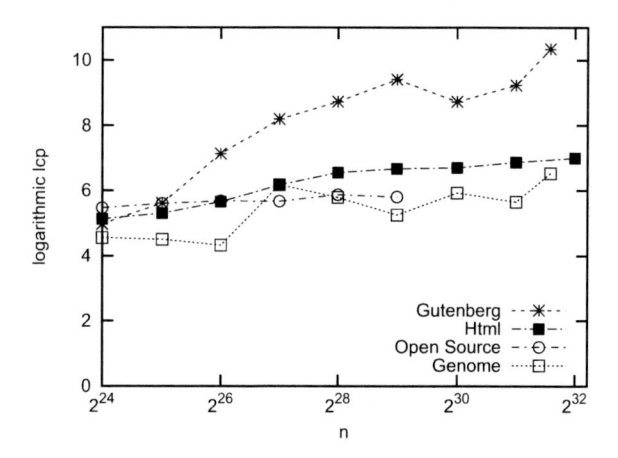

Figure 5.9: Statistics of the instances used in the experiments.

pling, pipelined quadrupling with discarding[2], and DC3 running on the Xeon machine. All ten plots share the same x-axis and the same curve labels. Computing all these instances takes about 14 days moving more than 20 TByte of data. Due to these large execution times it was not feasible to run all algorithms for all input sizes and all instances. However, there is enough data to draw some interesting conclusions.

Complicated behavior is observed for "small" inputs up to 2^{26} characters. The main reason is that we made no particular effort to optimize special cases where at least some part of some algorithm could execute internally. Sometimes STXXL makes such optimizations, e.g. automatically sorting small inputs in the internal memory. Another factor is the constant start-up overhead of `stxxl::vector`s which amortizes only with larger inputs. The granularity with which `stxxl::vector` loads and stores blocks from/to external memory was not optimized for small inputs.

The most important observation is that the DC3-algorithm is always the fastest algorithm and is almost completely insensitive to the input. For all inputs of a size of more than a GByte, DC3 is at least twice as fast as its closest competitor. With respect to the I/O volume, DC3 is sometimes equaled by quadrupling with discarding. This happens for relatively small

---

[2]The discarding algorithms we have implemented need slightly more I/Os and perhaps more complex calculations than the newer algorithms described in Section 5.3.

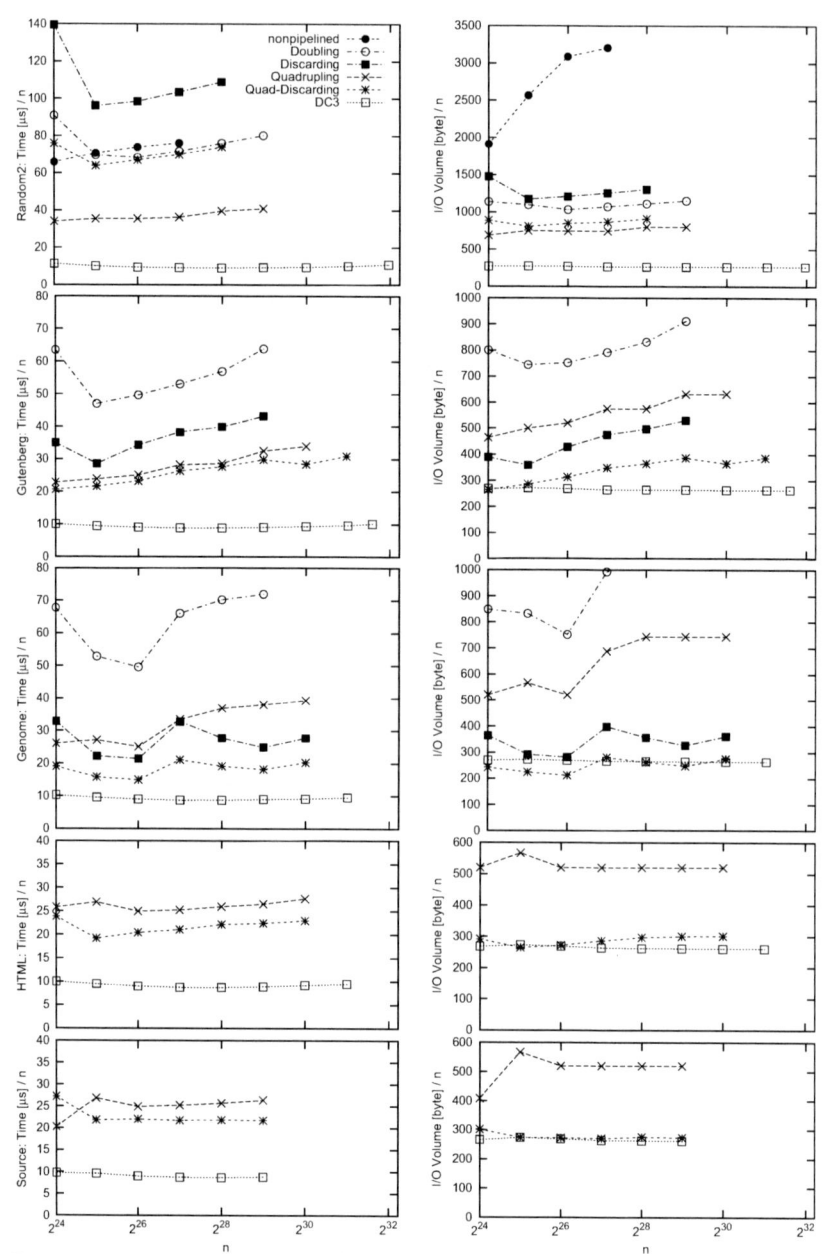

Figure 5.10: Execution time (left) and I/O volume (right) for Random2, Gutenberg, Genome, HTML (on the Xeon machine).

5.8. EXPERIMENTS

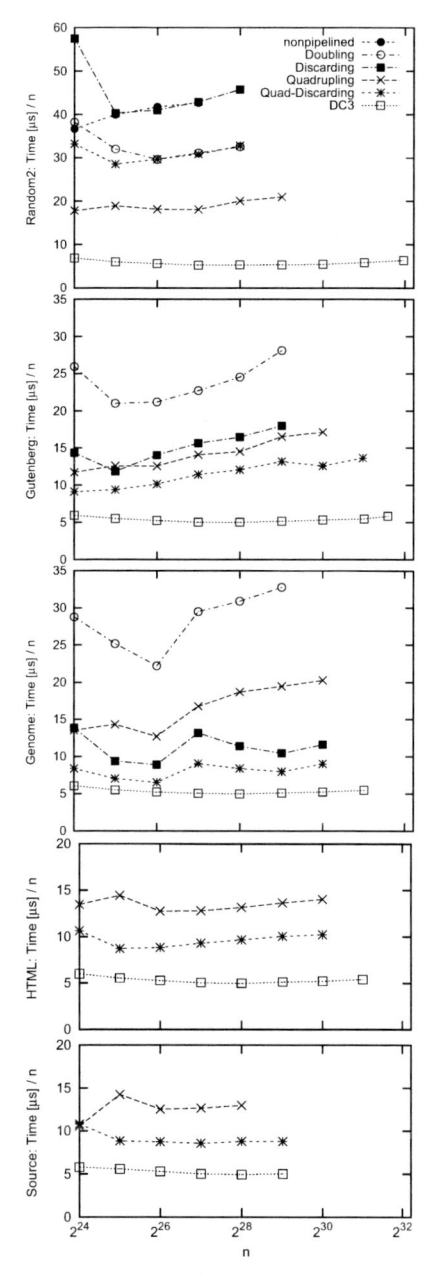

Figure 5.11: Execution time for Random2, Gutenberg, Genome, HTML (on the Opteron machine).

inputs. Apparently quadrupling has more complex internal work.[3] For example, it compares quadruples during half of its sorting operations whereas DC3 compares triples or pairs during sorting. For the difficult synthetic input Random2, quadrupling with discarding is by far outperformed by DC3. Even plain quadrupling, is much faster than quadrupling with discarding. This indicates that the internal logics for discarding is a bottleneck.

For real world inputs, discarding algorithms turn out to be successful compared to their nondiscarding counterparts. They outperform them both with respect to the I/O volume and the running time. This could be explained by the smaller log dps values according to Table 5.6. For random inputs without repetitions the discarding algorithms might actually beat DC3 since one gets inputs with very small values of log dps.

Quadrupling algorithms consistently outperform doubling algorithms as predicted by the analysis of the I/O complexity in Section 5.4.

Comparing pipelined doubling with nonpipelined doubling in the top pair of plots (instance Random2) one can see that pipelining brings a huge reduction of the I/O volume, whereas the execution time is affected much less — a clear indication that our algorithms are dominated by internal calculations. However, in a setting with a slower I/O subsystem, e.g. a system with a single disk, pipelining gives a significant speedup. Our experiments with $D = 1$ show that pipelined doubling is faster than its nonpipelined version by a factor 1.9–2.4. We also have reasons to believe that our nonpipelined sorter is more highly tuned than the pipelined one so that the advantage of pipelining may grow in future versions of STXXL. We do not show the nonpipelined algorithm for the other inputs since the relative performance compared to pipelined doubling should remain about the same.

A comparison of the new algorithms with previous algorithms is more difficult. The implementation of [CF02] only works up to 2 GByte of total external memory consumption and would thus have to compete with space efficient internal algorithms on our machine. At least we can compare the I/O volume per byte of input for the measurements in [CF02]. Their most scalable algorithm for the largest real world input tested (26 MByte of text from the Reuters news agency) is nonpipelined doubling with partial discarding. This algorithm needs an I/O volume of 1303 Bytes per character of input. The DC3-algorithm needs about 5 times less I/Os. Furthermore, it is to be expected that the lead gets bigger for larger inputs. The GBS algorithm [GBYS92] needs 486 bytes of I/O per character for this input in

---

[3]One might also conclude that a similar increase in internal work could be expected in an implementation of the DC7 algorithm.

5.8. EXPERIMENTS

[CF02], i.e., even for this small input DC3 already outperforms the GBS algorithm. We can also attempt a speed comparison in terms of clock cycles per byte of input. Here [CF02] needs 157,000 cycles per byte for doubling with simple discarding and 147,000 cycles per byte for the GBS algorithm whereas DC3 only needs about 20,000 cycles. Again, the advantage should grow for larger inputs in particular when comparing with the GBS algorithm.

The following small table shows the execution time of DC3 for 1 to 8 disks on the 'Source' instance on the Xeon machine.

D	1	2	4	6	8
$t[\mu s/\text{byte}]$	13.96	9.88	8.81	8.65	8.52

We see that adding more disks only gives a very small speedup. (And we would see very similar speedups for the other algorithms except nonpipelined doubling). Even with 8 disks, DC3 has an I/O rate of less than 30 MByte/s which is less than the peak performance of a *single* disk (45 MByte/s). Hence, by more effective overlapping of I/O and computation it should be possible to sustain the performance of eight disks using a single cheap disk so that even very cheap PCs could be used for external suffix array construction.

Figure 5.11 shows the execution times of the implementations running on the Opteron machine. The implementations need a factor of 1.7–2.4 less time. The largest speedup is observed for the quadrupling with discarding running on the largest source code instance. This might be due to the faster SCSI hard disks with higher bandwidth (70 MB/s versus 45 MB/s) and the shorter seek time (3.6 ms versus 8.8 ms on average), and perhaps a faster 64-bit CPU. However, the relative performance of the algorithms remains the same as in the experiments using the Xeon system.

5.8.1 The Checker

Figure 5.12 shows the execution time and the I/O volume of the suffix array checker from Section 5.7 running on the Opteron system. The horizontal axis denotes the size of the input string T. The curves for the other input families are not shown, since the algorithm is not sensitive to the type of input. The implementation only needs 1–1.2 μs per input string character.

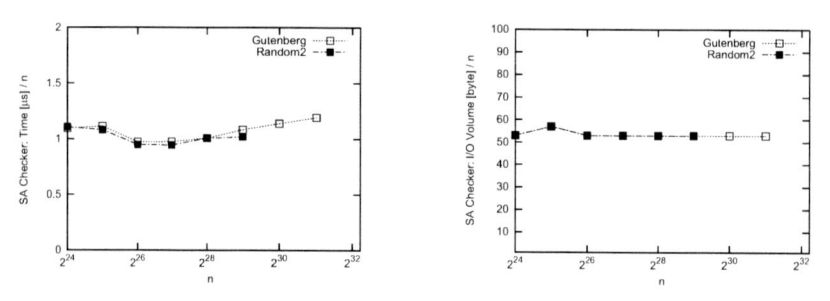

Figure 5.12: Execution time (left) and I/O volume (right) for the suffix array checker (Opteron machine).

5.9 An Oracle PL/SQL Implementation

In [Foy06] we have implemented the doubling algorithm using the PL/SQL language of the Oracle XE relational database system[4]. For I/O-efficient sorting, the Oracle data base engine has been used.

As an opponent we took the *pipelined* STXXL implementation of doubling. We have run both implementations on a 3.0 GHz Pentium 4 system with a single SATA disk. Oracle XE could use 1 GByte of main memory, the internal memory consumption of STXXL doubling has been limited to 512 MBytes. The source code instance has been chosen as the input.

Table 5.7 shows the results of the experiments. The PL/SQL implementation needs a lot of time even for small inputs: processing a 20 MByte input took more than 11 hours. PL/SQL could not avoid disk I/O despite the fact that the working space space for such small inputs fits into the internal memory. The observed CPU load has been about 40 %, which indicates that the implementation was indeed I/O-bound. Additionally, Oracle XE does not allow to change the block size for its tables: it is fixed to 8 KBytes, which is too small for our application, and makes it perform more I/Os than the STXXL implementation does. The STXXL implementation could save I/Os in sorting which can be done in internal memory for these inputs. Another source of inefficiency of PL/SQL is that the tables which store the S, T and P arrays can not use a fast and simple 32-bit integer type to represent their values. Only the heavy arbitrary-precision integer type NUMBER can be used in Oracle tables.

In order to see how much time must be invested for the STXXL doubling if

---

[4] http://www.oracle.com/technology/products/database/xe/

the sorting must work externally, we ran an experiment on 512 MByte input. Still, the STXXL implementation was faster by a factor of 65 if we assume that PL/SQL implementation needs 2662 μs per input character.

Table 5.7: Running times of PL/SQL and STXXL pipelined doubling implementations in μs per input character.

input size (MBytes)	PL/SQL	STXXL
1	2033	34
2	1307	30
4	2206	29
8	1836	27
15	2662	33
20	2662	33
512	—	41

5.10 Conclusion

The efficient external version of the DC3-algorithm is theoretically optimal and clearly outperforms all previous algorithms in practice. Since all practical previous algorithms are asymptotically suboptimal and dependent on the inputs, this closes a gap between theory and practice. STXXL implementation of DC3 outperforms the pipelined quadrupling-with-discarding algorithm even for real world instances. This underlines the practical usefulness of DC3 since a mere comparison with the relatively simple, nonpipelined previous implementations would have been unfair.

The suffix array construction algorithms are benefiting from the STXXL pipelining, saving huge amounts of I/Os. This is particularly important for the performance on systems with slow I/O. On systems with many parallel disks, the CPU-efficiency of the internal memory processing plays a bigger role in the performance.

The most important practical question is whether constructing suffix arrays in the external memory is now feasible. We believe that the answer is a careful 'yes'. We can now process $4 \cdot 10^9$ characters overnight on a low cost machine, Which is two orders of magnitude more than in [CF02] in a time faster or comparable to previous internal memory computations [ST01, LSSY02] on more expensive machines.

There are also many opportunities to scale to even larger inputs. In Section 5.6 we have outlined that for small alphabets, the generalized difference cover algorithm DCX, can yield significant further savings in I/O requirements. With respect to the internal work, one could exploit that about half of the sorting operations are just permutations. A better overlap between I/O and computation in future versions of pipelined STXXL sorters should speedup the implementations. More interestingly, there are many ways to parallelize. On a small scale, the pipelining paradigm allows us to run several sorters and one streaming thread in parallel. On a large scale, DC3 is also perfectly parallelizable [KSB06]. An MPI-based [GLT98] distributed memory implementation of DC3 [KS06] scales well up to 128 processors according to the experiments. It looks likely that the algorithm would also scale to thousands of processors. However, the parallel implementation does not use I/O-efficient processing, therefore this leaves room for further improvements which will enable a fast construction of even larger suffix arrays.

Chapter 6

Porting Algorithms to External Memory

It turns out that some algorithms designed for the internal memory or for parallel computers can be directly adapted to run efficiently in the external memory. Such adaptation only includes a replacement of few underlying non-I/O-efficient algorithms by corresponding I/O-efficient versions.

We have already seen a 2-coloring algorithm in Section 4.7.7 where the replaced algorithms were the spanning forest algorithm and the traversal of the trees using I/O-efficient Euler tour and list ranking algorithms. In this chapter, we show how to externalize a 5-coloring planar graph algorithm in Section 6.1 and an approximation algorithm for the maximum weighted matching problem in Section 6.2. An *extended* example of an externalization for an algorithm finding perfect matchings in bipartite multigraphs is shown in Section 6.3.

6.1 5-Coloring Planar Graphs

A PRAM algorithm [HCD89] for 5-coloring planar graphs can be adopted to run in $\mathcal{O}(\text{sort}(n))$ I/Os. It recursively colors the graph constructing a subproblem which has at most a *constant* fraction of nodes of the input graph. The algorithm identifies a set of *reducible* nodes which are candidates for the removal from the graph and also merges some of the nodes incident to reducible nodes, similarly to the algorithm in Section 4.7.6. The identification and the merging can be implemented in a constant number of sorting and scanning steps. Not all of the candidates can be removed in a recursion, because there might be conflicts, e.g. if many reducible nodes decide to merge the same node. However, these conflicts might be resolved filtering some candidate nodes out with a kind of maximal independent set computation in $\mathcal{O}(\text{sort}(n))$ I/Os [Zeh02]. The remaining node set is still large enough [HCD89] such that one has a constant-fraction graph reduction in each recursion.

6.2 1/2-Approximation of Maximum Weighted Matching

6.2.1 Definitions

A *matching* in graph G is a set of pairwise non-adjacent edges.

A *maximal* matching is a matching M of a graph G with the property that if any edge not in M is added to M it is no longer a valid matching.

A *maximum weighted* matching is a matching where the sum of the weights of the edges in the matching have a maximal value. There may be many maximum weighted matchings.

A *p*-approximation algorithm of a maximization problem is an algorithm that computes for any input instance I a solution with weight W, such that $\frac{W}{\text{OPT}(W)} \geq p$, where $\text{OPT}(W)$ is the weight of an optimal solution for I.

6.2.2 The Algorithm

The internal memory greedy algorithm [Avi83] grows a maximal matching, choosing in each step the *heaviest* edge currently available, i.e. an edge not incident to any of the already covered nodes. The algorithm runs in $\Theta(m \log m)$ time since it requires sorting the edges of the graph by decreasing weight. This greedy algorithm produces an $\frac{1}{2}$-approximation as shown in [Avi83].

The algorithm can be externalized as follows:

1. sort the edges by decreasing weight using the I/O-efficient sorting,

2. assign unique ids to the edges numbering them according to the obtained order,

3. run the maximal matching algorithm from [Zeh02], but instead of the edge numbering proposed there, use the edge ids computed in the previous step.

The maximal matching algorithm runs in $\mathcal{O}(\text{sort}(m + n))$ I/Os [Zeh02], therefore the 1/2-approximation algorithm for finding a maximum weighted matching only needs $\mathcal{O}(\text{sort}(m + n))$ I/Os.

6.3 Perfect Matchings in Bipartite Multigraphs

6.3.1 Definitions

A *multigraph* is a graph which is permitted to have multiple edges, (also called "parallel edges") i.e. edges that have the same end nodes.

A *perfect* matching is a matching which covers all nodes of the (multi)graph. That is, every node of the (multi)graph is incident to exactly one edge of the matching.

A bipartite (multi)graph is a special (multi)graph where the set of nodes can be divided into two disjoint sets U and W such that every edge has one end-point in U and one end-point in W.

An *Euler partition* is a partition of the edges into open and closed paths, so that each node of an odd degree is at the end of exactly one open path, and each node of an even degree is at the end of no open path.

An *Euler split* of a bipartite multigraph $G = (V_1, V_2, E)$ is a pair of bipartite graphs $G_1 = (V_1, V_2, E_1)$ and $G_2 = (V_1, V_2, E_2)$ where E_1 and E_2 are formed from an Euler partition by placing alternate edges of paths into E_1 and E_2.

A Δ-regular (multi)graph is a (multi)graph where each node has exactly Δ neighbors.

6.3.2 Introduction

Many efficient sequential algorithms for the problem have been developed. Cole [Col82] and Rizzi [Riz02] develop algorithms with a running time $\mathcal{O}(m + n \log n \log \Delta)$. There is also an EREW PRAM algorithm by Lev, Pippenger, and Valiant [LPV81] which requires $\mathcal{O}(\log \Delta \log^2 n)$ time and

$\mathcal{O}(n\Delta)$ processors. The fastest sequential algorithm is the $\mathcal{O}(m)$ algorithm by Cole, Ost, and Schirra [COS01] which has improved the $\mathcal{O}(m\Delta)$ algorithm by Schrijver [Sch98]. The algorithms are complicated and require efficient algorithms and data structures (e.g. depth first search, splay trees) to be available. Unfortunately the state-of-art external counterparts of those techniques are slow.

Recently two simple sequential $\mathcal{O}(m \log m)$ time algorithms [KM02, Alo03] have been presented that are easier to externalize. The only non-trivial subprocedure they require is the Euler partition computation. We will present a fast algorithm for finding an Euler partition of a multigraph that performs $\mathcal{O}(sort(m))$ I/Os. Then we show how to externalize the remaining subprocedures of Alon's algorithm [Alo03] efficiently. Finally we obtain a perfect matching algorithm performing $\mathcal{O}(sort(m) \log m)$ I/Os.

6.3.3 Euler Partition Algorithm

The algorithm chooses an arbitrary pair of incident edges (u, v) and (v, w) and replaces them by the single edge (u, w), also logging the action made. It continues doing that until no further replacement is possible, i.e. the remaining graph consists of node disjoint edges only (self-loops are allowed). Then, we assign each remaining edge a unique number. The number identifies the path represented by the edge. We undo the performed replacements playing back the logged history and transferring the path identifiers to the replaced edges. The order of edges in the path can be computed as a byproduct during unrolling of the edge replacements.

Since we have the freedom to choose in which order the edges are replaced, we perform replacements of *all* edges incident to a certain node *at once*. If the node has an odd degree, one edge is left. Fixing the order in which nodes are processed and using the time forward processing technique we obtain an I/O-efficient implementation of the algorithm.

Lemma 16. *An Euler partition can be generated with $\mathcal{O}(sort(m))$ I/Os.*

PROOF. An edge replacement operation does not increase the degree of any node. Therefore the number of total replacements is at most m. ∎

Lemma 17. *A bipartite multigraph can be Euler split with $\mathcal{O}(sort(m))$ I/Os.*

PROOF. We sort the edges from the output of the Euler partitioning algorithm by the path identifier and the edge identifier within the path lexicographically. Then we take every second edge into E_1, the rest is E_2. ∎

6.3.4 I/O-Efficient Perfect Matching Algorithm

We assume that the bipartite input multigraph $G = (V_1, V_2, E)$ is Δ-regular, where Δ is the maximum node degree. If it is not the case, we can extend the graph I/O-efficiently. Compute the degree of each node: sort list E lexicographically, then scan, counting consecutive edges that belong to the adjacency list of the same node. Add the degree information for lists V_1 and V_2 (constant number of sort and scan passes). Scan V_1 and V_2 and contract consecutive nodes into one node such that its degree is in the range $[\Delta/2, \Delta]$. This step makes sure that there is at most one node in V_1 and one in V_2 with a degree less than $\Delta/2$. Add nodes to the smaller side. Add edges until the obtained multigraph is regular. This can be done by parallel scan of V_1 and V_2: insert $\min\{\Delta - deg(v), \Delta - deg(w)\}$ edges between nodes $v \in V_1$ and $w \in V_2$. Since the number of edges in G is at most doubled, the following lemma holds.

Lemma 18. *A bipartite graph can be made Δ-regular with $\mathcal{O}(sort(m))$ I/Os.*

If a bipartite graph $G = (V_1, V_2, E)$ is 2^t-regular for a positive integer t then it is possible to find a perfect matching with $\mathcal{O}(sort(m))$ I/Os using the idea of Gabow [Gab76]. We compute an Euler split of graph G obtaining a 2^{t-1}-regular subgraph G_1. We repeat this procedure recursively on G_1 k times ending up with a 1-regular subgraph, which is a perfect matching. However, if a given graph is not 2^t-regular for some positive t, the above approach does not yield a *perfect* matching. Therefore for *any* regular multigraph, a different strategy is conceived.

First we externalize the *RegularSplit* subroutine of Alon's algorithm [Alo03] that splits the $2k$-regular bipartite multigraph $G = (V, E)$ into two k-regular spanning bipartite subgraphs $G_1 = (V, E_1)$ and $G_2 = (V, E_2)$. If the edge multiplicity $\mu(e)$ is given by the value associated with edge e, then the split can be performed with $\mathcal{O}(sort(m'))$, where m' is the number of distinct edges in G. We proceed as follows: Sort list E lexicographically, scan the result of the sorting, if edge e occurs multiple times ($\mu(e) > 1$) move its $\lfloor \mu(e)/2 \rfloor$ copies to E_1 and $\lfloor \mu(e)/2 \rfloor$ copies to E_2 as well, compute an Euler split on the remaining subgraph G' of G obtaining lists E_1' and E_2' and add E_1' to E_1 and E_2' to E_2. This can be done updating the edge multiplicities in a constant number of sort and scan passes. Since the number of distinct edges in graphs G', (V, E_1'), and (V, E_2') is at most m', and due to Lemma 17, the Lemma 19 follows.

Lemma 19. *The* RegularSplit *subroutine can be implemented to run in* $\mathcal{O}(sort(m'))$ *I/Os.*

With the help of our *RegularSplit* procedure the Alon's bipartite multigraph perfect matching algorithm works I/O-efficiently:

1. Construct an arbitrary perfect matching M' between two sides of G (which does not necessarily consist of edges of G).

2. Let $t = \min\{i \mid 2^i \geq m\}$, $\alpha = \lfloor 2^t/\Delta \rfloor$, and $\beta = 2^t - \Delta\alpha$

3. Construct graph $G' = (V_1 \cup V_2, E')$: for each $e \in E$ create α copies of e in E' (these are the *good* edges) and add β copies of each edge of M' (the *bad* edges). (constant number of sorting and scanning passes)

4. Run *RegularSplit* on G' obtaining subgraphs G_1 and G_2.

5. Count number of *bad* edges in G_1 and G_2 (scanning) and let G' be equal to the one with the smaller number of *bad* edges.

6. If G' does not contain *bad* edges return G', otherwise go to step 4.

Theorem 20. *A perfect matching in a bipartite multigraph with m edges can be computed with $\mathcal{O}(sort(m) \log m)$ I/Os.*

PROOF. Let $\hat{m}$ be the number of distinct edges in G'. Then each iteration takes $\mathcal{O}(sort(\hat{m}))$ I/Os (Lemma 19), note that $\hat{m} \leq m + n/2 = \mathcal{O}(m)$. Since there can be at most $t = \log(m)$ iterations (see [Alo03]), Theorem 20 holds. ∎

Chapter 7

Conclusions

We have developed STXXL: a library for external memory computation that aims for high performance and ease-of-use. It supports parallel disks and explicitly overlaps I/O and computation. STXXL processes data sets only limited by the capacity of hard disks. The library is easy to use for people who know the C++ Standard Template Library. STXXL supports algorithm pipelining, which saves many I/Os for many external memory algorithms. The library implementations outperform or at least compete with the best available practical implementations on real and random inputs. Several projects using STXXL have been finished already, among them are fast implementations of algorithms for graph and text processing problems. They include algorithms for computing (minimum) spanning forests, connected components, breadth first search decomposition, network analysis metrics, graph coloring and suffix arrays. With the help of STXXL, they have solved very large problem instances externally using a low cost hardware in record time.

This book emphasizes the importance of engineering for computing that deals with very large data sets. Our work indicates that for achieving a *high performance* the engineering should be done *vertically*, from the bottom to the top: starting from the hardware design and ending up with algorithmic decisions at the application level.

The experiments in the book show that the running time of I/O-efficient algorithms can be (significantly) improved by using parallel disks. However, the prerequisite of this speedup is the bottleneck-free *hardware I/O-subsystem* that allows to transfer the data from/to the hard disks without hindrance, at the full bandwidth of the disks.

At the *operating system level*, much attention should be given to the choice of the file system type and to the choice of the used I/O calls. File systems based on linear search data structures should be avoided. Overlapping of I/O and computation is important for the performance, since it can hide the disk latency. Operating systems offer the buffered I/O and the system–wide file caching to facilitate it, however, because of the lack of the access pattern knowledge, this way to overlap is suboptimal for the application. For the best results, one *explicitly* overlaps I/O with computation, invoking direct non-buffered I/O calls and using the multithreading mechanisms. The fine details of asynchronous I/O should be hidden in a library that provides high-level I/O objects to the application.

At the *algorithm implementation level* it is important to reduce constant factors in I/O volume. We have shown that one can save many I/Os avoiding the storing of the output and the retrieving of the input to/from the hard disks in many I/O-efficient algorithms. Instead, we directly feed the output of external memory algorithms to algorithms that consume the output. To facilitate *rapid* programming with this kind of pipelining one should provide out-of-box implementations of basic external memory algorithms having a *stream* interface, which does not require to store its data on disks.

At the *algorithm design level* the off-the-shelf RAID-0 solutions for disk parallelism can not achieve the best performance in I/O-efficient algorithms, neither theoretically nor (as shown in this work) practically: The algorithms should access the disks independently and balance the data between the disks on their own. Once the I/O-bandwidth scales well with the number of disks the performance can stagnate because of the bottlenecks in the internal memory processing. Possible inefficiencies might stem from cache/TLB faults, branch mispredictions in internal subprocedures (e. g. sorting) or from the saturation of the main memory bandwidth. It turns out that sometimes the bottleneck algorithms and data structures can be (easily) replaced by simpler and more CPU-efficient ones with the same (or smaller) I/O volume: e. g. replace an I/O-efficient priority queue with a bunch of I/O-efficient buckets, replace the internal quicksort by an integer sorting, replace integer divisions by logical shifts, avoid modulo computations, etc.

Much attention should be devoted to the tuning of the algorithm parameters (if there are any) and to the tuning of the parameters of the *underlying* basic I/O-efficient algorithms and data structures (i.e. block size B, buffer cache sizes, prefetch aggressiveness, etc.). The I/O-efficient algorithms can be very sensitive to these parameters since they must fit into the computer architecture and the input size range.

Directions for Future Work. The pipelined sorter can be improved with respect to better overlapping of I/O and computation: currently, the run formation algorithm has big fluctuations in CPU work while reading the input elements, since it sorts large data chunks of size $M/2$ at once. This results in a worse overlapping. Approaches that use fast priority queues can both reduce these irregularities and generate longer runs using the same memory size [Knu98]. The latter can improve the performance itself, since a larger block size can be used in the merge phase(s).

The library has room for a speedup by using parallel processing. We have already achieved good results with the MCSTL library [Sin06] parallelizing the CPU work in external memory sorters. Other possible improvements include task-based parallelism: the processing in the nodes of pipelined applications could be done in parallel.

Bibliography

[AAG03]   P. K. Agarwal, L. Arge, and S. Govindarajan. CRB-Tree: An Efficient Indexing Scheme for Range Aggregate Queries. In *9th International Conference on Database Theory (ICDT '03)*, pages 143–157. 2003.

[AAY05]   P. K. Agarwal, L. Arge, and K. Yi. I/O-Efficient Construction of Constrained Delaunay Triangulations. In *13th European Symposium on Algorithms (ESA '05)*, number 3669 in LNCS, pages 355–366. 2005.

[ABC+95] J. Allwright, R. Bordawekar, P. Coddington, K. Dincer, and C. Martin. A comparison of parallel graph coloring algorithms. Technical report, Northeast Parallel Architecture Center, Syracuse University, 1995.

[ABD+02] L. Arge, M. A. Bender, E. D. Demaine, B. Holland-Minkley, and J. I. Munro. Cache-oblivious priority queue and graph algorithm applications. In *Proceedings of the 34th ACM Symposium on Theory of Computing*, pages 268–276. ACM Press, 2002. ISBN 1-58113-495-9. doi:http://doi.acm.org/10.1145/509907.509950.

[ABH+03] L. Arge, R. Barve, D. Hutchinson, O. Procopiuc, L. Toma, D. E. Vengroff, and R. Wickeremesinghe. *TPIE: User manual and reference*, November 2003.

[ABW02]   J. Abello, A. L. Buchsbaum, and J. R. Westbrook. A functional approach to external graph algorithms. *Algorithmica*, volume 32:pages 437–458, 2002.

[ADM06]   D. Ajwani, R. Dementiev, and U. Meyer. A computational study of external memory BFS algorithms. In *ACM-SIAM Symposium on Discrete Algorithms (SODA-06)*, pages 601–610. ACM, Miami, USA, 2006.

[ADN+96] T. E. Anderson, M. D. Dahlin, J. M. Neefe, D. A. Patterson, D. S. Roselli, and R. Y. Wang. Serverless network file systems. *ACM Transactions on Computer Systems*, volume 14(1):pages 41–79, 1996. ISSN 0734-2071. doi:http://doi.acm.org/10.1145/225535.225537.

[AFGV97] L. Arge, P. Ferragina, R. Grossi, and J. S. Vitter. On sorting strings in external memory. In *29th ACM Symposium on Theory of Computing*, pages 540–548. ACM Press, El Paso, May 1997.

[Aga96] R. Agarwal. A super scalar sort algorithm for RISC processors. In *ACM SIGMOD International Conference on Management of Data*, pages 240–246. 1996.

[AGL98] S. Albers, N. Garg, and S. Leonardi. Minimizing stall time in single and parallel disk systems. In *Proceedings of the 30th Annual ACM Symposium on Theory of Computing (STOC-98)*, pages 454–462. ACM Press, New York, May 23–26 1998. ISBN 0-89791-962-9.

[AHVV99] L. Arge, K. H. Hinrichs, J. Vahrenhold, and J. S. Vitter. Efficient Bulk Operations on Dynamic R-trees. In *1st Workshop on Algorithm Engineering and Experimentation (ALENEX '99)*, Lecture Notes in Computer Science, pages 328–348. Springer-Verlag, 1999.

[AJR+01] P. An, A. Jula, S. Rus, S. Saunders, T. Smith, G. Tanase, N. Thomas, N. Amato, and L. Rauchwerger. STAPL: An Adaptive, Generic Parallel C++ Library. In *Workshop on Languages and Compilers for Parallel Computing (LCPC)*, pages 193–208. Cumberland Falls, Kentucky, August 2001.

[Ajw05] D. Ajwani. *Design, implementation and experimental study of external memory BFS algorithms*. Master's thesis, Universität des Saarlandes, 2005.

[AKO02] M. I. Abouelhoda, S. Kurtz, and E. Ohlebusch. The enhanced suffix array and its applications to genome analysis. In *2nd Workshop on Algorithms in Bioinformatics*, volume 2452 of *Lecture Notes in Computer Science*, pages 449–463. 2002.

[Alo03] N. Alon. A simple algorithm for edge-coloring bipartite multigraphs. *Information Processing Letters*, volume 85(6):pages 301–302, 2003.

[AMO07] D. Ajwani, U. Meyer, and V. Osipov. Improved external memory BFS implementations. In *9th Workshop on Algorithm Engineering and Experiments (ALENEX)*. ACM-SIAM, 2007. To appear.

[APV02] L. Arge, O. Procopiuc, and J. S. Vitter. Implementing I/O-efficient Data Structures Using TPIE. In *10th European Symposium on Algorithms (ESA)*, volume 2461 of *LNCS*, pages 88–100. Springer, 2002.

[Arg95] L. Arge. The Buffer Tree: A New Technique for Optimal I/O-Algorithms. In *4th Workshop on Algorithms and Data Structures*, number 955 in LNCS, pages 334–345. Springer, 1995.

[AV88] A. Aggarwal and J. S. Vitter. The input/output complexity of sorting and related problems. *Communications of the ACM*, volume 31(9):pages 1116–1127, 1988.

[Avi83] D. Avis. A survey of heuristics for the weighted matching problem. *Neworks*, pages 475–493, 1983.

[BCFM00] K. Brengel, A. Crauser, P. Ferragina, and U. Meyer. An experimental study of priority queues in external memory. *ACM Journal of Experimental Algorithms*, volume 5(17), 2000.

[BDIW02] M. Bander, Z. Duan, J. Iacono, and J. Wu. A locality-preserving cache-oblivious dynamic dictionary. In *13th Annual ACM-SIAM Symposium On Descrete Algorithms (SODA-02)*. 2002.

[BFMZ04] G. S. Brodal, R. Fagerberg, U. Meyer, and N. Zeh. Cache-oblivious data structures and algorithms for undirected breadth-first search and shortest paths. In *SWAT 2004 : 9th Scandinavian Workshop on Algorithm Theory*, volume 3111 of *LNCS*, pages 480–492. Springer, Humlebaek, Denmark, 2004.

[BFV04] G. S. Brodal, R. Fagerberg, and K. Vinther. Engineering a cache-oblivious sorting algorithm. In *Proc. 6th Workshop on Algorithm Engineering and Experiments*, pages 4–17. 2004.

[BGV97] R. D. Barve, E. F. Grove, and J. S. Vitter. Simple randomized mergesort on parallel disks. *Parallel Computing*, volume 23(4):pages 601–631, 1997.

[BJ85] F. Bauernöppel and H. Jung. Fast parallel vertex colouring. In *5th International Conference on Fundamentals of Computational Theory*, LNCS 199, pages 28–35. 1985.

[BK87]   J. F. Boyar and H. J. Karloff. Coloring planar graphs in parallel. *J. Algorithms*, volume 8(4):pages 470–479, 1987.

[BK03]   S. Burkhardt and J. Kärkkänen. Fast lightweight suffix array construction and checking. In *14th Symposium on Combinatorial Pattern Matching*, LNCS. Springer, 2003.

[BLMP06]   A. Z. Broder, R. Lempel, F. Maghoul, and J. O. Pedersen. Efficient pagerank approximation via graph aggregation. *Information Retrieval*, volume 9(2):pages 123–138, 2006.

[BM72]   R. Bayer and E. McCreight. Organization and maintenance of large ordered indices. *Acta Informatica*, page 173189, 1972.

[Bor26]   O. Boruvka. O jistém problému minimálním. *Pràce, Moravské Prirodovedecké Spolecnosti*, pages 1–58, 1926.

[BS03]   L. Bic and A. Shaw. *Operating Systems Principles*. Pearson Education, 2003.

[BW94]   M. Burrows and D. J. Wheeler. A block-sorting lossless data compression algorithm. Technical Report 124, SRC (digital, Palo Alto), May 1994.

[BYBC06]   R. Baeza-Yates, P. Boldi, and C. Castillo. Generalizing PageRank: damping functions for link-based ranking algorithms. In *SIGIR '06: Proceedings of the 29th annual international ACM conference on Research and development in information retrieval*, pages 308–315. ACM Press, New York, NY, USA, 2006. ISBN 1-59593-369-7. doi:http://doi.acm.org/10.1145/1148170.1148225.

[CC02]   G. Chaudhry and T. H. Cormen. Getting more from out-of-core columnsort. In *4th Workshop on Algorithm Engineering and Experiments (ALENEX)*, number 2409 in LNCS, pages 143–154. 2002.

[CCW01]   G. Chaudhry, T. H. Cormen, and L. F. Wisniewski. Columnsort lives! an efficient out-of-core sorting program. In *13th ACM Symposium on Parallel Algorithms and Architectures*, pages 169–178. 2001.

[CE00]   K. Czarnecki and U. Eisenecker. *Generative Programming: Methods, Tools, and Applications*. Addison Wesley Professional, 2000. http://www.generative-programming.org/.

[CF02]   A. Crauser and P. Ferragina. Theoretical and experimental study on the construction of suffix arrays in external memory. *Algorithmica*, volume 32(1):pages 1–35, 2002.

[CFKL96]   P. Cao, E. W. Felten, A. R. Karlin, and K. Li. Implementation and performance of integrated application-controlled file caching, prefetching and disk scheduling. *ACM Transactions on Computer Systems*, volume 14(4):pages 311–343, November 1996.

[CGG+95]   Y.-J. Chiang, M. T. Goodrich, E. F. Grove, R. Tamasia, D. E. Vengroff, and J. S. Vitter. External memory graph algorithms. In *6th Annual ACM-SIAM Symposium on Discrete Algorithms*, pages 139–149. 1995.

[Cha00]   B. Chazelle. A minimum spanning tree algorithm with inverse-ackermann type complexity. *Journal of the ACM*, pages 1028–1047, 2000.

[Chi95]   Y.-J. Chiang. *Dynamic and I/O-Efficient Algorithms for Computational Geometry and Graph Algorithms*. Ph.D. thesis, Brown University, 1995.

[Chr05]   F. J. Christiani. *Cache-Oblivious Graph Algorithms*. Master's thesis, Department of Mathematics and Computer Science (IMADA) University of Southern Denmark, Odense, 2005.

[CL91]   L.-F. Cabrera and D. D. E. Long. Swift: Using Distributed Disk Striping to Provide High I/O Data Rates. *Computing Systems*, volume 4(4):pages 405–436, 1991.

[CLG+94]   P. M. Chen, E. L. Lee, G. A. Gibson, R. H. Katz, and D. A. Patterson. RAID: High-Performance, Reliable Secondary Storage. *ACM Comput. Surv.*, volume 26(2):pages 145–185, 1994.

[CLR90]   T. H. Cormen, C. E. Leiserson, and R. L. Rivest. *Introduction to Algorithms*. McGraw-Hill, 1990.

[CM99]   A. Crauser and K. Mehlhorn. LEDA-SM, extending LEDA to secondary memory. In *3rd International Workshop on Algorithmic Engineering (WAE)*, volume 1668 of *LNCS*, pages 228–242. 1999.

[CM00]   A. Crauser and K. Mehlhorn. LEDA-SM a platform for secondary memory computations. Technical report, MPII, 2000. Draft.

[Col82]   R. Cole. *Two problems in graph theory*. Ph.D. thesis, Cornell University, Ithaca, NY, 1982.

[COS01]   R. Cole, K. Ost, and S. Schirra. Edge-coloring bipartite multigraphs in $O(E \log D)$ time. *Combinatorica*, volume 21:pages 5–12, 2001.

[Cul]   J. Culberson. http://web.cs.ualberta.ca/~joe/Coloring/.

[DC05]   E. R. Davidson and T. H. Cormen. Building on a Framework: Using FG for More Flexibility and Improved Performance in Parallel Programs. In *IPDPS*. 2005.

[Dem]   R. Dementiev. The STXXL library. Documentation and download at http://stxxl.sourceforge.net/.

[Dik86]   K. Diks. A fast parallel algorithm for six-colouring of planar graphs (extended abstract). In J. Gruska, B. Rovan, and J. Wiedermann, editors, *Mathematical Foundations of Computer Science 1986 (Proceedings of the Twelfth Symposium Held in Bratislava, Czechoslovakia)*, volume 233 of *LNCS*, pages 273–282. Springer-Verlag, Berlin, 1986.

[DKMS06]   R. Dementiev, J. Kärkkäinen, J. Mehnert, and P. Sanders. Better external memory suffix array construction. *ACM Journal of Experimental Algorithmics*, 2006. To appear.

[DKS05a]   R. Dementiev, L. Kettner, and P. Sanders. Stxxl: Standard Template Library for XXL Data Sets. In *13th Annual European Symposium on Algorithms (ESA)*, volume 3669 of *LNCS*, pages 640–651. Springer, 2005.

[DKS05b]   R. Dementiev, L. Kettner, and P. Sanders. Stxxl: Standard Template Library for XXL Data Sets. Technical Report 18, Fakultät für Informatik, University of Karlsruhe, 2005.

[DLL+06]   D. Donato, L. Laura, S. Leonardi, U. Meyer, S. Millozzi, and J. F. Sibeyn. Algorithms and experiments for the webgraph. *Journal of Graph Algorithms and Applications*, volume 10(2), 2006. To appear.

[DLMT05]   D. Donato, S. Leonardi, S. Millozzi, and P. Tsaparas. Mining the inner structure of the Web graph. In *International Workshop on the Web and Databases (WebDB)*, pages 145–150. 2005.

[DMKS05] R. Dementiev, J. Mehnert, J. Kärkkäinen, and P. Sanders. Better External Memory Suffix Array Construction. In *Workshop on Algorithm Engineering & Experiments*. Vancouver, 2005. http://i10www.ira.uka.de/dementiev/files/DKMS05.pdf.

[DS03] R. Dementiev and P. Sanders. Asynchronous parallel disk sorting. In *15th ACM Symposium on Parallelism in Algorithms and Architectures*, pages 138–148. San Diego, 2003.

[DSSS04] R. Dementiev, P. Sanders, D. Schultes, and J. Sibeyn. Engineering an External Memory Minimum Spanning Tree Algorithm. In *IFIP TCS*, pages 195–208. Toulouse, 2004.

[FGK+00] A. Fabri, G.-J. Giezeman, L. Kettner, S. Schirra, and S. Schönherr. On the Design of CGAL, a Computational Geometry Algorithms Library. *Software - Practice and Experience*, volume 30(11):pages 1167–1202, September 2000.

[FJKT97] R. Fadel, K. V. Jakobsen, J. Katajainen, and J. Teuhola. External heaps combined with effective buffering. In *4th Australasian Theory Symposium*, volume 19-2 of *Australian Computer Science Communications*, pages 72–78. Springer, 1997.

[FLPR99] M. Frigo, C. E. Leiserson, H. Prokop, and S. Ramachandran. Cache-oblivious algorithms. In *40th Symposium on Foundations of Computer Science*, pages 285–298. 1999.

[Foy06] E. N. Foyet. Konstruierung von Suffixarrays in PL/SQL. Studienarbeit, Fakultät für Informatik, University of Karlsruhe, July 2006.

[FPS05] I. Finocchi, A. Panconesi, and R. Silvestri. An experimental analysis of simple, distributed vertex coloring algorithms. *Algorithmica*, volume 41:pages 1–23, 2005.

[Fre84] G. N. Frederickson. On linear-time algorithms for five-coloring planar graphs. *Information Processing Letters*, volume 19(5):pages 219 – 224, November 1984.

[FS01] R. Farias and C. T. Silva. Out-of-core rendering of large, unstructured grids. *IEEE Computer Graphics and Applications*, volume 21(4):pages 42 – 50, July 2001.

[Gab76]   H. N. Gabow. Using Euler Partitions to Edge Color Bipartite Multigraphs. *International Journal on Computer and Information Sciences*, pages 345–355, 1976.

[GBYS92] G. Gonnet, R. Baeza-Yates, and T. Snider. New indices for text: PAT trees and PAT arrays. In W. B. Frakes and R. Baeza-Yates, editors, *Information Retrieval: Data Structures & Algorithms*. Prentice-Hall, 1992.

[GGKM05] N. K. Govindaraju, J. Gray, R. Kumar, and D. Manocha. GPU-TeraSort: High Performance Graphics Coprocessor Sorting for Large Database Management. Technical Report MSR-TR-2005-183, Microsoft, December 2005. Revised March 2006.

[GGL03]   S. Ghemawat, H. Gobioff, and S.-T. Leung. The Google file system. In *SOSP '03: Proceedings of the nineteenth ACM symposium on Operating systems principles*, pages 29–43. ACM Press, New York, NY, USA, 2003. ISBN 1-58113-757-5. doi: http://doi.acm.org/10.1145/945445.945450.

[GJS76]   M. R. Garey, D. S. Johnson, and L. Stockmeyer. Some simplified NP-complete graph problems. *Theoretical Computer Science*, volume 1:pages 237–267, 1976.

[GLT98]   W. Gropp, R. Lusk, and R. Thakur. Latest Advances in MPI-2. Tutorial on EuroPVM/MPI'98, 1998.

[GND99]   P. Gaumond, P. A. Nelson, and J. Downs. *GNU dbm: A Database Manager*, 1999.

[GPS87]   A. Goldberg, S. Plotkin, and G. Shannon. Parallel symmetry-breaking in sparse graphs. In *STOC '87: Proceedings of the nineteenth annual ACM conference on Theory of computing*, pages 315–324. ACM Press, New York, NY, USA, 1987. ISBN 0-89791-221-7. doi:http://doi.acm.org/10.1145/28395.28429.

[Gra]   J. Gray. Sort Benchmark Home Page. http://research.microsoft.com/barc/sortbenchmark/.

[Gsc01]   T. Gschwind. PSTL: A C++ Persistent Standard Template Library. In *Sixth USENIX Conference on Object-Oriented Technologies and Systems (COOTS'01)*. San Antonio, Texas, USA, January-February 2001.

[Haa04]   H. Haanpää. Minimum sum and difference covers of Abelian groups. *Journal of Integer Sequences*, volume 7(2):page article 04.1.8, 2004.

[Har69]   F. Harary. *Graph Theory*. Addison Wesley, 1969.

[HCD89]   T. Hagerup, M. Chrobak, and K. Diks. Optimal parallel 5-colouring of planar graphs. *SIAM Journal on Computing*, volume 18(2):pages 288–300, 1989. ISSN 0097-5397.

[HK79]   F. Harary and H. J. Kommel. Matrix measures for transitivity and balance. *Journal of Mathematical Sociology*, volume 6:pages 199–210, 1979.

[HKM+88] J. H. Howard, M. L. Kazar, S. G. Menees, D. A. Nichols, M. Satyanarayanan, R. N. Sidebotham, and M. J. West. Scale and performance in a distributed file system. *ACM Transactions on Computer Systems*, volume 6(1):pages 51–81, 1988. ISSN 0734-2071. doi:http://doi.acm.org/10.1145/35037.35059.

[HL04]   M. Henzinger and S. Lawrence. Extracting Knowledge from the World Wide Web. In *Proc. of the National Academy of Science*. 2004.

[HSV01]   D. A. Hutchinson, P. Sanders, and J. S. Vitter. Duality between prefetching and queued writing with parallel disks. In *9th European Symposium on Algorithms (ESA)*, number 2161 in LNCS, pages 62–73. Springer, 2001.

[Hum02]   A. Hume. *Handbook of massive data sets*, chapter "Billing in the large", pages 895 – 909. Kluwer Academic Publishers, 2002.

[Int]   Intel web site. http://www.intel.com.

[JP93]   M. Jones and P. Plassmann. A parallel graph coloring heuristic. *SIAM Joirnal on Scientific Computing*, volume 14(3):pages 654–669, 1993.

[KA03]   P. Ko and S. Aluru. Space efficient linear time construction of suffix arrays. In *14th*, volume 2089 of *Lecture Notes in Computer Science*, pages 200–210. Springer, 2003.

[Kar05]   B. Karlsson. *Beyond the C++ Standard Library: An Introduction to Boost*. Addison-Wesley, 2005.

[KK00] T. Kimbrel and A. R. Karlin. Near-optimal parallel prefetching and caching. *SIAM Journal on Computing*, volume 29(4):pages 1051–1082, 2000.

[KM02] S. F. K. Makino, T. Takabatake. A simple matching algorithm for regular bipartite graphs. *Information Processing Letters*, volume 84(4):pages 189–193, 2002.

[Kni] K. Knizhnik. Persistent Object Storage for C++. http://www.garret.ru/~knizhnik/post/readme.htm.

[Knu98] D. E. Knuth. *The Art of Computer Programming—Sorting and Searching*, volume 3. Addison Wesley, 2nd edition, 1998.

[Kru56] J. B. Kruskal. On the shortest spanning subtree of a graph and the traveling salesman problem. *Proceedings of the American Mathematical Society*, volume 7:pages 48–50, 1956.

[KS06] F. Kulla and P. Sanders. Scalable parallel suffix array construction. In *EuroPVM/MPI*. 2006. To appear.

[KSB06] J. Kärkkäinen, P. Sanders, and S. Burkhardt. Linear work suffix array construction. *Journal of the ACM*, 2006. To appear.

[KSPP03] D. K. Kim, J. S. Sim, H. Park, and K. Park. Linear-time construction of suffix arrays. In *14th*, volume 2676 of *Lecture Notes in Computer Science*, pages 186–199. Springer, June 2003.

[KST03] I. Katriel, P. Sanders, and J. L. Träff. A practical minimum spanning tree algorithm using the cycle property. In *11th European Symposium on Algorithms (ESA)*, number 2832 in LNCS, pages 679–690. Springer, 2003.

[KV01] M. Kallahalla and P. J. Varman. Optimal prefetching and caching for parallel I/O systems. In *13th Symposium on Parallel Algorithms and Architectures*, pages 219–228. 2001.

[Leo04] S. Leonardi, editor. *Algorithms and Models for the Web-Graph: Third International Workshop, WAW 2004, Rome, Italy, October 16, 2004, Proceeedings*, volume 3243 of *Lecture Notes in Computer Science*. Springer, 2004. ISBN 3-540-23427-6.

[LPV81] G. F. Lev, N. Pippenger, and L. G. Valiant. A fast parallel algorithm for routing in permutation networks. *IEEE Transactions on Computers*, volume C-30(2):pages 93–100, February 1981.

[LSSY02]   T.-W. Lam, K. Sadakane, W.-K. Sung, and S.-M. Yiu. A space and time efficient algorithm for constructing compressed suffix arrays. In *Computing and Combinatorics, 8th Annual International Conference COCOON '02*, volume 2387 of *Lecture Notes in Computer Science*, pages 401–410. 2002.

[Meh04]   J. Mehnert. *External Memory Suffix Array Construction*. Master's thesis, University of Saarland, Germany, November 2004. http://algo2.iti.uka.de/dementiev/esuffix/docu/data/diplom.pdf.

[MM93]   U. Manber and G. Myers. Suffix arrays: A new method for on-line string searches. *SIAM Journal on Computing*, volume 22(5):pages 935–948, October 1993.

[MM02]   K. Mehlhorn and U. Meyer. External-Memory Breadth-First Search with Sublinear I/O. In *10th Annual European Symposium on Algorithms (ESA)*, volume 2461 of *LNCS*, pages 723–735. 2002.

[MMI72]   D. W. Matula, G. Marble, and J. Isaacson. *Graph Coloring Algorithms*. Academic Press, New York, 1972.

[MN99]   K. Mehlhorn and S. Näher. *The LEDA Platform of Combinatorial and Geometric Computing*. Cambridge University Press, 1999.

[Moo00]   R. W. Moore. Enabling petabyte computing. http://www.nap.edu/html/whitepapers/ch-48.html, 2000.

[MR99]   K. Munagala and A. Ranade. I/O-complexity of graph algorithms. In *10th Symposium on Discrete Algorithms*, pages 687–694. ACM-SIAM, 1999.

[MSS03]   U. Meyer, P. Sanders, and J. Sibeyn, editors. *Algorithms for Memory Hierarchies*, volume 2625 of *LNCS Tutorial*. Springer, 2003.

[MT03]   R. J. T. Morris and B. J. Truskowski. The evolution of storage systems. *IBM Systems Journal*, volume 42(2):pages 205–217, 2003. ISSN 0018-8670.

[Nao87]   J. Naor. A fast parallel coloring of planar graphs with five colors. In *Information Processing Letters, Vol. 25, issue 1*, pages 51–53. 1987.

[NBC+94] C. Nyberg, T. Barclay, Z. Cvetanovic, J. Gray, and D. Lomet. AlphaSort: A RISC machine sort. In *SIGMOD*, pages 233–242. 1994.

[Nel98] T. Nelson. Disk-based container objects. *C/C++ Users Journal*, pages 45–53, April 1998.

[Neu45] J. v. Neumann. First draft of a report on the EDVAC. Technical report, University of Pennsylvania, 1945. http://www.histech.rwth-aachen.de/www/quellen/vnedvac.pdf.

[NKG00] C. Nyberg, C. Koester, and J. Gray. Nsort: A parallel sorting program for NUMA and SMP machines, 2000. http://www.ordinal.com/lit.html.

[OBS99] M. A. Olson, K. Bostic, and M. Seltzer. Berkeley DB. In *USENIX Annual Technical Conference*, page 183192. June 1999.

[OBS00] M. A. Olson, K. Bostic, and M. Seltzer. Berkeley DB White Paper. http://dev.sleepycat.com/resources/whitepapers.html, 2000.

[Osi06] V. Osipov. personal communication, 2006.

[PAAV] O. Procopiuc, P. K. Agarwal, L. Arge, and J. S. Vitter. Bkd-tree: A Dynamic Scalable KD-Tree. In *8th International Symposium on Spatial and Temporal Databases (SSTD '03)*, pages 46–65.

[Pat04] D. A. Patterson. Latency lags bandwith. *Communications of the ACM*, volume 47(10):pages 71–75, 2004. ISSN 0001-0782. doi:http://doi.acm.org/10.1145/1022594.1022596.

[PGK88] D. Patterson, G. Gibson, and R. Katz. A case for redundant arrays of inexpensive disks (RAID). *Proceedings of ACM SIGMOD'88*, pages 109–116, 1988.

[PR00] S. Pettie and V. Ramachandran. An optimal minimum spanning tree algorithm. In *27th ICALP*, volume 1853 of *LNCS*, pages 49–60. Springer, 2000.

[PV92] V. S. Pai and P. J. Varman. Prefetching with multiple disks for external mergesort: Simulation and analysis. In *ICDE*, pages 273–282. 1992.

[Raj98] S. Rajasekaran. A framework for simple sorting algorithms on parallel disk systems. In *10th ACM Symposium on Parallel Algorithms and Architectures*, pages 88–98. 1998.

[Riz02] R. Rizzi. Finding 1-factors in bipartite regular graphs and edge-coloring bipartite graphs. *SIAM Journal on Discrete Mathematics*, volume 15(3):pages 283–288, 2002.

[RSST96] N. Robertson, D. P. Sanders, P. Seymour, and R. Thomas. Efficiently four-coloring planar graphs. In *Twenty-eighth annual ACM symposium on Theory of computing*, pages 571 – 575. 1996.

[San00] P. Sanders. Fast priority queues for cached memory. *ACM Journal of Experimental Algorithmics*, volume 5, 2000.

[Sch98] A. Schrijver. Bipartite edge coloring in $O(\Delta m)$ time. *SIAM Journal on Computing*, volume 28:pages 841–846, 1998.

[Sch03a] D. Schultes. External memory minimum spanning trees. Bachelor thesis, Max-Planck-Institut f. Informatik and Saarland University, http://www.dominik-schultes.de/emmst/, August 2003.

[Sch03b] D. Schultes. External Memory Spanning Forests and Connected Components. http://i10www.ira.uka.de/dementiev/files/cc.pdf, September 2003.

[SH02] F. Schmuck and R. Haskin. GPFS: A Shared-Disk File System for Large Computing Clusters. In *FAST '02: Proceedings of the 1st USENIX Conference on File and Storage Technologies*, page 19. USENIX Association, Berkeley, CA, USA, 2002.

[Sib97] J. Sibeyn. From parallel to external list ranking. Technical Report MPI-I-97-1-021, Max-Planck Institut für Informatik, 1997.

[Sib04] J. Sibeyn. External connected components. Technical report, Fachbereich Mathematik und Informatik, Martin-Luther-Universität, Halle, Germany, 2004. http://users.informatik.uni-halle.de/~jopsi/dps/si54.ps.gz.

[Sin06] J. Singler. MCSTL: The Multi-Core Standard Template Library. http://algo2.iti.uni-karlsruhe.de/singler/mcstl/, 2006.

[SKS01] A. Silberschatz, H. F. Korth, and S. Sudarshan. *Database System Concepts*. McGraw-Hill, 4th edition, 2001.

[SKW92] V. Singhal, S. V. Kakkad, and P. R. Wilson. Texas: An efficient, portable persistent store. In *Fifth International Workshop on Persistent Object Systems*. September 1992.

[SL94] A. A. Stepanov and M. Lee. The Standard Template Library. Technical Report X3J16/94-0095, WG21/N0482, Silicon Graphics Inc., Hewlett Packard Laboratories, 1994.

[SM02] J. Sibeyn and U. Meyer. External connected components and beyond, 2002. Unpublished.

[ST01] K. Sadakane and T.Shibuya. Indexing huge genome sequences for solving various problems. *Genome Informatics*, volume 12:pages 175–183, 2001.

[Ste98] A. Stevens. The persistent template library. *Dr. Dobb's*, pages 117–120, March 1998.

[Str] The STREAM Benchmark: Computer Memory Bandwidth. http://www.streambench.org/.

[SW05a] T. Schank and D. Wagner. Finding, counting and listing all triangles in large graphs, an experimental study. In *4th International Workshop on Experimental and Efficient Algorithms (WEA'05)*, volume 3503 of *Lecture Notes in Computer Science*. Springer, 2005.

[SW05b] T. Schank and D. Wagner. Finding, counting and listing all triangles in large graphs, an experimental study. Technical report, Universität Karlsruhe, Fakultät für Informatik, 2005.

[Tar75] R. E. Tarjan. Efficiency of a good but not linear set merging algorithm. *Journal of the ACM*, volume 22:pages 215–225, 1975.

[Unia] University of California, Berkeley. *dbm(3) Unix Programmer's Manual*.

[Unib] University of California, Berkeley. *ndbm(3) 4.3BSD Unix Programmer's Manual*.

[vdBDS00] J. van den Bercken, J.-P. Dittrich, and B. Seeger. java.XXL: A prototype for a library of query processing algorithms. In *International Conference on Management of Data*, volume 29(2), page 588. ACM, 2000.

[Ven94] D. E. Vengroff. A Transparent Parallel I/O Environment. In *Third DAGS Symposium on Parallel Computation*, pages 117–134. Hanover, NH, July 1994.

[VH01] J. S. Vitter and D. A. Hutchinson. Distribution sort with randomized cycling. In *12th ACM-SIAM Symposium on Discrete Algorithms*, pages 77–86. 2001.

[Vit01] J. S. Vitter. External memory algorithms and data structures: Dealing with MASSIVE data. *ACM Computing Surveys*, volume 33(2):pages 209–271, 2001.

[VS94] J. S. Vitter and E. A. M. Shriver. Algorithms for parallel memory, I/II. *Algorithmica*, volume 12(2/3):pages 110–169, 1994.

[VV96] D. E. Vengroff and J. S. Vitter. I/O-Efficient Scientific Computation using TPIE. In *Goddard Conference on Mass Storage Systems and Technologies*, volume 2, pages 553–570. 1996. Published in NASA Conference Publication 3340.

[WP67] D. J. A. Welsh and M. B. Powel. An upper bound for the chromatic number of a graph and its application to timetabling problems. *Computing Journal*, volume 10(85), 1967.

[WS98] D. Watts and S. H. Strogatz. Collective dynamics of "small-world" networks. *Nature*, volume 393:pages 440–442, 1998.

[Wyl99] J. Wyllie. SPsort: How to sort a terabyte quickly. http://research.microsoft.com/barc/SortBenchmark/SPsort.pdf, 1999.

[Zeh02] N. R. Zeh. *I/O Efficient Algorithms for Shortest Path Related Problems*. Ph.D. thesis, Carleton University, Ottawa, April 2002.

Appendix A

Notation

If not stated explicitly, the symbols below have the following meaning:

Symbol	Definition
N	The input size in bytes
M	The main memory size in bytes
B	The block size in bytes used for transfers between main memory and hard disk
D	The number of disks
$\text{scan}(N)$	The number of I/Os required to scan N items
$\text{sort}(N)$	The number of I/Os required to sort N items
G or $G = (V, E)$	Denotes a graph which consists of a set of nodes V and a set of edges E
V	The set of nodes in a graph
E	The set of edges in a graph
n	The number of input items, or the number of nodes in the input graph ($n = |V|$)
m	The number of edges in the input graph ($m = |E|$)
$deg(v)$	The degree of node v
Δ	The largest node degree of the graph

VDM

Verlag Dr. Müller

Wissenschaftlicher Buchverlag bietet

kostenfreie

Publikation

von aktuellen

wissenschaftlichen Arbeiten

Diplomarbeiten, Magisterarbeiten, Master und Bachelor Theses
sowie Dissertationen und wissenschaftliche Monographien

innerhalb von Fachbuchprojekten
(Monographien und Sammelwerke)

in den Fachgebieten Wirtschafts- und Sozialwissenschaften
sowie Wirtschaftsinformatik.

Sie verfügen über eine Arbeit zu aktuellen Fragestellungen aus den genannten Fachgebieten, die hohen inhaltlichen und formalen Ansprüchen genügt, und haben **Interesse an einer honorarvergüteten Publikation**?

Dann senden Sie bitte erste Informationen über sich und Ihre Arbeit per Email an info@vdm-verlag.de. Unser Außenlektorat meldet sich umgehend bei Ihnen.

VDM Verlag Dr. Mueller e.K. · Dudweiler Landstraße 125a
D - 66123 Saarbrücken · www.vdm-buchverlag.de